IOTA

OFFICIAL ORGAN OF THE 500 CLUB

ONE SHILLING AND SIXPENCE MONTHLY

APRIL 1947

Iota
1947-1953
EDITED HIGHLIGHTS OF F3
500 c.c.

Published 1980

ISBN 08518 40345

Printed by Unwin Brothers Limited,
The Gresham Press, Old Woking, Surrey

TRANSPORT BOOKMAN PUBLICATIONS LIMITED
8 South Street, Isleworth, Middlesex TW7 7BG

INTRODUCTION

To write an Introduction before an Introductory Editorial might seem at first glance to be rather a waste of time and space, but I believe the background to the first and subsequent editions of 'Iota' deserves some explanation, if only to younger readers. The production of any magazine in 1947 was a triumph, let alone a club motoring journal. Factories had only just returned to peacetime conditions, raw materials including paper were desperately short, and stringent rationing was the norm. Food, clothing and indifferent quality 'pool' petrol were all subject to 'points' and 'coupons'. Despite this background of austerity a small number of 500 c.c. racing cars had already been completed by 1946 and others were under way, the primary aim being for a low-cost racing formula to compete in hill climbs and sprints; circuit racing was to follow a little later. A club had been formed and the cars were to conform to the National 500 c.c. Formula unsupercharged which was eventually to become International Formula 3 with events being held all over Europe.

Certainly building motorcycle-engined cars was not new; the construction of 'cyclecars' had started before the first world war and they were prolific in the 'twenties and 'thirties. Racing versions were competing regularly during those years, one of the most notable being John Bolster's 'Bloody Mary' which must have served as inspiration to many post-war amateur constructors. For one family of builders at least the long road to World Championship success had started and it proved the perfect nursery for young drivers like Stirling Moss, Peter Collins and many others whose names became household words. It is significant that many of these exciting little racing cars can be seen regularly competing in Historic events today in pristine condition and going just as fast as ever; surely a fitting tribute to the durability and skill of their construction.

'Iota' in its original form had a life span of approximately six years and eventually in the Spring of 1953 it was merged with 'Motor Racing'. In choosing the articles and photographs for the book, I have tried to recapture the atmosphere and excitement of this period in motoring history. So much for the background and now I think 'Iota' can speak for itself.

JOHN WARD
Christmas 1979
Oxfordshire

PUBLISHER'S FOREWORD

In this day of computerised control, preplanned strategy and perfection-honed organisation, it is difficult to appreciate thoroughly the truly amateur way in which many of the best-known names in yesterday's and today's motor sport scene began to channel their enthusiasm for things mechanical. In the U.K., the years immediately following the Second World War were ones of considerable monetary and material austerity, but, to these people, their hobby was truly their passion and, whilst those whom Fate was pleased not to snatch from the scene have mellowed through the years, their early infectious enthusiasm still lives through the pages of 'Iota'.

Some few years ago, I began to come into contact with some of those people connected with the half-litre movement. I learned of their deep affection for the little homespun '500s' (from which eventually 'big time racing' extrapolated the rear engine location and reaped the concomitant benefits). With their encouragement and through the invaluable position in the motor literature scene of Chater & Scott (in whose racetrack and motor museum establishments I have met so many motor sport and motor book devotees), I was able to assemble a complete collection of the magazine, with the valued help of Peter Richley. This has allowed John Ward to reduce an otherwise daunting task into a manageable editorial labour of love.

It should be borne in mind that, here, we are considering a publication whose lifespan encompassed but a few short years over a quarter of a century ago. Although it has been possible to count on the assistance of—amongst others—John Bolster (technical editor of 'Autosport'), Dean Delamont (R.A.C. Motorsport Division) and John Webb (Motor Circuit Developments)—it has not been possible to contact everyone I would have liked to. I would welcome constructive comments from anyone whom time and movement have prevented me from contacting and who, after reading this book, may be in a position to assist in some way.

It is pertinent to refer particularly to the high standard of photography in the original magazine, which was unusual for the period. The names of Guy Griffiths and Geoff. Goddard appeared regularly alongside many of these—and this reminds us that they were the official photographers to the magazine. Both of these enthusiasts still have a large selection of the original photographs as well as many others of the era, and copies can be obtained from them. Guy is now at Bedfont House, Chipping Campden, Glos. GL55 6HJ, and Geoff's address is 55c Fernbank Road, Ascot, Berks. SL5 8HA. To these two, in particular, I owe a debt of gratitude for their generosity in foregoing their professional fees and in allowing their work to be reproduced once again.

Perhaps nowadays karting comes closest in enthusiasm to the '500' days, but the machines are light years apart. The golden age of the half-litre lightweights has passed irrevocably, although some examples are still soldiering on, through the enthusiasm and dedication of the 500 c.c. Association. The originality and humour of 'Iota' is a tribute to those far-off golden days; I feel privileged to have been in a position to nurture this legend from another time.

FRANK STROUD
(Publisher)

Introductory Editorial

The main object of "Iota" is to provide interesting literature to the enthusiast.

At the moment, I think I am right in saying, there is no magazine which caters completely for the amateur builder of motor cars. It is hoped, therefore, that "Iota" will provide for the amateur builder that very necessary requirement.

I, as Editor, am an amateur builder—I have also a certain amount of experience in print—these are my only qualifications for the job. I am, therefore, very much open to constructive criticism and definitely want readers to state their requirements and give opinions on the various articles which they will see each month.

The Club's primary function is to assist the ordinary man in the street to obtain motor racing at something like an economical cost. This is an ideal which we hope will be very shortly attained, and the magazine will be working along these lines, in order to assist both the Club and the reader.

It is going to be, sometimes, rather difficult to get results, photographs and write-ups of the various meetings in which 500's and "Specials" will be competing. Any member or reader, who feels the slightest inclination to assist will be more than welcome, and is requested preferably to get in touch with the Editor before the meeting in question, or if this is not possible, after is not too late.

This month's illustration on the cover is of Colin Strang at Prescott, 1946.

The magazine will be divided, after the first issue, into four main headings:—

1. Reports on Meetings.
2. Technical Panel reports and comments.
3. Central Club News.
4. Articles of general constructional interest.

THE 500 c.c. FORMULA UNSUPERCHARGED

A Simple Explanation of the National Unsupercharged Formula

By A. C. H. Harding, Secretary of the Technical Panel.

Engines.—Engines may be of any type, any number of cylinders, providing that the capacity does not exceed 500 c.c.

Superchargers will not be permitted.

It was decided that any type engine, up to 500 c.c. capacity, could be employed providing that it is naturally aspirated. This rule was made for several reasons:—

(a) The use of a supercharger enables the enthusiast with unlimited capital to gain considerable advantage over those less fortunate. Multi-cylinder engines, designed for use with high boost pressure give exceedingly high power output but may easily entail expenditure amounting to thousands of pounds.

(b) Considerable difficulty is experienced in supercharging single cylinder engines without adding undue weight and cost. Here, again, the advantage is on the side of the more costly multi-cylinder units.

(c) The availability of power units suitable for use with superchargers amounts to less than five per cent. that of the more general type of unit, not to mention the extreme difficulty of obtaining superchargers. Again the advantage would go to builders who are either in the trade or have trade contracts.

(d) Considerably less difference exists between performance figures of naturally aspirated engines in any one class compared with the results obtained from engines of similar capacity but with differing boost pressures.

The barring of superchargers, for the purpose of the 500 c.c. Formula should, therefore, enable the impecunious enthusiast to compete with the more fortunate on equal terms. To put the whole thing in the simplest way. We may say that power or horse-power per litre remains remarkably consistent on naturally aspirated engines but increases with supercharged engines in an ever diminishing proportion to the capital outlay.

Fuel.—Any Type of Fuel. The decision not to restrict the fuel was arrived at after exhaustive discussion. There are several excellent fuels obtainable by any competitor at a cost which is not beyond the reach of anyone; the slight extra cost is more than offset by the saving in engine components.

Almost all the engines within the capacity of the Formula can be run on petrol, petrol-benzol, or alcohol, without very much alteration. The use of an alcohol fuel is of the utmost assistance to builders of cars, especially designs with air cooled rear engines. The evaporation of the fuel in the cylinders of dope engines is extremely useful to the internal combustion engineer, providing internal cooling, preventing detonation and enabling the working pressures to be raised with consequent increase in available horse-power.

The case for a standard pump fuel restriction condemned itself from the outset. Pump fuel would not be cheaper than special fuel if cost in engine components could be considered; and the extra supervision which would have to be provided by hard worked organisers of events coupled with the almost impossible question of defining pump fuel made such a restriction pointless.

Fuel Tanks.—Fuel Tanks to be of one Imperial Gallon Capacity.

The use of small capacity tank has a number of advantages which may be summed up as follows:—

(a) Minimum of risk from fire. Although one gallon of fuel can be extremely dangerous the risk is obviously very small compared with a crashed machine with a full 10-gallon tank.

(b) The use of a minimum weight of fuel is essential for all types of sprint events and a tank of one gallon capacity is sufficient.

(c) Racing on circuits can be greatly enhanced by the use of suitable pit accommodation. The employment of a small capacity tank will enforce, at least, one pit stop in a race of 50 miles length if the machine is running on petrol and considerably more if a dope motor is in use.

A pit stop takes time and it will readily become obvious that the faster the machine, the greater the horse-power output of the engine. Fuel consumption can, therefore, provide an automatic handicap to the machines using alcohol and enable the competitor, using a machine running on petrol to offset the gain in speed and power from the use of an alcohol fuel.

Minimum Weight.—A Minimum Weight of 500lbs. Dry. with Tyres, but without Fuel and Oil.

A minimum weight of 500 pounds will allow builders of 500 c.c. cars to construct wheels, chassis and other highly stressed parts, from materials which have been adapted from parts already in existence. There is, of course, nothing to prevent the construction of cars from light alloys; in fact builders are advised to incorporate as much light alloy as possible, always providing that the correct grade is used and that it is handled in the correct manner. This minimum weight was fixed after consideration of facts and figures obtained from specials already in existence. A machine, built down to the limit of 500lbs. will need careful thought and design to ensure that useless material is not left in places where a little extra hard work can affect its removal. On the other hand, the limit does, definitely, exclude attempts to beat the power weight ratio figures by the construction of cars which would endanger both the lives of drivers and spectators and the sport in general.

It may be stated that a figure of 650lbs. for a finished car, built to the formula would be in line with machines built to really sound engineering standards.

Gearboxes.—Any Type of Gearbox may be used and the incorporation of Reverse is optional.

No limit, whatsoever, is put on the transmission of cars built to the Formula. The cars, unless built for use on the road, will not normally be influenced by such matters as the laws under the Traffic Act and even if used on the road, they would not be required to be fitted with reverse gear unless the weight exceeds 8cwts.

Brakes.—Brakes must operate on all four wheels with independent hand operation of brakes on one pair of wheels.

This rule makes it clear that in addition to the normal brakes operating on all four wheels, a separate hand brake must be provided to ensure that a failure of the foot brakes system does not render the car absolutely devoid of brakes.

It should be stressed that this rule will be most rigidly adhered to by all scrutineers acting on behalf of the Club. Although brakes are such an important item of equipment, the number of cars which come to the line in sprint races with defective brakes is most surprising. The brakes should be regarded as the most important single item of equipment and builders will do well to concentrate on retardation at the expense of a little acceleration. Mistakes in acceleration may be made as many times as the car is moved from rest, but a mistake in the fitting of a brake pin, brake pipe or cable, may possibly prove to be the first and last.

Bodywork and Body.—Bodywork is Optional—but desirable.

It may be said that a car body has little effect on its performance; that statement is, to some extent, true. Included in the term bodywork, such matters as chain guards, seating and general protection to the driver, must be considered.

Too many Specials are apt to just "happen" when it comes to the finishing stage. Too often there is insufficient time to complete anything in the way of seating or protection from the potential dangers of whirling chains, spinning wheels and bare exhaust pipes, to say nothing of the extreme discomfort of the combined results of the elements and track surface.

A workmanlike body is a most desirable asset; it most certainly enhances the appearance of a machine and, what is more, from the public angle, is most essential. From the builders' point of view it provides comfort, protection and that sense of satisfaction, derived from the knowledge that a job has been designed, manufactured and above all, finished.

APPLICATION FOR MEMBERSHIP

Name (in full) ....
(Please use Block Letters)

Address..

....

....
(If in the Services, please give Permanent Address)

To The Secretary, The 500 Club,
Milford House, Lansdown, Bath:

1. I wish to become a Member of The 500 Club.
If elected, I undertake to abide by the Rules of The Club.

2 I enclose Cheque/Postal Order for..
(All Cheques or Postal Orders should be crossed and made payable to The 500 Club).
Subscription £1 1s. 0d. to cover One Year.

3 It is NOT a condition of Membership to construct or intend to construct a 500 c.c. Car, but if you own, or are building a Car, it will be necessary to complete a card which will be sent on request.
Description of other Car/s suitable for Racing:

....

....

Date.............................. Signature..

THE BIRTH OF THE COOPER 500.

Character and ambition are said to be formed by environment and by some hereditary process of which I know nothing. I can only say that from the age of nine years when my father was mechanic to " Kaye Don " until the present day my whole interest has been centred around racing cars and their intestines. At the tender age of nine I became the proud possessor of a real midget car powered by a 175 c.c. Villiers Two Stroke with a three speed gear box which at the crack of dawn could be heard tearing up and down the local road at the rate of knots—

The Cooper 500 at Prescott
[Reprint by courtesy of " The Motor "

at least 40 anyway. Latterly my attention was again arrested by the " Midget Car " and as soon as I heard of the 500 c.c. class, I decided to build one. Amongst other considerations the low running cost made me decide to concentrate on this size.

With great enthusiasm my father and I put our heads together and after much struggling with knotty problems evolved the " Cooper 500 " which we commenced building in June and completed after five weeks, in time to enter for the Prescott Hill Climb. Our " Child Car " as some newspaper disparagingly described it, was constructed around two Fiat 500 front suspension assemblies and was powered by a Jap 500 c.c. engine.

I said we completed in time for the July Prescott Hill Climb but only just. The meeting was held on a Sunday but our first test run wasn't completed until the previous Friday, and that was carried out on the local highway, causing much annoyance to the public in general and more especially to the " Cops." During that first run I developed " Gearbox Mounting " trouble which necessitated slaving into the early hours of the morning before it was rectified. After a few short hours of beauty sleep, my friend Eric Brandon and I loaded the car on to our truck and drove the hundred miles to Prescott.

We arrived at 11 o'clock on the Saturday morning and immediately set out to familiarise ourselves with the course, noting with some trepidation the odd hair-pin and sudden steep gradients. Nevertheless we were in a confident mood as we plodded back to the paddock, drenched to the skin, and decided to have a crack at the trial trip there and then. What optimism —The car even " shied " at the starting line and with a good old " buck " and heart rending accompaniment left the engine hanging by its " sprockets." The engine mountings had sheared. This occured at about three o'clock in the afternoon and as " Tempus " has a way of " fugiting " we knuckled to and sorted out the debris. Not much could be done at the paddock however, so we loaded the car back on to our truck with disgust and returned to our hotel for dinner.

Whilst satisfying the " Inner Man," Eric suddenly hit on a brain wave which necessitated driving sixty miles to his friend's garage in Hereford. Being a country garage we turned to the land for assistance, and after much thought, beer and sandwiches, supplied by our host, rammed two plough handle struts through the broken tubes of our original engine mountings, which we drilled, pinned, and re-assembled. The job completed we drove back to Cheltenham to try and make up for lost sleep, the time being about 4.30 a.m.

Sunday morning dawned fine and clear and although Eric and myself were still suffering from a slight hammering on the temples there was a pleasant feeling of tingling anticipation coursing through us. My father arrived at about 9 o'clock complete with two new engine bearers made up of $1\frac{1}{8}''$ solid bar, reamers and all the necessary for making a good sturdy job. We decided that ours was solid enough however and left it at that.

The trials started at about 10 o'clock, and with pent up excitement I drove slowly up to the line and awaited the signal. With the roar of 500 c.c.'s pulling their weight I shot off with a good start, this time crossing the line. I took the first bend in " third " and held her nicely prior to changing down to " second " for the next, which I remembered was rather deceiving. Reving her smartly to find my gear, I took the bend without trouble, but to my utter chagrin suddenly found I had lost all power. On investigation we discovered that valve bounce had occured due to excess reving with consequent damage to the exhaust valve.

Fortunately that happened to be a practice trial, the first official one being held that afternoon, so we had time to whip the head off, and strip down the valve assembly, have the valve trued up in Cheltenham, and reassemble in time for the two o'clock meeting. With some concern I again faced the starting signal and as I feared, maximum power was not to be had that day. The valve was not as true as the manufacturers had intended it to be. I finished the run, however, and let Eric have a shot in the second event. No further damage was likely to occur to the engine and experience in handling was valuable to both of us.

During the following few weeks until the next Prescott meeting I got down to a spot of real maintenance. The engine bearers of solid 1⅛″ bar my father had prepared were fitted, together with a new valve, etc., and the car was dusted, spat upon and polished until it seemed as though nothing could possibly prevent us from walking off with the fastest time.

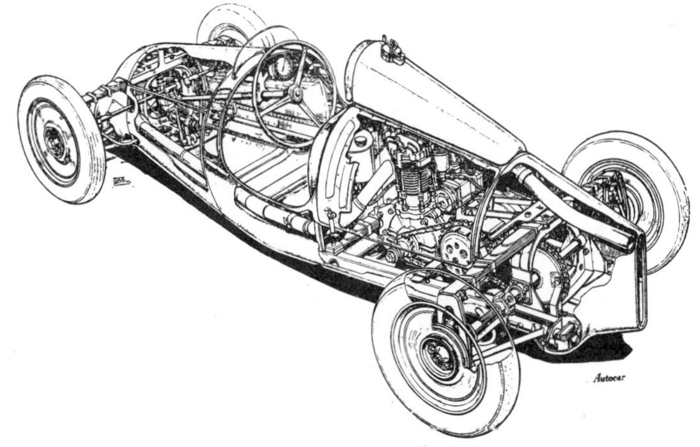

Cut Out Drawing of the Cooper 500

[Reproduced by courtesy of "The Autocar"

Again disillusionment! The second Prescott meeting we attended surprisingly enough dawned fair, and Eric and I set off in high spirits, but this time with our fingers crossed; we weren't quite the same optimistic amateurs that had sallied forth for the previous meeting. Maybe we were still a trifle too optimistic however, as Mother Nature stepped in as is her wont, and promptly damped our spirits, and us, more than a trifle. We arrived in good time and at about 11 o'clock I found myself in the now familiar position facing the starter. The sun was shining anæmically but with hope, though the ground was still wet and muddy. Given the signal I was off, and eating up the yards to the first bend. I went into it at speed and with a little extra throttle to take the next gradient skidded beautifully until I found myself facing the way I had come. The spectators were rather surprised to see me back so soon, but instead of a radient glow of triumph beaming from my face, I fear it must have appeared a trifle " sheepish." Happily that was a practice run, so my prestige suffered little. Eric had a practice run next and then I was permitted to have another, the car going like a bird with nothing unusual occuring.

Fairly satisfied with ourselves Eric and I covered up the car, parked it in the Paddock and went off for some food. After lunch the first official runs took place. My turn came approximately half way through the programme, and with even my toes crossed I approached the line and was off—for about twenty yards! Again my engine bearers had gone, solid 1⅛″ bar snapped clean through added to which we found that the gearbox bearers had fractured. Some Torque!

Teething trouble were by now becoming somewhat monotonous and my little car should have felt very small under the withering glances and scathing remarks we rained upon it. Still my father and I persevered, and after reinstating it in its " Home Garage " really got down to some serious thinking to rectify this trouble for good and all, and thank goodness met with success. We fitted two leaf springs transversly across the frame and bracketed the engine to them. This modification we completed as usual on the " Eve " of the Brighton Speed Trial in September. What a rush that was. Early on the Saturday morning at about six o'clock with a clear sky and a promise of a good day ahead, Eric Brandon and myself rolled out the 500 and made our way to the Kingston By-Pass. Eric followed in his T-Type M.G. and when all was ready we opened the " Taps " and fairly belted the car down the deserted highway. The Cooper 500, minus silencers really excelled herself that morning. Without a hitch we flew down the road with the tuneful crescendo of power echoing back from the houses on either side. It was a joy to be alive though the occupants of the houses probably thought otherwise, and I believe blamed the " Hellish " racket on to Jeff Taylor whose works are situated nearby and who was also racing at Brighton that day.

Our practice runs complete, Eric and I, offering up a silent prayer, loaded the car on to our truck and proceeded to Brighton. I was running with M. Chambers in the 850 c.c. class and this time felt on top of the world. With a really clean start I got away smartly, changing rapidly up the gears and then giving her everything she had for the full kilometer. All our troubles were repaid as we won the 850 c.c. racing class by a clear two seconds.

Eric drove the car in the 1000 c.c. class competing against H. C. Lones in his 1000 c.c. " Tiger Cat." Our previous success egged us on to hope for victory in this race also but as luck would have it he came in fourth. Nevertheless for the first time in our short career with the 500 c.c. we felt we had earned at least one leaf from the laurels of victory and celebrated that fact well and truly on our way home.

The next fortnight was spent in generally overhauling the machine in preparation for the " West Court " speed trial in which we gained a further leaf to our laurels. We entered for the 1100 c.c. class and after a practice run each without trouble, settled down for the official trials in the afternoon

I decided to have the first crack in the 1100 c.c. event, and kicked off in fine style. Everything was going according to plan. The engine was crackling at full power, the gears were sweet, in fact there wasn't a cloud on my horizon. Suddenly out of the blue they began to gather. The engine coughed and spluttered and with dismay I watched the rev. counter drop 2000.

Resplendent in the Paddock

I did my damndest to clear her, but to no avail, she wouldn't go one rev. over 4000. I finished the course and handed the car over to Eric, with the advice that he should try and keep her as much as possible in top to counteract our " Rev. rationing." This he did and completed in very good time.

We employed the same tactics in our final two runs and to our gratification discovered that Eric had made the fastest time in our class at 24.42 and I came second at 24.73.

So ended my first year's experience of Hill Climbing and Speed Trials and for some reason that last meeting at West Court gave me the greatest amount of satisfaction, and was a grand " Finale."

I sincerely hope that the 500 c.c. class has now come to stay for if it really catches on I am sure great sport at low cost will be available to all enthusiasts, and the greater the number of enthusiasts, the greater will become the scope for extending our activities. The anticipation of inter-club meetings, circuit racing and more and still more hill-climbing and speed trials makes me yearn to get things cracking.

At the present moment my father and I have a new design under construction. An aerodynamic 500 c.c. two-seater which we hope will be completed within a few weeks. Also nearing completion is another " Cooper 500 " for Eric Brandon who will be competing during the coming season. Then, in the not so far distant future we hope to have twelve more " Coopers " under construction at the same time. You can see the idea has had a good reception in this part of the world.

To conclude, I should like to say that I shall be only too willing to extend the advice, encouragement and good fellowship that was extended to me by C. H. Strang and H. C. Lones, to any new enthusiast who may find himself in difficulties.

J. N. COOPER.

500 REFLECTIONS.

By Colin Strang

During a good many years service abroad while Hitler was doing his stuff, I often wondered in what form, if any, it would be possible to get some kind of motor racing in our post war England. An essential was that it would have to be done on a strictly limited budget, and with this in view I never ventured to hope that my first season would provide such good sport and so many cheerful outings.

I had never contemplated using a small capacity car, looking upon them as small in swept volume only and Goliath in cost, but George Mullett, one of our directors was very keen, and after reviewing the matter in the light of the suggested use of a motor-cycle engine as put forward by the Bristol enthusiasts, I found the idea very attractive. Now, after a season's sprints with the Strang 500, I am convinced that this class really is the answer for the man whose racing has just got to be done on a strictly limited cost basis.

After spending some considerable time grubbing about in breakers' yards, searching for what we hoped would be suitable components for the proposed car, and getting an engine promised to us by Vincent H.R.D. of Stevenage (an old T.T. unit), we got to work, and completed the little car in four months. This meant my working almost exclusively on the model often late into the night, and much hard work and enthusiasm from G. Mullett and N. Shorrock who of course had their normal work to attend to. Hours were spent in discussion and I was most grateful for their helpful advice as well as hard graft, and to L. Frazer Barnes, who during the war was our works manager, for his great assistance in this field. As we had garage and machine shop facilities you may think that we took a long time. For my part I think that many people are extremely optimistic in assessing the amount of work involved in building a 500, and I feel sure that the builders of those now under construction will probably endorse this view. It must be remembered that a 500

[Photo by Thomson, Glasgow

Colin Strang at Bo'ness, the Scottish Sporting Car Club's Open Hill Climb, September 7th, 1946

although a very small car is still a racing car and thus has just got to be a right job throughout. Any poor construction or questionable parts incorporated can easily have unfortunate consequences, and would quickly give this class a bad name in a country so lacking in understanding of motor racing. By the same token, although I would urge collaboration in the building of the cars, I think that it is very desirable that the driving and testing in the early stages should be done by those with some experience of high performance cars if possible. One of the snags of the sprint job is getting to know your car; one drives it such a little way, so get just as much practice as you possibly can on an airfield before running it in competitions.

Unless you are prepared to spend a lot of money, or have adequate technical knowledge and facilities, don't be tempted by over complication in construction; it is much better to build and compete with a straightforward and not too ambitious machine, than to start something really super that through cash running short or difficulties of manufacture does not reach completion. It is certainly a fact that far more Specials have been started than have ever been completed and run.

It has been said before, but it is worth repeating, that it will pay to get out drawings of your proposed car. Even if you are not much of a draughtsman, quite rough drawings will be of great assistance. If you cut out in cardboard or plywood a profile from drawings of the engine and other main components, it will give you a line as to where these can be disposed in your chassis.

If you can find something standard in the way of a chassis, there is a great deal to recommend its use. You can quite likely adapt it and improve over its known weaknesses. If the steering layout is satisfactory—leave it alone! Of course the more ambitious will be building up their own chassis, and its advantages particularly from the weight saving point of view are considerable, but my opinion is that to build up a chassis from scratch and obtain satisfactory road holding and teering is not easy, and is likely to result in subsequent modifications which may prove costly.

In the Strang 500 I have used a 1938 Fiat 500 chassis with quarter eleptic rear springs. As the bodies on these cars provide additional strength to the chassis, I have supplied this extra rigidity by welding in 18G sheet steel right along the side members (thus converting it into a box section), and a light tubular steel member of 2⅜ dia. brazed in position 17 inches from the front member which carries the transverse spring. The standard single acting hydraulic shockabsorbers are used on the front end, and I have found these satisfactory, their main handicap being their weight. Both front and rear springs have their standard number of leaves, but I have found it an advantage to bind the front springs. In the early part of the season the standard Fiat steering box was used, but later we found that a higher geared steering made for rather more peaceful motoring. You will find that an extension of 1½ inches on the Fiat drop arm will give a ratio of approx. 1¾ turns of the wheel from lock to lock. This can be achieved by bolting on an extension to the drop arm. Incidentally, regarding the quoting of the number of turns of the steering wheel from lock to lock, it does occur to me that this only gives a rough indication of the steering gear ratio owing to the variation in steering lock on different cars.

The idea that a heavy car was necessarily a good road holder was a falacy exposed years ago, but I believe the point can be reached with an ultra light weight vehicle when to obtain something approaching satisfactory roadholding is a major problem. It is far easier to get the results with, say a 12cwt. job than with the 500lbs. minimum weight as laid down by the 500 Club. I think it was John Bolster who said " there is no such thing as roadholding with a very fast light car." Nevertheless with the limited power of the 500 it is yet absolutely essential that everything be done to reduce weight. Now, this weight saving is inclined to be an expensive, or at any rate a tedious job. If you have seen my little car you have probably noticed that there are a few holes drilled here and there! I will have the greatest admiration and envy for anyone who approaches the 500lbs. mark.

When my car was completed I found that I had underestimated the weight by about 60lbs. Somehow, when you put the bits together, they seem to get heavier! However, when you are working away to reduce the weight of your car, it is worth remembering that, with the approximate power to weight ratio of a 500, every 10 to 12 pounds you save is worth 1 h.p. Weight distribution in the Strang 500 entailed lengthy dis-

cussions. As eventually evolved and run last year it was approx. 80lbs. less on the front wheels than the rear with the driver seated. This was found to be satisfactory.

On the question of brakes. I don't think there is anything to touch hydraulic operation, and from a constructors point of view it is easier to lead pipe lines along your chassis than to cope with cables or rods. Brakes are a pest the way they increase your unsprung weight, and I like very much the inboard brakes as incorporated in the new Lagonda. We did toy with the idea of a chain driven rear brake, and which I believe could be quite satisfactory, because after all a chain can cope with the engine torque well enough, but the idea was not carried out for a variety

[Photo by courtesy of "The Motor"

Close up of Strang's interesting lay-out

of reasons. Unfortunately efficient brakes are heavy, and it is not advisable to reduce the drums in weight as they generally distort easily enough already, but a useful improvement can be obtained by using aluminium back plates. There seems a good deal of doubt about aluminium drums and cast iron liners. It can certainly save some weight, and should be of help in heat dissipation; I am going to try it when I have time.

I suppose that many others like myself long to obtain the light alloy wheels which they can even in these times apparently produce in Italy. Making the best of a bad job last season we used motor-cycle rims and fitted 18 × 3.25″ tyres in front and 4″ on the back. To start with the pressures we used were too high as we had not fully appreciated the very low loading per wheel. Later for runs in the wet we came down to as low as 12lbs. in the rear wheels—low enough to give Messrs. Freeman and Smetz, of Dunlops, heart failure! Security bolts were used in the back wheels, and incidentally the tubes as well as the tyres were synthetic and gave no trouble. This combination of tyre sizes was fairly satisfactory, although really the motor-cycle tyre is too rounded in the tread for good results with a car as the consequent small area of tread in contact with the road is not ideal for adhesion, particularly in the wet. For this season I am going to try car type 4.25 tyres, and with which I anticipate some improvement.

A good many people have asked if we get any clutch trouble, as we use the normal type of heavy weight motor-cycle clutch. So far it has done all that we could ask, which includes letting in the clutch at 4,000 to 5,000 r.p.m. to make a reasonable get away. The Ferodo linings look as good now as they did at the beginning of the season. It is important, by the way, to check the clutch springs to see that their tension is equal.

Regarding engine mountings, however carefully balanced, motor-cycle singles and twins have an inherent lack of balance, and varying degrees of vibration are unavoidable, and if you are going to use a rigid engine mounting, it has just got to be extremely robust, or else you will find that your engine mounting, etc., will quickly fracture. Cooper on his very nice little car now mounts his engine on a couple of leaf springs, which in turn are mounted on rubber, and he tells me that it gives excellent results.

In engine tuning I think there is a tendency to go to all sorts of elaborate lengths (and which of course are really necessary to get a high power output) and rather neglect or overlook the more mundane attentions which a normal road car in good trim should receive. I refer to such things as contact breaker points, float level, etc., etc. Observation does show that cars come to the line in competition with such things as carburettor mixture miles out, and yet the owner has probably spent many hours polishing ports and doing the many other things which experts advise the searcher after speed to do! Remember that in racing it is far commoner to see a car eliminated through a minor mishap such as a plug lead coming off, than from spectacular engine failures. I strongly advocate using alcohol fuel for the motor-cycle type of engine as you are far less liable to experience piston and other allied troubles as when using a petrol benzole mixture. Regarding mixture, it is generally accepted that it is better to err on the rich side, as a weak mixture will burn through a piston very quickly.

One of the fascinations of the 500 Class will undoubtedly be the diverse types of machines competing, as there are obviously so many ways of going about the building of these cars. The foregoing notes are based simply on one season's sprint experiences with one of these little cars so I certainly don't pose as an expert on the class, but if any of the points I have mentioned prove of interest or use to 500 constructors, I shall be delighted. In conclusion, the best of luck to all 500 constructors. I look forward enormously to meeting them, together with my old friends Lones and Cooper next season. And may we have some decent weather!

* * *

Y.M.C.A.,
Colston Street, Bristol.
17th October, 1947.

Dear Sir,

May I encroach upon the pages of "Iota" to endorse Mr. Matthews' suggestion in his letter published in the September issue, that an "Iota" team of mechanics should be available to help all "500" competitors at meetings? Probably one of the very capable gentlemen on the Technical Panel would be glad to lead the venture which could develop into a complete mobile workshop, and in its service to members yield invaluable help to the "500" movement.

One would infer from Mr. Whiteley's letter, had he not mentioned it, that he was occupied in structural engineering. He appears quite unfamiliar with the dynamic loading of a vehicular chassis, and I consider his letter wholly misleading to the builders of 500 c.c. competition cars.

The suggestion in Mr. Pritchard Lovell's second letter, would, I think, add unnecessary entanglements to 500 c.c. racing. Apropos his opening remarks, may I cite the modest examples of Messrs. Bacon and Bosisto, both of whom, no doubt, have thoroughly enjoyed themselves this season.

In conclusion, may I express my appreciation of the informative articles by Messrs. Gordon Jones, Horstman and Harding. These bear the mark of men who thoroughly know their subject. I feel, however, that any "special" builders who could learn anything from the first half of Mr. Harding's last article would do better to pay an expert to weld for them, or at the least they could commence operations by taking out a comprehensive insurance policy.

Yours faithfully,
R. W. Houghton.

THE CLUB.

I have heard that quite a number of enthusiasts still think it is a condition of membership to be an owner or builder of 500 c.c. cars. THIS IS NOT SO. The Club exists solely to develop inexpensive racing and is open to all who have the need for recognition of the importance of motor racing at heart.

One has only to consider logically that if 40 cars of 500 c.c. are constructed and their owners pay one guinea a year to the Club (which includes 18/- worth of Iota) and they constitute the entire membership of the Club, we would be in Queer Street right away.

The Club has been of service in answering many technical questions not even remotely connected with 500's. This has been a great achievement particularly when it is borne in mind that the members of the Technical Panel have worked on an honorary basis.

A s the Club grows it will become necessary to put the whole thing on professional lines, but in the meantime I am sure you will wish me to thank, on your behalf, all those who have worked so hard to make the Club a success.

The Vintage Sports-Car Club have also invited us to compete in their race meeting at Grensden Lodge on July 15th. Anyone who intends to compete is requested to get in touch with the Hon. Secretary, T. W. Carson, Esq., " Mellaha ", Pack Lane, Kempshott, Basingstoke.

(By courtesy of " The Light Car "

Roy Clarkson casting envious eyes over the Strang motor

DON'T . . .

By Jack Moor

Punch's famous advice to those about to marry is the same as mine to those about to " Special-ize."

After 23 years at the game I can think of no hobby which offers such a poor return for such an expenditure of cash, care and time as sprint motoring.

The most one can hope for is a collection of plate to add to the already over-burdened house-hold cleaning, but the most likely reward is that of disappointment, to which can be added the ridicule of one's acquaintances.

Unless great tact is exercised, one is likely to find oneself at cross-purposes with the rest of the family, who do not look favourably on those irregular appearances for meals, the dirt and noise which usually accompany the pursuit.

One is liable to get at loggerheads with the local authorities and to graduate from " a hare brained young ass " to " a silly old fool, who ought to know better " amongst the local population.

Again, the type of person who is likely to be the most earnest and useful helper, is generally the sort whom the family " can't stand at any price."

Having got the affair finally constructed, then the troubles really start.

By paying a goodly sum as entry fee, you are allowed to attend an event, but whether you actually compete is in the hands of the R.A.C. Scrutineers, who, to my mind, carry their demands to a degree not at all warranted, by a record of former accidents.

The only one I remember caused by mechanical failure was when a fly-wheel of unsuitable metal burst, and this would not have been apparent beforehand to any scrutineer.

I do not agree with the ruling that all vehicles must have front wheel brakes.

In all the years I have competed I have never felt the need for these, even when breaking the course record at Weatherby, where the finish is down hill, between trees, I have never had an anxious moment. It is worth recording that the car which took the record from me did hit a tree, in spite of his F.W.B.

I maintain that a high geared steering is absolutely essential on a high speed light weight, intended for competing on tricky, bumpy courses, where the whole run is taken up by connecting power slides almost before they begin. I always feel that the sensation of a fast man at Shelsley must be very much akin to the experience of a tight-rope walker.

Unless perfect in every respect F.W.B. systems can be very dangerous when used in conjunction with high geared steering. You only need a brake to " pick up " slightly to cause a very awkward situation. In addition there is the extra unsprung weight, which is bad from the suspension point of view.

Referring to entry fees, I can never see why we should pay out such sums merely to be allowed to entertain the spectators, who in turn, pay considerable sums and car parking fees to see us.

I find the practice day very entertaining, much better than the event itself, as it is much more informal.

The trouble here is that you are apt to over-do the practice business, with the result that something unfortunate occurs, necessitating loss of sleep, on just the night you really should have complete rest.

I remember having worked all one night, feeling tired and " scruffy," with an engine with which I was far from happy, being accosted by a bright young thing for an autograph, who remarked, " . . . it must be so exciting to have a real racing car ! " To which I made no reply !

Having avoided all family, police and scrutineers complications, and having survived the practice runs, you come to the big moment, when you wish you were anywhere else except about to get into your car, which you feel sure will let you down and bring ridicule on your head. Your knees feel weak and your stomach queer.

I used to think that my feelings were unique until a fellow-sufferer confided in me how he felt, adding that he envied me because nothing ever worried me ! I probably felt worse than he did.

I remember one wet Shelsley, when the course was anything but nice, wishing I could gracefully back out of driving and vowing I would never run again.

I got as far as the Kennel Bend, when " bang " went the crank shaft. I returned sorrowfully to the start, where my mechanic Bill reminded me that we had a complete assembly at home—39 miles away.

I was told that I could have 2 hours before my next run, so the engine was completely stripped down in the long wet grass, the pilgrimage home was made and I was ready for my next run within 2 hours. We had had to straighten a bent valve on a brick with a hammer, but I only missed my class award by less than a second.

The margin between failure and success is very slender. I have performed twice at Saltburn, the first time the engine kicked back just once against my pushers, and sheared a key in the works, this caused much local amusement.

Next year I returned with the identical machine and got F.T.D. by a clear 10 miles an hour.

It is extraordinary what havoc can be created in a short space. In 1938 I had spent a lot of time on a new engine and I was very pleased with my start at Shelsley and was going well round Kennel Bend, when the hair pin valve springs, coupled with higher lift cams proved too much for the front of the crank shaft, which drove the tuning gear.

A piston detached itself and inserted itself between the connecting rods at about 7,000 r.p.m. It was a classical blow up !

I think the most extraordinary sensation was when I bent a propeller shaft accelerating out of a corner. One moment all was serene, the next a terrifying feeling coupled with an inability to see anything at all clearly. It was an experience to be felt to be believed.

Silly things are liable to happen. I remember compressing the clutch spring up to such an extent, to overcome slip, that I could scarcely hold out the pedal. Finally the clutch pedal cross shaft bent to such an extent that it got mixed up with the clutch toggles and there was no more motoring that day !

I may be considered ghoulish but I keep a collection of relics, among them a gudgeon pin shaped like a banana, a cramp pin with rollers welded on to it, con rods in all fantastic shapes, a steering wheel which disintegrated between the S bends of Shelsley.

There is another hazard I have omitted, that of getting the car to the course. Poor old Wasp I was a complete write off, having detached itself from the tow bar at a speed I dare not mention, after having towed for 210 miles during the night.

The Wasp

One year the car had behaved well at Shelsley, so we towed on to Brighton. Here she proved short of power to such an extent that cars I knew to be much slower than mine just walked away and I was unable to find the reason.

The following week the experts got busy, but were also unable to find any fault. Finally the tank ran dry—another tin of " dope " opened and off she went like a scalded cat. All that way, to be let down by a dud tin of dope.

I started in 1923 with an O.H.C. (chain driven cam shafts) G.N. Vitesse model with racing shell 2 section body.

I competed in a few events with the car as it was but the following year the wheel base was shortened by 12 inches and the front track widened (?) A narrow very amateurish body with central steering column.

After meeting Basil Davenport at Surton Bank I decided to go 1,500 and increased bore stroke accordingly.

Some time later I found the 2 litre class always slower than the 1½ litre so I increased my bore to give me 1,510 c.c.

In 1928 at Shelsley, Sharpe, Davenport and I won the 1,100, 1,800 and 2,000 classes, all with twins.

Shortly after this I acquired one of the Skila 4 valve shaft driven O.H.C. cars in quite good condition for £30 !

This was rebuilt into Wasp III and on its first appearance broke the class record at Shelsley.

I persevered with this car until I felt that I had reached the limit of power from the existing engine.

I approached Nortons who were very helpful and up to the present time I am using Norton components, which have given every satisfaction.

I am at the moment working on a new car, and I have put a good deal of time and money into it.

I am very disappointed to find that in the new Shelsley regulations the unblown cars have to compete on even terms with the supercharged jobs and there is no award for the fact unsupercharged car or for the fastest "special." This is a blow indeed.

I started this article with "DON'T," I end with the same word.

If you ask me why I am spending more time, money and energy on the game, I must answer I really. DON'T know !

★ ★ ★

Strang, Bo'ness 1947

by courtesy of the Light Car

by courtesy of Alex Thomson, Glasgow.

SHELSLEY WALSH—JUNE 21st, 1947

The International Meeting at Shelsley Walsh attracted an entry of 76 Racing Cars, and the pick of the Country's Racing drivers.

It was of course typical, that as soon as the Meeting was due to start, down came the rain. There was a smaller crowd than was expected for such an important meeting, but the old 'Shelsley Sweats' were seen hurrying along to their positions at the start of the proceedings, clad in gum boots, oilskins, and Sou'-Westers.

Frank Bacon at Shelsley, June 21st, 1947

Raymond Mays, the racing Vice-President of the 500 Club made fastest time of the day, in both of his two magnificent runs. In the appalling conditions the two-litre E.R.A. now painted Electric Blue, was going true to form, and came up to the expectations of the crowd. Mays has truly mastered the hill, and close observers say, that wet or fine, he invariably takes exactly the same line.

The five fastest in order of merit were :—

Raymond Mays	E.R.A.	41.50 secs	(2nd run)
K. Hutchinson	Alfa Romeo	43.21 ,,	(2nd run)
B. Bira	Maserati	43.30 ,,	(1st run)
F. R. Gerard	E.R.A.	43.31 ,,	(2nd run)
J. V. Bolster	"Bloody Mary"	43.80 ,,	(2nd run)

The 500's were the first to make the ascent, and all eight of them completed their two runs. The strange ailments that always attend a collection of specials at a race meeting, afflicted a number of them as can be readily seen from the results.

Once again Colin Strang showed himself to be the best of the 500's and his two runs of 49.65 and 49.43 were so consistent that there is no doubt that he employs the same technique, and this has undoubtedly shown him profit. The Strang was exceedingly steady and in fact went up so smoothly that a vast number of spectators did not realise just how good his time was.

Frank Aikens was driving his Triumph engined special and improved his time on his second run by a shade over 3 seconds, finally recording 50.52.

Eric Brandon was the fastest of the cooper 500's and is driving very nicely indeed. It was noticeable that his cut-off point on the esses was some 10 yards later than any other competitor. He brakes smoothly and very nicely indeed while he is changing down. Brandon's time on his second run was 50.60 secs. which was 2.31 seconds faster than John Cooper in the sister car. COOPER had bad luck in his first run by losing a major part of his sparking apparatus.

Then came a really incredible car, manufactured and driven by J. Bond, and surely this was the strangest that hard-bitten Shelsley had ever seen. To be quite honest, a large proportion of those who saw it could not believe that this was a serious racing machine as it appeared to be a child's toy, and was in fact referred to as the " fair-ground special ". Completely unsprung and having front wheel drive, not more than 4-ft. long and 2-ft. high, it leaped up the hill in a series of hops to record 54 seconds dead. The scrutineers on the day previously, requested Mr. Bond to go very slowly up the hill before his practice run was allowed. But to the astonishment of all but the driver and his wife, it performed all the functions required of it exceedingly well, and of course, was accepted. It is nice to know that Laurence Bond has two other 500's, to the unblown formula under construction, which will be finished in a very short space of time and he hopes to compete in some of the 500 Club events this season.

Frank Bacon was very steady in his Austin chassis'd special but found that his gear ratio was not quite right for the hill, in spite of which he went up in 55.78 secs. For the first time out, this was exceedingly good.

★ ★ ★

IN THE PADDOCK

Friday was just every bit as bad as Saturday, in fact as soon as most of the cars had arrived the rain started and it continued on and off all day.

The M.A.C. use an extremely efficient method of giving every competitor three practice climbs, by issuing, as soon as the car has passed the scrutineers, three tickets. Before each run the driver of the car hands up a ticket, thus obviating any question of one driver getting any more than his three practice runs. The only really objectional part of the practice is the fact that one has to queue up throughout the afternoon, and hang about waiting, which, when the day comes is all made very much easier as all the cars are run off class by class.

The pits themselves are extremely good and are well covered with reasonably leak proof corrugated iron sheeting, the only snag being that the floors of the pits are dry mud and once having dropped a nut, bolt, or sundry other bits of motor car, it is extremely difficult to regain them. Several remarks were heard in the 500 pits about bringing fine rakes to the next Shelsley in order to collect some much needed bits. For those who did not have the opportunity of getting into the Paddock, the competitors' bar was right next door to the 500 stables, which considerably eased the minds and the wheels of both drivers and mechanics.

There were three newcomers to 500 c.c. competition. No. 2 on the Shelsley programme being Frank Bacon. This car was described on Page 7 of the May issue. He did remarkably well and as far as was seen did not have any serious teething troubles.

The next new car on the list was No. 6 Stromboli, which was reviewed in the June issue of Iota. There seemed to be an endless buzz of activity around this car more or less continuously the whole time it was in the pit. Troubles mainly consisting of carburation, magneto, and back axle, which caused quite a large amount of midnight oil to be burnt.

Car No. 7 has not previously been described in Iota, so a short description of its construction will be given here, and possibly an article by the owner will be included at a later date. The front end consists of Morgan front suspension with rather large oversize tyres. The back end is a very cleverly converted B.S.A. front, giving

The "Guts" of Jim Bossisto's Buzzie

independent suspension and two universals connected by a splined cross shaft on which are mounted final drive sprocket and brake drum. The chassis is fairly normal, using mild steel channel. The Dirt Track Douglas engine is fitted on a sub frame extended from the back end to the cross member, which drives through a Norton gear box on to the back axle, using a Norton clutch on the kick change gear box.

The gear change itself is worked by a hand lever to which the clutch itself is fitted. The whole car is very light, and the body which is of light alloy is extremely effective.

There is also a very clever form of wind conveyance to the front cylinder head, this being done by forming a type of double under-shield. The car ran reasonably well at Shelsley, but unfortunately it still experiences missing as soon as revs start getting anything over 55, this the builder attributes to fuel and carburation—which no doubt will soon be cured.

The last and certainly the least was No. 8. This incredible little car, built by Mr. Bond, was not built in conformity with the 500 c.c. National Class I formula as drawn up by the 500 Club. This car undoubtedly earned considerable praise for its owner. It has front wheel drive and no suspension, the alloy wheels relying entirely on the tyre section for any springing effect which it might get. It certainly surprised and startled a number of the more serious 500 c.c. builders and made some, I think, feel even a little ashamed. All the 500 c.c. enthusiasts, however, will undoubtedly feel a lot more friendly towards Mr. Bond, when they hear that he has practically completed a car to the 500 c.c. National Class I formula.

* * *

BROUGH, JUNE 28th

The first road race of the 500 Club, organised with the co-operation of the Blackburn Welfare Motor Club, should have attracted 16 entries. However, for one reason or another, only four can manage to get up to Yorkshire. It was very disappointing indeed to a large number of North Countrymen, many of whom were looking forward to their first sight of a 500, when they heard that the event might be scratched.

We have been pursuaded to continue with the meeting, in the hope that it will spread the fever up north, from which part many invitations to race have recently come, but we have cancelled the arrangement to make a film.

The main trouble seems to be that the Calendar is so full of attractive events in the South, where the majority of completed cars reside, that it has been impossible to pursuade the drivers to motor the 400-500 miles to a meeting these hard times.

* * *

FUTURE EVENTS

July 26th, 1947. Cofton Hackett Circuit Race, organised by the Midland Motoring Enthusiasts' Club. The course will consist of four short straights, two S bends, and two hairpins. The track is 50 ft. wide, and three cars will run at the same time, cars being required to cover 3 laps (1½ miles). There will be Heats and Finals.

Entry forms, etc., from :

W. H. Faulkner, Esq., 40 Sandford Road, Moseley, Birmingham, 13.

September 6th, 1947. Sand Races at Filey, Yorks, organised by the Scarborough & District Motor Club. Sprints and races on sand, with two mile-long straights. Entry forms, etc., from :

J. Claxton, Esq., Lancesund, Mill Lane, Cayton Bay, Scarborough, Yorks.

Sunday, 10th August, 1947. Southampton Car Club Speed Hill Climb. Further details, entry forms and regulations, from :

R. Bowyer, Esq., 26 Glen Eyre Road, Bassett, Southampton.

Regulations can also be obtained from J. Siddall, Milford House, Lansdown, Bath.

POWER PER LITRE.

No. 3: What a c.c. tax would mean.

Contributed by R. P. Gordon Jones.

Will the c.c. basis of taxation stand close scrutiny ? The answer is, of course, in the negative for, as was shown in the first of these articles, power does not vary directly as the capacity. The larger the cylinders, so inevitably, the lower the power per litre. In other words the c.c. basis discourages the engine with large cylinders—the "big four" type which is not without popularity. To discourage the large cylinder ultimately turns into discouragement of the large engine.

"Stromboli" at Shelsley 1947 (Photo by John Browning).

For many years there has been a considerable outcry against the R.A.C. rating, primarily on the score that it has prevented the building of reasonably large engines; that the c.c. tax should have been chosen, or even considered, in its place appears paradoxical. Clearly those who put their weight behind such a choice were not studying design.

A few simple calculations will show just the type of engine which such a system will foster under the stress of competition. (In passing, any really moderate form of tax will have an almost negligible influence on design ; but then if it is moderate it might with advantage be nominal and free of any taint—none of us like even the slightest trace of milk in our drinking water).

Take the modern 8 h.p. (R.A.C.) engine : 57 by 93 mms. ; 950 c.c.'s ; giving 30 b.h.p. at 4,200 r.p.m. with a b.m.e.p. of 100 lbs. per square inch. Assuming the tax incidence is the same on 8 h.p. (R.A.C.) as on 950 c.c.'s capacity, the designer has two possible lines of reconstruction : (1) He can produce an engine of the same power, but of greater life expectancy or (2) he can get more power for the same tax, at the cost of longevity. (That looks as though the c.c. basis is advantageous either way, this is partly because we have equated 8 h.p. (R.A.C.) to 950 c.c.'s and partly . . . but wait.)

Taking the first choice : by decreasing the stroke to 80 mms., a bore area of 18½" is obtained ; running the engine at the same r.p.m. and maintaining the b.m.e.p. at 100 pounds per square inch (there should be no difficulty here) the same power is on speed of 2,200 feet per minute in place of 2,500 feet per minute.

(It is a rather unfortunate trait of this country that we speak of capacity in litres, bore area in inches, bore diameter and stroke, invariably in mms. and piston speed in feet per minute. The use, however, of the same measure throughout would render some of these terms almost meaningless to most and cause the writer, at any rate, to turn to his slide rule for translation.)

By all standards the above is a more pleasant power unit than its predecessor. Unfortunately it does not represent an economical utilization of 950 c.c.'s, when each c.c. may cost 2½d. More power can be claimed.

In taking the second line the designer can increase the r.p.m. to 5,000—probably the present day practical limit—shorten the stroke to 67 mms. and extract 36½ b.h.p. Such an engine would have a stroke-bore ratio of 1 : 1 ; a power per litre of 38½ b.h.p. and an R.A.C. rating of 11 h.p. It illustrates well the opposite swing of the pendulum. It has the complementary, and equally nasty, ingredients found in those engines reared by the R.A.C. tax ; and the sterner the competition the nastier it is likely to become, for such an engine will not run into the limiting piston speed for another 1,000 r.p.m. And the chief criticism of this unit is aimed at its r.p.m.

A high rotational rate is very injurious to the life of the valves, distortion and stretch cause loss of compression, excessive guide wear, hard starting, noise, an engine which loses " tune ". The desire to maintain the b.m.e.p. calls for increases in valve overlap for, although the piston speed is modest, the " time " period is very short This valve spread creates a brittle type of engine : starting will require a rich setting to compensate for the low gas velocity and a high speed of turning to compensate for the low nominal compression ratio, outcome of a late inlet valve closing point. This characteristic will live through the speed range, and case-harden out what little elasticity the small unit might have had.

The increase in speed will excite sympathy to vibrate in engine, chassis and body components which previously lay above the synchronous range. The short stroke, together with the small cylinder, make insoluble the problem of combining good combustion shape, high compression ratio, and adequate bronchial tubes. Indeed, the whole question of obtaining a satisfactory compromise between combustion chamber space, valve area and required compression ratio, is fraught with interest without the added complication of the concertina effect of very small stroke-bore ratios. The combustion space for the suggested unit, with a 7–1 compression ratio, would only be some 40 c.c.'s, and this must be considered in conjunction with a piston area of 35 square centimetres.

An increase in maximum bearing load—on a basis of pounds per square inch of piston area—of some 20% is paid by the high speed unit. This is due to the fact that weight of reciprocating parts increases faster than the square of the bore and also to the fact that although the stroke has been reduced the r.p.m. have been increased —and the maximum load varies directly as the stroke, but as the square of the r.p.m. This, however, is no reason why the *specific* bearing load should be higher as the increase in bore diameter permits an increase in bearing length.

The Aikens Machine minus Body
by courtesy of the Light Car

None of these disadvantages are any more than just that—disadvantageous. Furthermore, they are not levelled at the short stroke engine *per se*. However, under the c.c. tax system, short stroke engines would come to be operated in just this manner and although, at first sight, it might appear that we would receive more b.h.p. per pound sterling than before, this would have no lasting value. Should someone tomorrow produce a one litre car capable of fulfilling all that the present day two-and-a-half litre can accomplish, and should all the population invest in such a car, then the tax incidence would immediately be shifted to once again bring the motorist's contribution back to its previous level.

There is, in fact, no " through " road, *via* design, to tax evasion ; such a road, once the financial dust has settled, is but another cul-de-sac.

ERIC BRANDON

Peter Garnie has very kindly consented to produce an original painting of one 500 each month. This painting will be available to the owner concerned. For the first month the 500 King of the moment was chosen as the subject.

CLUB NEWS AND GOSSIP

By the Secretary, J. O. H. Siddall,
Milford House,
Lansdown, Bath.

The Annual General Meeting has now been fixed for Saturday, December 13th, at the Surbiton Corporation Assembly Rooms at 4.00 p.m. The Annual Dinner will be held in the same building at 7.30 for 8.00 p.m. and arrangements have been made by Councillor Brandon, to have an extension applied for until 12 midnight. During the evening, Mr. Curtis of Antone's will be showing his complete films of the 500's up to date, and this season's racing films, all of which should make a remarkably good evening.

(By courtesy of the Auto Car)

Gerald Spink's motor rumoured for sale

Surbiton is on the best service line from London, and there should be no difficulty about travel, however late the hour. Tickets will be limited to the statutory 100, and will be £1 0s. 0d. sold in strict order of receipt. If there is an overwhelming demand, then we shall have a buffet supper, reduce the price and throw away our forks. Such are the laws of England. Details are being mailed to all Members.

The meeting of the North Eastern Centre will be reported elsewhere but at the time of writing, our President, Mr. S. C. H. Davis, has found that he is unfortunately unable to be present. Whilst on the subject of the activities of the North East, a most welcome letter has just been received from Mr. Leavy of the Blackburn Aircraft Motor Club. He says, " we are considering plans for the future so that as soon as the basic petrol ration is restored, we can continue to hold race meetings on the aerodrome here. Despite our disappointment earlier this year, we should still like to see some 500 cars on our circuit which we consider emminently suitable for them. Since approaching you previously, we have held another very successful motor cycle meeting on October 5th, during which, the lap record was put up to 60.3 m.p.h. by George Brown on a 500 Norton, so that you will see that despite its small size (0.65 miles), it is not a slow circuit.

" Again, we should like to include the 500 cars during a Motor cycle meeting as a start, and possibly if sufficient 500's become available, we might consider a ' car only ' meeting, later on."

Well, there you are, North Countrymen, let us see if we cannot have a decent turn out next year, to make up for our failure to appear this season. The track is a honey and has been approved by the R.A.C.

Without doubt, the greatest news which has burst upon the 500 world is the decision of the Federation Internationale de l'Automobile to include in the new International Formula 2 a special class for supercharged racing cars up to 500 c.c. This is recognition with a vengeance ! When it is recalled that it is scarcely 13 months ago that the 500 Club's fight for recognition was at its height, as we were then considered to be dabblers in slightly grown up toys, the startling fact that members of a poor man's racing Club find themselves possessing the ingredients of the most up-to-date Grand Prix racing car is an astounding achievement unparalleled in racing history.

I humbly submit that this reflects great credit on the founders of the movement and the 500 Club.

Doubt is expressed as to whether there will be any new blown 500's forthcoming to compete with the unblown " up to 2 litre " cars next season, but there is nothing to prevent certain mods. being made to our existing National Class cars, to enable them to compete on pretty equal terms with the big stuff on a power to weight ratio. One thing is certain, however, when the " 2 stage blown 500's " make their appearance, we shall retire into the shell of our National Class again, and what is still more likely, we shall howl for protection. Still and but, it would be nice to be a real Grand Prix Racer for a season.

Personalia

Welcome to England, member No. 1. Roy Clarkson will be robbing Scotland of their one Iota 500, as he has now settled down in Halstead, and bought himself an Elizabethan Mansion complete with Ghost ! according to Alex Bruce. We have certainly gained an experienced dicer and enthusiast ; we shall see at least a pair of Iotas in Southern events next season.

I hear that Gerald Spink is embarking on another special, but in order to do so, will have to part with his first one. He is also prepared to help with starting a centre of the Club in London. All those who are interested should write to him at Flat 2, 9, Avenue Elmers, Surbiton, Surrey.

Lord Strathcarron went out for a merry dice the other day in his newly acquired Marwyn. Unfortunately he forgot about a really nasty pot hole which should have been approached at a tick-over. The story goes that he negotiated it at full chat, was airborne for 40 feet, and was visibly in full flight, half a mile away. Fortunately neither the driver nor the car were very seriously damaged although Strathcarron received a bang which gave him delayed concussion.

Major Persse is off to Canada in the new year, and is contacting a number of enthusiasts over there, in order to start up the Canadian Centre of the Club.

Lt.-Colonel Goldie Gardner has been having a high time in London just lately. The R.A.C. gave a reception for him and John Cobb in honour of their amazing record attempts. We hope Goldie will be able to come to our Dinner too.

YOUR 500 c.c. CAR

By A. C. H. Harding, Technical Panel Secretary

The question of brakes.

Brakes, without any doubt, form the most important detail of any vehicle enjoying any measure of free movement relative to mankind, his property or living creatures in general.

We have come to regard brakes as just methods of preventing unwanted progress; a pedal which when stamped upon, unquestionably prevents the accident. When, for any reason whatsoever, the brakes do not perform the task required of them, their owners shower all manner of old English sayings upon them—if they are still in a fit state to do so. Seldom, if ever, does the driver ask himself whether he has carried out the few adjustments necessary to enable this invaluable item of equipment to carry out its job in the way its designers intended it to do.

When we approached the subject from the 500 c.c. Car designer's angle, we ask ourselves firstly, just what we expect our brakes to do and secondly, how best to enable them to do it.

The task of stopping an ultra-light weight racing car, which has attained a speed of, shall we say, one hundred miles per hour, is not at all easy. It is far less easy if deceleration is coupled with a time limit, limited space and another vehicle doing precisely the same thing within a few feet, each driver hoping that the other will give way and allow him a good position for the nasty corner at the end of the straight.

The potential racing driver should realise that a speed of one hundred miles per hour represents almost the speed he would attain if he jumped from an aeroplane without a parachute, from a height of say, five hundred feet.

Let us consider some of the qualities we expect from our braking system. From a purely mechanical angle it is abvious that deceleration imposes a tremendous torque on the suspension units and their anchorage or mountings ; more severe than that caused by the most violent acceleration. We must, therefore, ensure that these stresses are suitably catered for in the mountings which have to cope with them but—if these items are not to weigh more than necessary, then our brake system must be so designed that the torque on the components concerned is applied smoothly. Again, it is equally obvious that the loading must be shared evenly between the wheels on either side of the car.

Now for the actual driving and steering side of the matter. A maximum rate of deceleration which may be expressed in terms of " G " or the force of gravity implies that a state of slip between tyres and track has almost been reached. This condition reduces the handling qualities of a car to a point where the slightest fault, snatch or unbalance between the brakes on opposite sides of the car will produce a serious skid with subsequent loss of control and waste of valuable seconds.

Assuming that a vehicle is equipped with brakes capable of retarding its progress in a satisfactory way, that is, smoothly and evenly ; the question of reliability raises its ungainly head. Years of research work have enabled brake designers to produce equipment which does not " fade." The ability of brakes to go on working under the gruelling conditions caused by continual fierce application depends on designand manufacture in the same way that high speed reliability can be designed and built into an engine unit.

Because the application of brakes has been, generally speaking, one of the driving jobs which calls for muscular effort on the part of the driver, it stands to reason that this effort must be kept to a bare minimum if the desired results are to be achieved without fatigue. In races of any length, physical fatigue may be the deciding factor and any saving of a driver's strength by good braking design may more than affect the disadvantage of a few miles per hour less maximum speed.

If we sum up the points just mentioned, we realise that our brakes must incorporate all the advantages offered by good design and robust manufacture coupled with the lowest weight possible. They must be capable of frequent applications without any increase in the power needed to apply them ; they must absorb a large amount of energy and convert it into heat without loss of efficiency ; they must operate with a minimum of effort on the part of the driver ; they must weigh the least possible and yet remain comparatively simple to install and service.

There is one point which deserves mention before we leave our list of desirable features, and one which is often passed over by designers and builders of " Specials." In many cases the parts are adapted to fit the specials, but some sort of modification is hurriedly carried out " for just one car only." There is often a very serious if unconscious tendency, to " design out " all the maker's accessibility and simplicity in an attempt to make unsuitable components do something that they were never designed to do. Far better to put up with a few extra pounds in weight than to provide your machine with mutilated " touring " components at the expense of reliability and easy replacement.

So much for the things we expect from our braking systems ; let us see what steps can be taken to get the desired results and briefly refresh our minds with the points of design that our brake manufacturing friends have made available over a period of development covering a considerable number of years.

The simplest form of brake that the special builder is ever likely to be concerned with consists of a pair of brake shoes swinging about a common pivot at one end and provided with a simple cam to force the opposite ends apart, so bringing the friction surfaces of the shoes in rubbing contact with the inner surface of a drum attached to the rotating wheel in the usual way.

The operation of the cam by rod or cable and later by " Bowden " type cable assemblies enabled this brake to remain popular with some car manufacturers for a great number of years.

This type of brake construction forms the basis upon which the majority of modern brake designs are based and even in its simple form is capable of a reasonable range of usefulness providing that suitable provision to balance the separate assemblies is incorporated in the chassis layout.

The next development step was to introduce methods of adjusting the ends of the shoes remote from the operating cams to facilitate accurate positioning of the shoes and thereby reduce the amount of lost travel in the operating system. Many modifications were built into the brakes of different car builders and as was to be expected the thoughts of many were concentrated on the provision of braking systems which are now universally referred to as " servo systems." Many and varied were the methods adopted ; some designers introduced a third " servo " shoe whilst others proved that power taken from the vehicle's transmission system could be made to apply the brakes without the expenditure of much of the driver's energy.

Millington on arrival at Towcester, 1947.

Many large commercial vehicles were designed to make use of manifold suction, small vacuum pumps and compressors to actuate pistons which were placed in positions where they could add the required power to enable the weaker drivers to decelerate heavy vehicles without fatigue.

Whatever system of braking was incorporated in cars, it became obvious that a very careful balancing of the braking effort of the different wheels was necessary if the final result was to be satisfactory. This necessity prompted the inclusion of more and more cabled rods and pulley arrangements and in some cases elaborate designs of numerous levers to ensure that each brake would do its job.

The next major advance was hydraulic operation of the brake shoes. This method of operation was greeted with mixed feelings by some of the old motoring " diehards," but it quickly established its place in the car world and has now become " the thing " or the operation of the brakes on some of the fastest cars in existence

Next month's issue will contain a further article on brakes and braking and it is hoped that suitable drawings and sketches will be included.

THE ANNUAL GENERAL MEETING

On December 13th, at the Assembly Rooms at Surbiton, Surrey, about seventy members crammed themselves into a somewhat small room, in the afternoon prior to the Annual Dinner, to attend the First Annual General Meeting of the 500 Club.

The President, Mr. S. C. H. Davis, was in the Chair, and in addition to the Officers and a large proportion of the retiring Committee, there were in attendance the following notable people.

Vice-President F. J. Findon, Editor of the " Light Car."
Mr. and Mrs. C. I. Craig, all the way from Jersey.
Major Persse, the future Canadian Secretary.
R. R. Jackson, a Founder Member of the Technical Panel of the Bristol era, and a dozen well-known builders and drivers of 500's.

Far reaching decisions were taken at this meeting, affecting not only the re-organisation of the Club, but three items of the National Class Formula. Here they are in brief, make a note of them.

THE CLUB. New Officers and a Main Committee were elected, based on the general approval that a British Club of an International nature should have its head-quarters in London.

Patron : The Rt. Hon. The Earl Howe, P.C., C.B.E., V.D.
President : S. C. H. Davis, Esq.
Vice-Presidents : F. J. Findon, L. H. Pomeroy, Raymond Mays.
Secretary : J. F. Gale.
Temporary and Assistant Secretary : J. O. H. Siddall.
Temporary Hon. Treasurer : M. A. Nedham.
Main Committee : J. Cooper, C. H. Strang, G. Spink, Cdr. G. A. Yorke, R.N., R. V. Palmer, N. Mulligan, J. O. H. Siddall, R. D. Caesar, B. E. Martin, I. K. Gough, A. H. G. Butler, M. A. Nedham, A. C. H. Harding.

It was unanimously decided, that the existing (Bristol) organisation should carry on until the London Centre can be formed. The Officers of each sub-Centre shall be ex-officio members of the Main Committee, and the Main Committee shall meet quarterly in the various districts in which centres are active. This of course is in addition to the meetings of the Main working Committee.

In about three months therefore, the Bristol pioneers will become the South-western Centre of the Club. Mr. Gale will then take over the reins of the Secretary-ship, and appoint a Treasurer.

SUBSCRIPTIONS. The Annual Subscription will be raised in 1948, to £2 2s. 0d. which shall cover the existing amenities of the Club, and the free issue of the Iota Magazine to members, every month. This reluctant but unanimous decision was reached because the present cost to the Club per Member was 31s. 9d. It was very necessary to put the Club on a sound financial footing, in view of the future activities, which would include the organisation of Races. Further, it was desirable that the issue of the IOTA Magazine should remain a part of the Club's service, and not a separate item one could buy for an additional subscription.

Members who have joined the Club between September 27th (Shelsley), 1947, and December 31st, remain unaffected by the rise in subscriptions which entitles them to membership until December, 1948.

This group is a few of the members who attended the Annual General Meeting at Surbiton. Unfortunately, there are one or two members who are unknown to us, and if they will send their names to the Editor, our records can be completed.

From left to right.—
John Siddall, Colin Strang, S. Edwards, ? ? ? Eric Brandon, W. L. Grose, John Cooper, ? C. A. Yorke, C. Lang, L. B. T. Stallwood, C. Cooper.

★ ★ ★

FORMULA.

Tank Size. Item 3 of the Regulations of the National 500 c.c. Class should be altered to read " UNLIMITED."

In races organised by the Club for Members only, some form of handicapping by means of limited fuel supplies may easily be introduced. The exact amount depends on the length and nature of the course, and this condition can be inserted as a supplementary regulation.

Brakes. Item 7 of the Regulations of the National 500 c.c. Class, should be altered to read : " Efficient means of braking on all 4 wheels, with an independent means of operation of the brake shoes of either Front or Rear pair of wheels."

Bodies. The Committee is to draw up a Ruling on this subject. Some sort of enclosed bodywork will be required, even if it is only canvas. All the builders at the meeting agreed that full, or half chassis on view, will not be acceptable in future.

The revised Formula is therefore as follows :—

1. ENGINES
Unsupercharged 500 c.c.

2. FUEL
Any type.

3. FUEL TANKS
Any capacity.

4. MINIMUM WEIGHT
500 lbs. Unladen Wet Weight.

Reprinted by permission of the Autocar.

THOUGHTS ABOUT 500 c.c. CARS

ADVICE ON THE MORE OBVIOUS MISTAKES IN DESIGN AND CONSTRUCTION

By S. C. H. Davis

Now that several excellent performances have been put up by the first of the 500 c.c.-engined racing cars, it may help to carry the matter a short stage further in regard to design and construction, because enthusiasm is not enough to guarantee success.

The point is that these cars must be well designed, for anything really bad, however inadvertant the errors, may give the whole class a bad name. Therefore I strongly advise the constructor to plan the chassis properly. Much time is saved, for example, if a general arrangement drawing is prepared before manufacture starts, because that gives a clear idea of what is necessary, whilst introducing quite early those little problems which may cause endless expense if not tackled at a very early stage.

Doubtless the main components will be obtained from outside suppliers, even if some alteration may be necessary afterwards, and that economizes time greatly. But all makers of components have general arrangement drawings available, so the whole chassis can be assembled on the drawing board. Even so one or two points must be borne in mind the whole time, points that need a rigid restraint lest eagerness to see the vehicle in being leads to the use of unsuitable material or incorrect design.

The success of the car depends upon the fact that it will sit down properly on the road and possess a natural stability at full speed. It is useless to contrive a machine which remains on the road only by reason of its driver's exceptional skill plus hard work with the steering. Equally with the land speed record cars, these little machines must be able to hold themselves straight within a reasonable limit. There is considerable freedom as to the proportion of track to wheelbase which will produce this result. Yet advice from someone who has many years' designing experience with cars is likely to be of benefit on this matter.

Importance of Steering Layout

The geometry of the steering is a matter which repays deep thought and also benefits from the advice of experience, since on the successful solution of this problem everything depends. By taking the stub axle axis pins and imagining that the pin has a line drawn through its centre and prolonged, one finds the important point at which this line would touch the road relative to the centre of the tread of the tyre. If the two are too close the steering is unduly sensitive ; if too far apart the car will be heavy to handle and possess a will of its own.

Apart from this, the upper end of the axis pin should be nearer to the driver than the lower end, to give caster action. On this angle depends the fact that the wheels prefer to travel in the straight-ahead position, but too much angle brings wheel flap, which is deadly, while too little destroys the automatic stability of the machine ; a reverse angle makes the car highly dangerous at speed.

Obviously the constructor would know that a tie in front of the axle is in tension and one behind the axle in compression, but a seemingly small point often escapes attention, in that the socket at each end of the tie-rod for the ball joints on the steering arms should rest on the ball and not hang from it, in order to avoid any chance of the rod falling off, particularly when the car is older and the ball or joint may be worn. The same applies to the fore and aft rod, which should rest on the drop-arm ball joint rather than hang from it. And there is a great deal to be said for a fore and aft rod parallel with the chassis side-member, rather than one carried athwartwise, which sometimes tends to induce wheel flap and generally gives a spongy feeling to the steering itself. Remember that the front axle moves up and down against the springs, but that this movement must have the minimum effect on the steering for obvious reasons.

The Power Unit of the Monaco

Again, it is never wise to use too much old material, however inexpensive and convenient it may be. Steel, like man but unlike wine, does not improve with age. The small crystals of which it is composed alter their character as a result of age and impact, until what had been a strong beam is all set to fracture.

Do not be tempted to make ball joints and sockets for the steering yourself, but obtain them from a maker of repute, for however handy one may be with a lathe it is all too easy to make an error in the character of the steel used, and if so be a ball joint is made of high carbon steel and then case hardened it will be glass hard all the way through and all too ready to snap off. It pays very often to polish the drop-arm and steering arms, the better to discover any cracks therein.

Weight Distribution and Braking

Weight distribution is a very big factor in road-holding, so avoid the temptation to make the car look fascinatingly fast by pushing the front axle too far forward relative to the radiator. Remember that the weight is thrown forward on to the front axle when the brakes act, and the more weight per wheel the better the adhesion and the stronger the brake power available.

For a vehicle of 500 c.c. there might be some merit in the crab track—that is, a narrower track for the rear than for the front wheels—because the shorter the rear axle the stronger it is. But do not be tempted to play with odd radius rods or torque tubes. More than one man has contrived that the rear axle must move in an arc controlled by two centres, which is catastrophic. Chain drive, incidentally, may make it a little more difficult to evolve a really strong back axle, but chain drive offers excellent advantages in the construction of these small cars.

Suspension, though important, often has to be of the type that the layout dictates, in spite of what one may wish to use, and remember that to make independent suspension in front successful is a good deal easier than to contrive a successful independent suspension for all four wheels.

Brakes are important, naturally, but do not economise too much in weight by trying to be ingenious with very small drums, even if there is no differential. And do not design a brake of your own ; the suppliers' article is the result of years of experience. Probably the simplest layout means operation by rods with independent adjustment for each set of brakes and no compensation, but, again, the layout must not fight against the steering.

Isolate the Fuel Tank

The fuel tank needs sufficient thought to avoid encouraging a bad fire if anything happens. If you can avoid placing the tank directly above the carburettor, so much the better, but in any case isolate it from vibration and make sure that the fuel pipes can flex without breaking, while the fuel tap should be within reach of the driver if that is at all possible.

Welding is another trouble. All kinds and manner of men find that acetylene or electric welding is easy ; but quite a number of them do not remember that to heat metal intensely is to change its character and strength, with the result that what looks a good welded joint becomes in fact the weakest part of the work.

Room to Move

In the layout of the cockpit give yourself room to sit naturally with all controls handy, avoiding those items which are likely to be unpleasant to contact if you do make a mistake.

All this does not cover real design, but the object is merely to point out one or two mistakes which have appeared in designs in the past and marred otherwise excellent machines. Avoid at all costs some skimped job, to rectify which would involve a task of extreme weariness, and remember to lock every single thing which is likely to come loose. Make sure of every fuel and water joint and study detail. Just as one small example, if the fuel tank has to be filled in a hurry as much air has to come out as fuel goes in, so that a small filler and a large funnel are not the correct answer.

LIVE LETTERS

"Emerald Isle,"
Crescent Road,
Lutterworth,
Near Rugby, Warwickshire.
20th January, 1948.

Dear Sir,

I wish to make a few comments on the revised 500 c.c. formula, which to me is not altogether quite clear.

Item 3—Fuel of any capacity seems to me to be the only solution, but why certain regulations should be included to limit the capacity in certain cases would seem very unfair to certain entrants who may have motors more thirsty than others.

Item 4.—Minimum weight. This also needs some explanation. Does 500 lbs. unladen wet weight cover water-cooled engines only or does it include petrol and oil as well ? If the latter, this surely opens a wide field for car builders with money and facilities to bring the weight of their cars well below the average. For example, a car with a 10-gallon fuel tank and 2-gallon oil tank would actually only weigh approximately 410 lbs. less fuel and oil and would, therefore, appear to me to be a loop-hole in this particular section of the formula.

Comments on this subject would be appreciated from you or any of the Members.

Yours faithfully,

A. Martin.

* * *

Ashleigh,
Romilly Rd., Cardiff.
27th February, 1948.

Dear Sir,

On reading the February number of IOTA, I was interested in the paragraph by Mr. J. O. Siddall concerning the badge of the 500 Club. I am sure that most members of the Club will enjoy "sporting" the 500 Car Club Badge when they duly arrive. But in these days of "basic uncertainty" and for those who do not own cars to "sport" the badge on, is it possible to obtain miniature badges of brass and enamel so that members may wear them in their coats, etc.

They seem to be easily obtained since most of the R.A.F. Squadrons have them, as do other services and clubs.

Yours faithfully,

(Sgd.) W. M. Harrison Woodrouffe.

* * *

The 500 Club Car Badges are now in the process of being finished. The makers, Messrs. Marples & Beasley, Ltd., have promised them by April or May.

Hooper's Cottage,
Leigh Sinton,
Nr. Malvern, Worcs.

Dear Sir,

I was extremely interested in Mr. Woolley's letter in the December issue and it may be of interest to him that I have (on paper) a Scott engined " 500."

Considering the '39 Scott Clubman would do about 90 then it wouldn't be unreasonable to expect it to give a useful speed in a suitable " chassis."

I imagine a Clubman engine would cost a packet, too !

Like Mr. Woolley I am rather concerned about that !

I shall definitely fit my own " 500 " with a neat aluminium single seat racing body and very definitely Lockheed brakes.

In my opinion the 500 Class has *not* been boosted by those blokes who would race without a decent body to cover the bits and pieces if nothing else. I am pleased to see there is now a ruling on this.

Can anyone tell me why a diff. should *not* be fitted except as a weight-saving factor ?

Yours sincerely,
(Sgd.) S. S. Smith.

*   *   *

26, Mansfield Avenue,
Weston-s.-Mare,
Som.
18th January, 1948.

Dear Sir,

In wishing you and the Club success and greetings for 1948, I must apologise for my delay in writing to you. Thank you for your help with my difficulty arising from Mr. Bosisto's article. On looking through the IOTA Magazine, I have noticed that there have been no photographs of the specials built by Mr. Clarkson and Mr. Bond. I often wonder why ? My special is progressing and with no snags arising, I shall have it finished by June. Work is limited to weekends because of my late hours at my job. I have a difficulty which I find very hard to overcome. When I purchased my Sturmey Archer engine I noticed that an oil pump and rocker box were missing. I cannot obtain spares from the large " spares " firms. Do you think that you know any m/c enthusiast who has any " gen " on Sturmey Archer racing engines, or can you please find out the address of the Sturmey Archer Co. ? Local m/c dealers cannot help me at all. If you have any forms for a competition licence I would be glad if you would forward me one of them.

Thanking you in anticipation,
Yours faithfully,
(Sgd.) M. F. Matthews.

Answer to the above question. Would Mr. Clarkson please oblige ? Mr. Bond and his cars are not members, as they do not comply with the Formula.

With regard to your engine information—will some member please oblige ?

EDITOR.

This month's reproduction of Peter Garnier's work is of Colin Strang in his famous little motor. What will he do this Season ?

LUTON HOO—THE EVENT

By R. D. Cæsar.

Eric Brandon had the distinction of making the first competitive run of the season. If it lacked the fire we often saw last year, it was a very competent effort all the same and took only 93.5 seconds.

Cooper followed in his new car and drove on the limit of control with great dash and determination. It looked decidedly faster than Brandon and was in fact the fastest Class I climb of the day in 89.57 secs. The two Cooper exponents seem to have exchanged roles during the winter !

An announcement that Frank Bacon could not run introduced Lord Strathcarron and the latest Marwyn, engined like the Coopers with a J.A.P. Strathcarron has shown himself to have a good heavy foot and his runs promised to be interesting. Naturally he is not yet as much at home in his car as the Cooper drivers and his performance accordingly had a less practical look, but he got up in 97.7 secs. which was faster than a good many larger cars.

Hartwell in the Monaco came next. The small size of the car and the hearty smack of the Norton exhaust after the crackle of the J.A.P.'s gave a great impression of speed and the car was undoubtedly going very well. After the roundabout at the top, however, something went wrong with an upward gearchange and the time was 96.48 secs.

Sir Francis Samuelson came last in another new Marwyn and had an unlucky run. He cut off too early for the first corner, cut in again, ran wide on the later corners and generally seemed to be having one of those runs where nothing goes right. Even his engine didn't seem quite happy.

Among the larger cars that followed it was interesting to notice how many failed to beat the better 500's and to find that the doyen of them all, Clutton's gigantic Itala, twenty-four times their size and forty times their age could just about compete with them on equal terms !

After the interval Brandon made a fine clean run with no fireworks and knocked exactly a second off his time. Cooper followed with another very fast run steadier than his first but .03 secs. slower.

Strathcarron made a poor getaway but afterwards diced with great vigour to make up for it. The Marwyn seemed to hop about rather more than the Coopers and he was pretty busy with the steering wheels, particularly during a very fast descent through the "esses."

Considering the bad start 94.12 secs. was good going and after more practice he should run the Coopers close, especially if the Marwyn can be made a bit more stable.

Hartwell in the Monaco made another fast and steady run, cutting each bend smoothly right in the gutter. There was no more trouble with the gearchange and the time came down to 94 secs. dead. The Monaco is a car to watch ; its ingenious and original chassis layout seems to work remarkably well. In sprints it just seems to lack the last horsepower or two, but in a race of any length, it might take a great deal of beating.

Then came Samuelson. Determined to get it right this time he made an excellent start—came cracking down the course and into the first bend with hardly a lift of the foot. It looked as if he might almost make it, but the tail came out too far to be recalled and he stopped facing his own dust. His Luton Hoo-Doo had got him again. Well, we all have days like that, especially at the beginning of the season.

Richard Dimbleby, John Shuter and Dick Caesar (left to right) standing round the microphone making the recording for the programme "Down Your Way", broadcast on Sunday the 21st March, at 10.30 a.m. Mr. Dimbleby, as you know, did the interrogation and between him and Dick Caesar they managed to get in a remarkable amount of information about the Movement, as a whole. It is surprising the number of enquiries we have received as a result of this broadcast addressed direct to the 500 Club, Bristol. It is also interesting to note that the address was interpreted correctly at the G.P.O.

The corner looked a very sporting one for drivers and the combination of fairly high speed with a rather dumpy surface made it an excellent place to do some field work on suspension. The fact that the best of brakes and steering only work when the wheels are touching the ground was nicely demonstrated by many and cars like Richardson's Riley showed how well softish I.F.S. does keep the wheels down. The 500's have a difficult problem here owing to their low total weight, and development must aim at still softer springs and lighter unsprung masses.

Excellent as these sprint meetings are we come away from each more convinced than ever of the urgency of starting some kind of circuit racing where every member who has a serviceable car can compete unharassed at first by the need to entertain the public and encouraged by a small and sympathetic audience of fellow members.

The search for circuits is priority one and *everyone's* job.

HAVE A GO

by John Bolster

Designing " Specials " is the greatest fun in the world. All you need is a piece of paper, a pencil, and a lively imagination. You might just as well incorporate all the latest ideas while you are about it. Of course, you will have independent front suspension and all the best people have torsion bars, don't they ? A De Dion rear end would be nice, wouldn't it ? A superbly streamlined body will give you that New Look, because you couldn't be seen in a rough looking thing like a Shelsley Special, and altogether this business of designing racing cars is pretty easy for a talented young chap like you.

Yes, designing 'em is un morceau de gâteau, but building 'em is quite another thing. You and I know the formulæ for calculating the length of a torsion bar, but who is going to pay for splining the ends of the thing ? Those forgings for the wishbones and steering arms will look beautiful when they are polished, and by the time we have made all those bushes, reamed and fitted them, and organised that geometrically perfect rack and pinion steering, we will be much poorer, and much older. After all that, the thought of all those tubes and joints and splines and things which compose the Margins De Dion's rear end will fill you with alarm and despondency. I once saw a most interesting picture, which had nothing whatever to do with motorcars, labelled " easy to draw but hard to get ", and that slogan should at all times be in the designer's mind.

If you have a great deal of money, unlimited workshop equipment, all the time in the world, and then a lot more money, you will be able to build the kind of " Special " that I should like to build. If, on the other hand, you are very poor, have to work for your living, and own a spanner and a screwdriver, you would be well advised to leave those higher flights of fancy alone and give birth to the crude sort of " Special " that I have perpetrated.

" Bloody Mary " is my pride and joy, and I wouldn't swop her for all the Maseratis or Alfas, but it must be admitted that when one sets oneself the task of producing for £70 a car to take on the £2,000 brigade, one has to abandon all the more elaborate features of design, and the resulting vehicle may lack none of the glamour of " a real one."

My car is propelled by two 1925 J.A.P. twin cylinder engines, which cost me £12 10s. 0d. each. I have, of course, played with these engines to some extent, but even so the power developed is much less than that of any supercharged racing car. Accordingly, I had to achieve the desired performance by making a carriage of approximately half the weight of my competitors, and as I couldn't afford expensive light alloys, the only method of making it twice as light was to make it twice as small.

My two litre car is therefore smaller than most " 500's," and weighs some 7 cwts. ready for the road. Another thing on which I concentrated was keeping down the frontal area ; and this necessitates squeezing the driver into an extremely small space very adjacent to the machinery. The discomfort is more than worth while, though, because the maximum speed is extremely satisfactory, to say the least. Old " Bloody " was, of course, built very many years ago, and her rather spidery appearance has not the voluptuous curves of the modern racers, but I still think she has a fierce and purposeful look about her which would be spoilt if I modernised her.

The gearbox is an old Sturmey Archer that I bought for £7 10s. 0d., but it has had to be modified to take the power of the two engines. The standard pinions were perfectly adequate once one had moved off, but a really fierce getaway sometimes chewed a tooth or two off the cogs. Accordingly, some very special pinions were secured by back door methods, and overcame that weakness.

The clutch was, at first, a constant source of worry, and we even had to fit new plates for each run at Shelsley. Eventually, we found that the trouble could be cured by enormously strong springs and very careful assembly. The important

Stirling Moss—Prescott, 1948.

thing is not only to make the clutch grip, but to make sure that it frees completely. If the clutch does not free instantly, heat will be generated, and once the clutch gets hot it will give trouble. It is essential that normal freeing of the clutch should cause the springs to become coil bound, i.e., go up solid. That is the only way to ensure that it doesn't behave like a swash plate at speed. A careful check must be made to ascertain that all the springs have exactly the same length when fully compressed (their free length is of minor importance). I have a grinding rig on a high speed drill for the Ferodo plates, which consists of a disc to which emery cloth can be stuck. I grind the Ferodo inserts most carefully, stopping at once if they warm up, and I do not allow a variation of more than .002". I have also put a spring steel band round the outside of the clutch to stop it from opening up like a cauliflower, and it is now 100% reliable.

The solid axle is a highly debatable point of design, and I don't think that its best friend would deny that it is at a disadvantage on sharp corners. The whole point about it is that it consists of a bar of steel with a wheel on each end, and that is so much cheaper than any other form of construction that it must commend itself to the impoverished amateur manufacturer. Chain drive is a convenient method of transmission, but it has a bad reputation for reliability. It is absolutely essential that the geometry of the rear suspension shall ensure that the tension of the chain does not tighten or loosen on spring deflection. Furthermore, axle location must be much more rigidly carried out than is usually the case, or the theoretical geometry will not be achieved. It is extremely easy to calculate the forces involved by elementary mathematics, and if a suitable chain size is chosen for the power and weight of the car, absolute reliability will be secured.

A good deal of nattering has taken place about bodies on " Specials," and personally I think that the object of a racing car is to go like blazes, and who cares what it looks like when it is standing still. Panel bashing is an extremely specialised job and the knack definitely cannot be acquired without expert tuition and long practice. To have an elaborately shaped body built professionally is a most expensive undertaking, and I certainly wouldn't spend money on the bodywork at the expense of the machinery department. Herr Uhlenhant has stated that over the standing kilometre, no streamlined car is as fast as a bare chassis, so don't imagine that that seductive, all enveloping shell you had in mind will do your time up Shelsley any good. Then there's all this bull about wearing white overalls, but I was driving in a red jersey almost before some of you blokes were born, and I don't suppose I'd drive any better if you dressed me up to look like a virgin.

I don't set myself up as being any sort of an expert, because the more one gets mixed up in this racing game, the less one finds one knows. Nevertheless, I have realised that the most important thing in racing is the meticulous preparation of the car. Very few cars in private ownership are as thoroughly prepared as they should be, simply because the classical type of racing machine is such a devil to pull to pieces and put together again. Most racing motorcycles are much better prepared than cars, because they are so much more get-at-able, and one can whip them to bits in a matter of minutes to check the condition of all the most important bits. If you are designing a motorcycle engined " 500," you have every chance of arranging the major components so that their accessibility is up to bike standards.

If you find you have a few pennies to spare, don't waste them on cellulose and chromium plating. Spend as much as you can on buying, or making up, spare parts, because you always break the one bit for which you haven't got a replacement.

To sum up, build yourself a simple, reliable, accessible motor car, and after you've got it dead reliable you might even consider making it go fast. Nothing is so distressing, though, as having a very fast car that nearly always lets you down. I could quite easily make old " Bloody " go a good bit faster, but I have just sufficient self control to resist the desire. In her present tune, she has given me many years of completely reliable dicing, and her bill for replacements has been negligible. I suppose that one day something must wear out or break in one of her marvellous old J.A.P. engines, but if they both flew into a thousand pieces tomorrow, I would still be eternally grateful to them for all the fun they have given me.

SHELSLEY—JUNE 12th, 1948

Most outstanding item of interest to Club members at the recent Shelsley meeting was the remarkably good performance put up by John Cooper in his 1,000 c.c. J.A.P.-engined Cooper. He succeeded in making 5th fastest time of the day and also making the fastest time for an un-supercharged car. A really remarkable piece of work.

Bacon—F.H.B. 500, Shelsley, June, 1948. What's bothering him?
(By courtesy of A. R. Coates)

Once again Eric Brandon has succeeded in coming back to the limelight by winning the 500 c.c. class in 44.16 secs. Colin Strang was a very close second with 44.78 secs., and then Lones in " Tiger Kitten " in 46.05 secs.

There were several new cars running, making altogether a total of 11 in the class.

There is no doubt that the 500's are making themselves known in no uncertain fashion. It is rather interesting to compare the times of the winner of the 1,500 c.c. class and the 500 class, the difference being only .51 secs.

It was a great shame that we were unable to get the IOTA Stand to Shelsley due to lack of help at the last moment. Ex-Secretary John Siddall just couldn't take his usual place due to petrol shortage.

PRESCOTT—JUNE 13th, 1948

Here again Cooper in his 1,000 c.c. car lowered the standing record for the 1,500 c.c. class and Eric Brandon succeeded in easily breaking the 50 secs. in the under 750 c.c. class. Lones beat his old rival Colin Strang by .06 secs.

CLIVE LONES AND OTHERS

By GREGOR GRANT, of "The Light Car"

WELL, well, well ! At last the Cooper-Strang stranglehold on B.T.D.'s has been broken, and by a true amateur at that ! At Prescott on May 15th, the tartan shirt came into its own. Clive Lones not only picked up the premier 500 c.c. award, but set up a new class record of 49.98 secs.—to crack 50 secs. for the first time with a D-Wagon.

Now records are what Clive Lones knows about. Some of the newcomers to the business might be interested to learn that our man from St. Melons still holds

Lones, Shelsley, June, 1948. *(By courtesy of A. R. Coates)*

a string of International Class Records with Morgan three-wheelers. These range from things like a hundred miles at 64.09 m.p.h. with a "350," to 86.723 m.p.h., and 101.154 m.p.h. with a "500" and a "750" respectively over five kilos.

So you see the wee man is no stranger to rapid achievements. Wherever there was a chance for some three-wheeler dicing, Lones was there. Donington, Brooklands, Southport—H. C. Lones (Morgan) was a conspicuous and successful performer. When the fast Morgans were doomed to do battle with sidecar outfits, except in events like the late-lamented L.C.C. Relay Race, Lones looked around for some other outlet for his enthusiasm.

"Tiger Cat" was the result, a machine which was as near a four-wheel Morgan as anything else, and which closely resembled the old G.N. idea of a big lusty twin in a lightweight frame. Many folk have thought along the same lines. Frank Spouse fabricated a similar machine for Bo'ness, and, if memory serves me right, I believe Sid Allard had something to do with a Morgan which sprouted a fourth wheel. There were, also, a few lash-ups created for the early Speedway days when anything went, from converted B.S.A. f.w.d.'s, cut-down Riley Nines to Elto marine-engined f.w.d. efforts ; the last-named made a lovely yowl from their two-stroke motors, but were made to look very slow when the four-wheel-drive Skirrows came along.

Anyway, when Caesar and Co. converted pipe dreams to realities, Lones was early in the field with one of Great Britain's two post-war D-wagons. The other was, of course, the Strang. As Clive will readily admit, " Tiger Kitten " in its original form was slightly underpowered and carried a trifle too much weight to see the Harrow projectile off. After all, the Lones effort was nothing more than none-too-new T.T. J.A.P. in a modified Ulster Austin chassis—even to the extent of an electric starter, which actually worked. Nevertheless, the feline device wasn't all that slower than the Vincent-H.R.D.-propelled Strang.

Eventually the glamorous Coopers entered the arena. Both Strang and Lones had to withstand the onslaughts of the Cooper-Brandon set-up, with the flying Winco Frank Aikens also figuring in the struggle. The Iotas began to appear ; the Norton-engined Monaco took shape ; Frank Bacon's F.H.B. was produced ; Spink's G.S.I. was completed ; the Marwyns swelled the entry lists.

In this free-for-all, Strang and the Coopers were the main contenders. Strang would set up B.T.D. ; Brandon would pinch it from him ; John Cooper would snatch some of the honours. Invariably it lay solely between the two marques for the D-wagon bun-fight.

Quietly Lones set about re-creating " Tiger Kitten." The Austin transverse front was chucked away. Clive went back to his first love Morgan for a suspension lay-out. The Kitten underwent a course of slimming, and a 5-stud Speedway J.A.P. motor was procured, from which Clive extracted a lot more poke from its already impressive stableful of horses.

With modest equipment, much hard work, and assistance mainly coming from his wife and daughter, Lones eventually produced a car with a dual personality—Cat or Kitten. With big twin power plant it was, until the advent of the new Cooper " 1000," possibly the fastest unblown eleven-hundred in these islands in sprint events.

The Kitten was nearly right at Poole last year, being only .19 secs. slower than John Cooper's Cooper. His Prescott showing this year has certainly given the boys to think. If anyone had said a year ago that a D-wagon would soon crack the half-century they'd have created the large and derisive guffaw. Why, even the fabulous Lightweight Special hasn't been pushed up under 50 secs ! The magic figures have been cracked just once in the post-war series of Prescott climbs by anyone with a car of under 1,100 c.c. At the same May 15th meeting, Ken Wharton did a remarkable 49.58 secs. with his blown J.3-powered Austin—another triumph for the home-built brigade.

Speaking off-hand, I should say that Lones' 49.98 secs. is the fastest climb ever achieved at Prescott by an unblown car of under 1,500 c.c. Indeed, I can think of only two unblown 2-litres that have bettered this—Frankie Penn (Riley) and the one and only John Vary Bolster (" Bloody Mary ").

I am willing to wager that Lones would welcome the addition of a Junior class to the movement. A 350 c.c. limit would suit him fine. Some of the bike boys might be interested to learn the amount of good solid b.h.p. that Clive has tickled from the smaller edition of the 5-stud J.A.P.

While Lones, Brandon and Strang were having their titanic battle, another D-wagoner took the eye. This was young Moss in his new, cream Cooper. Driving in his very first major speed event, this youngster recorded 51.01 secs., which, not so very long ago, would have been quick enough for a record. Over the difficult Stanmer Park course on June 5th, Moss shocked many of the more experienced hands by running away with the 500 c.c. class with an extraordinary 58.78 secs., to beat Brandon by over half a second. This performance is all the more remarkable, in that only nine folk out of 65 starters beat 59 secs.

Lones' Prescott record was short-lived. At the Bugatti O.C.'s Members' event on June 13th, Brandon, during one of the most savage assaults on the hill yet, returned 49.22 secs.—a new class record. He took Pardon Hairpin at a really shattering pace in one long controlled slide, treating his long-suffering gearbox very roughly as he cracked up to the Esses—a really magnificent effort !

Colin Strang, Shelsley, June, 1948. Time 44.78 secs.
(By courtesy of A. R. Coats)

Clive had previously equalled his own figures, but had trouble on his second run. Try as hard as he could, Strang could not get below 49.71 secs. (event for "specials") and could not break 50 secs. in the class event. The new alloy D.T. Vincent-H.R.D. motor, appears to have tremendous urge at the bottom end, but is not quite so quick at the top compared with his pre-war T.T. engine. Frank Aikens had a curious hiccup developing in his Triumph Twin as he reached peak revs. Nevertheless, the Wingco returned 51.22 secs. Curly Dryden is getting used to his Cooper, and his 51.28 secs. puts him amongst the fast boys.

The day before, all Shelsley 500 c.c. records went by the board when Brandon returned the amazing time of 44.16 secs. with the Cooper. Shelsley was a true Cooper Occasion, with John Cooper breaking the long-standing Wilkinson unblown record by the handsome margin of 1.34 secs., with the J.A.P. "1,000." Another miracle drive was that of John Bolster, who conducted "Bloody Mary" in 40.97 secs., to place Her Sanguinary Majesty in the honoured category of fastest-ever, unblown Shelsley Special. This was some consolation for the pinching of the Bolster Jeep from the car park at a Shrawley hotel later in the day. Two ruffians, who had been imbibing freely at the local, " boorowed " the Jeep, and ran it smack into a bank, fortunately damaging themselves as well as the car. " Bloody Mary " was eventually towed back to London behind my own car, John very rightly not caring to leave such valuable property lying around the countryside.

Before leaving Shelsley, I would like to draw attention to a plucky effort. Antony White had the bad luck to break an arm a few days before, and persuaded R. L. North to drive his new White-Lloyd, tubular backbone Lloyd " 350 " frame, all independent springing, J.A.P. Speedway motor. North, a complete stranger to Shelsley, got down to 47.99 secs., which, for a newcomer is stout piloting. Sad to think that North is by now on his way to Canada. Still and all, bones mend, so doubtless we will soon see Antony himself at the wheel.

Shelsley Walsh, is, of course, reported in more detail elsewhere, and the foregoing is by way of commentary.

It was at Stanmer Park that the new Cooper " 1000 " came into its own by setting up best unsupercharged time, and being fourth fastest of the day, with John Cooper at the wheel. This car has immense possibilities as a sprint-car, and, with cooling troubles overcome, might be a possible contender for Formula B honours.

Over in the Isle of Man, Spike Rhiando's golden Cooper " 1000 " (" The Banana Split ") was beset by cooling difficulties. Bill Pitcher, the Belle Vue dirt-track star, thought that the initial seizure might have been the outcome of mixing castor oil and methanol. Bill says the Speedway boys have long ago used nothing but " green " oil. He added that the J.A.P.'s are pretty ideal for short-distance stuff, but are definitely not designed to operate over road-race distances.

Undoubtedly the Spike machine was quick. I should put its pace past the stands in practice at rather over one-two-O, than under it. Some of the other competitors weren't over-enamoured of the Rhiando driving technique. In fact, I should say that the breezy American put the wind up everyone except himself—and even he couldn't have been too happy when the motor seized solid on him at over the " ton."

Unfortunately " Curly " Dryden pranged his Norton-engined Cooper in practice. The " 500 " was obviously very rapid—a lot quicker than Dryden expected. It held the road really well on the all-too-few occasions I was able to have a looksee at it in action, but it would seem as if Mr. Dryden had attempted to indulge in a spot of private dicing, which is not always a good plan in practice lappery. Maybe I have done him an injustice. The evidence of my spies may be none too reliable. Possibly he was just a shade over-enthusiastic with the boot !

Now where do we go from here ? Will road-racing 500's be developed, or will the types be reserved for sprint events. We still have absolutely no clue as to whether D-wagons will last a full-distance road event. Most of the boys cannot afford to do the obvious thing—have two different power-plants. A suitable sprint motor costs something like £75, and I have heard tell that characters have parted with two hundred smackers for an alloy Norton road-race unit.

I will quote Dick Caesar's remarks in his extremely sensible article in the May issue of " IOTA." " *Unless something can be done, the ' impecunious enthusiast ' will be left behind again, and* 500 *c.c. racing will become as expensive as any other class.*" The italics are Caesar's as well as mine.

Dick goes on to explain the difficulties of grading and handicapping, also the impossibility of setting any price limit on the cars. His conclusions regarding a system of promotion and relegation are searching and show the puzzles which will beset if such a system were adopted.

How about the segregation of "production" 500's and home-brewed specials, which might spring to mind as a possible solution ? In my opinion this would be extremely unfair to all concerned. Merely because someone has put by sufficient scratch to acquire a Cooper or a Marwyn isn't sufficient reason for such a drastic step. After all, there is no guarantee that the owner can drive the thing.

Then there is the idea of creating two separate awards in each event, one for "Professionals" and one for "Amateurs." This would lead to frightful complications. Even if you manage to define a Professional as one who makes his living directly or indirectly by means of the motor trade, there is no way to stop a fairly wealthy "amateur" using all the resources of the trade, whilst still retaining his amateur status.

It may be quite feasible to introduce a "Novice" and "Expert" class in events organized by the 500 Club, but it will be difficult to persuade other clubs to fall into line. Quite rightly, they will refuse to countenance the idea of complicating awards by the inclusion of a "two events in one" class. They will argue that this would not be fair to other classes, which have the identical problems.

There is bound to be lots of beefing from impecunious builders. On the other hand, many special builders have successfully weathered the storm. Wharton doesn't let the presence of factory-built cars worry him over-much in the 750 c.c. class ; the 1,500 c.c. category has long been a happy hunting ground for the "special," while I don't suppose John Bolster has ever bothered over much about Mays, Gerard and Co. providing the opposition in the 2-litre classes.

When the highly-specialized business of record-breaking in the 750 c.c. class was at its height, and M.G.'s and Austins were putting all their resources into building special cars, it was a then comparatively unknown amateur who shocked the factory boys be setting up new 750 figures. I refer, of course, to Viscount Ridley and that incredible twin-cam "750" he built to his own designs.

In the hurly-burly of professional motor-racing, the big European factories had to bow to a private-builder in the "little cylinders" race preceding last year's French Grand Prix. Eugene Martin and his B.M.W.-engined "special" defeated the famed Gordini Simcas and the much-publicised Cisitalias. Also, in that same event, the British Emeryson, another home-constructed effort, came pretty near breaking the lap record, being only fractionally slower than Bira's Simca.

No, it would be a disastrous thing if 500 c.c. racing were to become divided in itself. If it is felt that something will have to be done for the impecunious enthusiast, it will have to be attempted on the lines of "meritorious performance" awards, or by a system of personal handicapping for special awards by the 500 Club itself.

It is obvious that very little can be done until the parent body is in a position to organize its own events. Then, of course, it should be comparatively simple to work out a system of personal handicapping without altering the nature of scratch racing. For instance, at the first 500 Club meeting, there will probably be several events. Each of those should be duplicated. One class should be reserved for "experts," to be designated as drivers who have competed in a stated number of events and/or have gained any awards. The opposite class should be made up entirely of newcomers and/or those who have never gained an award in any previous events.

Consequently the "experts" have nothing to lose. The "fastest novice" will then be automatically promoted to the big-time class. Eventually, of course, the "experts" class will be filled to capacity, and the opposite class contain practically nothing else other than beginners. Which will make it so that we shall have to start from the beginning again. So now you can see Dick Caesar's points.

Peter Garnier has chosen for his subject for the anniversary issue, the most prominent of all the truly amateur constructors.

THE SECRETARY'S COLUMN

Forest View,
Cleaver Hill Road,
Windsor, Berks.

The first point I will deal with concerns IOTA or to be exact—the lack of it.

A lot of members have written to me letters and post cards couched in terms far from complimentary, so I will answer them all now.

Our Magazine is prepared by Adrian Butler our Honorary Editor, and NOT by the CLUB Secretary, and the honorary editor has to obtain suitable copy regularly

G. R. Hartwell warming up his "Monaco" at Shelsley—12th June, 1948
(By courtesy of John Browning)

to enable the publishers to go to print on the correct day. This copy is very difficult to come by, and entails a lot of hard work by the editor in persuading people to produce it and by the people themselves who actually write it. I know because I've tried.

The solution is for YOU to help fill the Magazine either by producing some copy yourself or obtaining it from some interesting source. If every member wrote a two page article every THIRD YEAR the Magazine would always have sufficient to fill it. It is your Magazine so I leave it to you. Secondly, I will deal with the member who wants to know if the Club is alive (I don't mean YOU only, there are several like you).

Well, for the benefit of recent members I will go back to the last Annual General Meeting in December when it was decided by the members that the control of this

Club should be administered by a Committee based in London. A Committee prepared to meet this condition was elected and it was agreed that the hand over of control should take place in about three months time.

This new Committee, or Council, as some people call it, started to get together to sort out basic principles and after several meetings and also discussions, and lengthy correspondence with such key men of the first Committee as Caesar, the founder of the Club, Siddall, the first Secretary, Nedham, the treasurer, and Adrian Butler, the Magazine editor, a general plan was agreed and control was handed over on May 1st. Our first aim is to foster motor racing in the 500 " National " class as a means of providing less expensive racing.

Secondly we aimed to ensure that the Club was run on a sound financial basis.

I will now try to explain how we are endeavouring to achieve these two aims.

Taking the racing side first we try to ensure that all promoters of events include a class for our members, and there is no doubt that promoters of all hill climbs and sprint events are well aware of the potency of some of our cars in this respect and this side of the sport is well established for us. Circuit racing however, is a very different picture. In 1947 we had a chance of racing at Brough, but due to lack of entries this did not materialise, and our only showing was at Gransden which was a failure. The cars were unreliable.

The entrants cannot be blamed as the difficulties confronting a man who wants to test his racing car were then, and still are, appalling.

This year the race at Brough was again offered us—thanks to the Blackburn Welfare Motor Club and to Mr. Leavy their own Chairman, and excellent sport was enjoyed as well as many lessons learned.

Before this season ends there are two more circuit races for us.

The R.A.C. " 500 " race at Silverstone on October 2nd, and the 500 Club race at Dunholme on October 9th. The Dunholme event was proposed many months ago by the British Motor Cycle Racing Club, who are running a motor cycle race meeting at Dunholme, near Lincoln, on October 9th, and very kindly asked us if we would like to run a car race in their Meeting. This proposition was of course approved by the 500 Club Committee, and draft regulations and a plan of this course have been approved by the R.A.C. who are issuing the permit. The Silverstone race has just appeared out of the blue, it is the work of the R.A.C. Silverstone Sub-Committee, one of whom is our Chairman, and is an opportunity for which we are deeply grateful. It is limited to thirty entries so the proximity of the two events should not affect entries for Dunholme, which is 32 miles, and Silverstone 50 miles.

With these two events I suggest this season has offered the Club member who has built a car a wide variety of opportunities for indulging in motor racing.

Turning to the financial side—our only expenditure so far has been on IOTA and fees in connection with the R.A.C. permits for Brough and Dunholme, and we feel confident that there will be a positive balance at the end of the year.

In case you are still reading here is some general news :—A new Centre has formed with H.Q. at NORTHAMPTON—will all members in that district contact the Secretary—W. L. Grose, " Sundial," Billing Road East, Northampton.

Club Badges are becoming available and a statement on this will be in the next issue.

CRAIGANTLET, 1948

If ever interest was aroused in Belfast in connection with Motor Sport, it was so during the week of Craigantlet Hill Climb when the Marwyn, driven by W. Lee, was first shown to the public. At the scrutineering all eyes were on the " amazing little machine " which one leading newspaper described as " The car with the Two Way Look," displaying a very good photograph of the car in action. Needless to say on the day of the event the car and crew were surrounded and bombarded with questions. The car itself finished in silver certainly looked grand and it will be surprising if in future events there is not a contingent of 500's competing.

Although being unfortunate in not being able to use the car during the official practise, due to gear trouble, Lee, a newcomer to racing and to the hill really showed the many thousands on the day of the climb just what could be done. Making only one climb he returned the amazingly good time of 1 minute, 36.1/5 secs., which compared with many of the blown 1,500's and was in fact a good deal faster than many. It was indeed a pity that there were not more 500's present.

Plans are being made to run the car in the next Ulster Climb, at Knockagh in late September when, with teething troubles over, the car should amaze a good many. We wish Lee every good luck.

* * *

At a gathering of The 500 Club of Ireland on Friday, 27th August in the Grand Central Hotel, Belfast, members and friends enjoyed a most interesting talk given by Mr. Raymond Mays, who most generously consented to give the talk despite being fully occupied during his period in Belfast with preparations for Craigantlet Hill Climb, at which, we are happy to say, Mays recorded the amazing time of 1 minute, 15.1/5 secs. A new record.

In his talk Mr. Mays stressed the great value of the 500 movement as being one of the chief ways in which young and coming drivers could train to take their places in upholding British prestige in motor racing. Some most interesting personal accounts were also given of past events and a most clear picture of the way in which one requires to go about the sport, being methodical and with much hard work. The great value of pitwork and of the great work of the team behind the driver was also stressed. Those present also had the opportunity of learning first hand of the progress of the B.R.M. and of the work entailed in the launching of such project.

Mr. W. Lee, the only 500 c.c. entrant at Craigantlet and a member of the Council of the Club presided and passed a vote of thanks to Mr. Mays on behalf of the Club.

MOTOR
RACING
IS
DANGEROUS
Brockbank

R.A.C. "500" c.c. RACE, SILVERSTONE

Of the 35 Entrants for the R.A.C.'s miniature 50 mile Grand Prix for National 500's over the identical course used by the Formula cars later in the day, 28 started and 8 completed the Course. There might have been more but for those unforeseen difficulties arising on the last day of practising the previous day.

No less than 7 of the Entrants were unable to present themselves in time for practice, and were therefore disqualified. Lones, Bacon, Hartwell and Davison did not bring their cars to the course. The remaining two, Bond and Sparrowe, were just too late to put in any laps, the latter having the misfortune to break a chain in the pits as the official practice was finishing.

Had it not been for the delayed appearance of Villoresi and Ascari, the two champions who motored from Milan without a pause, and who came in First and Second in the Grand Prix, it is possible that Bond and Sparrowe would have been given the chance to qualify. The Maseratis had to put in their practice laps during the time available, and there was therefore no more to be said.

Bond has a very interesting machine which performs very well indeed. Built to the National Formula, it is a front engined Front-Wheel-Drive car, finished beautifully, and which we hope to see more of, in the future.

Practice

On Thursday and Friday, practice times of the 500's astonished not only the drivers of the " big stuff," but also the Officials of the R.A.C. They revealed that they were not far short of G.P. times for the circuit, and the technique of the drivers was highly commended. Moss, Strang, Rhiando, C. F. Smith, Aikens and Cooper were particularly fast, and Coward, Bosisto, Grose and Dryden were all well up in the list.

Moss's 3 m. 17 secs., averaging 67.07 m.p.h. was the high light of the performance in the 500's, his time comparing most favourably with Lord Selsdon's Talbot, 3 m. 42.6 and Salvadori (Maserati) 3 m. 13.6.

Various troubles set in as speeds increased. Bosisto stripped his gears. Flathers was not going full chat. Gibbs was somewhat unstable, and Wharton was missing badly. Grose was busy on final preparations on his Manx Norton-engined Special and very nice looking indeed it is. Aikens was hard at work devising a new pressure system to his fuel tank.

Complete re-build

First prize for courage and initiative must undoubtedly go to the cousins, David and Joe Fry. The Cross rotary valve engine which they had installed (very ancient, and a hack mount), finally blew up. One suspects overheating possibly by insufficient exit ducts as the cause. So at 4 p.m. on Friday, the Frys, together with their indomitable helpers, decided to get a new J.A.P. from John Cooper, and re-design the mountings. It was all-night work. Jeremy Fry built and braised in four hours, a new 6 gallon tank made of three old oil drums. New engine plates had to be designed and made from anything handy. The car had to be left untouched from midnight to six a.m. on Race Day, owing to a police shut down of the very helpful garage

The Fry Freikaiserwagen being unloaded after having the "J.A.P." engine fitted over night—they would appear to be still working.

in Brackley. —BUT—the car was started up at the pits, and the bonnet clapped on, Two Minutes before the Start !

The Race

John Cobb having opened the course, the 500's started up from the pits, which were well forward of the starting line, and assembled on the Grid. It was impossible for the drivers to hear the commentator through the P.A. systems saying " Three minutes, . . Two . . . One . . .Half . . .to go," owing to the noise of their engines.

Probably owing to bad briefing as to the procedure of the Start, many competitors were still being wheeled and ordered to their respective starting grids, as Earl Howe, exactly at zero hour, 12.00 Noon, dropped the Union Jack.

The resulting confusion produced a debacle which will remain in memory for a long while. Some drivers watching the flag made perfect getaways, and the order passing the pits into the first bend was :—Strang, Moss, Dryden and Cooper. A pause, then came Rhiando and Strathcarron.

One's reactions were curious at this unexpected spacing, particularly as the leaders slowed right down, looking anxiously backwards. As other cars were soon to be approaching, Moss, who had taken the lead from Strang, signalled him to pass and resumed his place behind him. A nice gesture, and very good racing manners.

To go back to the starting line. Of those who had not made themselves aware of " Official Time," Brandon, Bosisto and Fry, were caught changing to " hard " plugs. " Spike " Rhiando—the ultimate winner—was standing beside his car (surely the first time this has ever happened) and Page, called upon to start suddenly, broke a chain and pushed into the pits a hundred yards away.

Cooper, who was scheduled to start in a leading row and was well in the rear, weaved neatly through to a good start, as also did Strathcarron in the Marwyn.

Underwood motored slowly into the pits, changed a plug and was away in seven minutes. Fry was on his first lap, seen hurrying along with " something trailing behind." This turned out to be his rev. counter drive, which he had not had time to fit before going to the line.

Twelve minutes after the start, Saunders (Cooper) broke down and retired, and Underwood having failed to improve his engine with plugs, retired also.

After three laps, Moss took the lead at a speed of 60.67 m.p.h. Strang having gone very fast indeed, found he was getting no oil, and on the point of seizing up, retired. After Moss and only 0.7 secs. behind, came Rhiando followed by Dryden (Cooper), John Cooper and Coward in the Cowlan.

Messenger's special packed up on the course, and at 12.13 p.m. he was seen returning dejectedly to the pits. One minute later Dryden was in trouble. The front engine bearing collapsed and " Curly " was out of the race.

Clark (A.S.A.) was seen to be in difficulties, and he pulled off the course, whilst Rhiando was making a supreme effort to wrest the lead from Moss, and was gaining steadily. On his third lap, Spike, driving his golden coloured Cooper—known amongst the boys as the " Banana Split "—very forcefully made the fastest lap in 3 m. 29 s. (63.22 m.p.h.), John Cooper being only .32 secs. behind in the race position. Bosisto retired after one lap with his gearbox stripped, for the second time.

Calamity in various forms

At the pits, Pa Moss was anxiously waiting for young Stirling who failed to arrive as the seconds ticked by, and Rhiando took the lead followed by Cooper, Coward, S. Coldham (Cooper) and C. Smith (C.F.S.), the last three being within ten seconds of each other.

Moss was seen at Seaman's Corner, frantically examining his Cooper. Fry's Iota was overdue as also was Flather's Marrott, and there was rising excitement at the pits as the cars failed to report.

Rhiando was still in the lead with the order unchanged, when Smith, who was lying 5th and going extremely well, suddenly spun round on a corner and had done with his dicing for the day. Samuelson then nipped smartly into fifth place.

Joe Fry appeared at his pit with a seized engine. This was not very surprising considering it had been started for the first time just prior to the race. Flather's magneto had " had it," so there was no joy in his camp.

Samuelson, driving imperturbably, had by now worked his way past Coldham and was awaiting his chance to pass Coward into third place. The latter wasn't having any, however, and continued at full chat.

The leader had started to slow down perceptably, and was exceedingly uncomfortable, as his petrol tank, not quite recovered from the upset at BO'ness, had started to leak onto Spike's shoulders and back. Anyone who has had Methanol-nitric-benzine on his skin should know just how bad this can be, but he carried right on determined to remain in the lead !

By now, Brandon, who it may be remembered, was caught napping at the start with a fistful of plugs, had worked his way steadily up through the field and was lying placed behind Coldham. Coward was still going like a bomb.

Grose warming up his beautiful "Merc-like" 500.

Gibbs came into the pits with his M.A.C. looking for some vanished horses. They had left the stable however, and he retired after a gallant effort.

Grose had a nasty moment when nothing occurred as he braked hard for a corner. After the excitement had died down, he stopped and discovered that one of his brake fluid lines had been cut clean through by a flying stone or other sharp hazard met on the track. Re-starting, he came into the pits and perforce retired after six laps.

Moss by now had reached the pits with the news that his driving sprocket had come adrift. Seizing various tools, he set off again at a run for Seaman's Corner.

Rhiando was not the only one to suffer with tank trouble, and K. W. Smith went out of the race with a split fuel tank. Three minutes later, Frank Aikens seized up his Triumph. The field was thinning out !

Moss decided to retire thinking that the race was over, but managed to repair the Cooper in time to drive it to the pits, at the end of the dice.

Samuelson was now close behind Coward, .25 secs. after Cooper, who was lying second, with Brandon coming up steadily.

Wharton, after losing 18 minutes at the pits with fuel and plug trouble, resumed racing with five minutes to go.

W/Cmdr. F. Aikens (plus Hat) himself.

Phillips (Fairley) was driving steadily, bent on finishing at all costs, and F/Lt Stoop (Spink Squanderbug) who was handling his good looking car very well indeed, shared the same notion.

Within two or three minutes of the finish, Coward suddenly ceased to revolve round the track. He got going again without too much delay but this involuntary breakdown may have cost him a place.

The Cooper's Outing

Sore and weary, not knowing if he could complete his final lap through loss of fuel, Rhiando saw the chequered flag as he flashed over the line to win the R.A.C. 500 Race at 60.68 m.p.h. in 47 mins. 10 3/5 secs., with Cooper Second, and Sir Francis Samuelson Third.

Pa Cooper was in great form after the race, as five out of nine of his machines completed the course, with a 1, 2, 3, 4, Victory.

Final Placings for the eight finishers

	Driver.	*Car.*	*Speed.*	*No. of laps.*
1.	S. Rhiando	Cooper	60.68 m.p.h.	13
2.	J. Cooper	Cooper	60.55 ,,	13
3.	Sir F. Samuelson	Cooper	59.90 ,,	13
4.	E. Brandon	Cooper	59.87 ,,	13
5.	R. L. Coward	Cowlan	60.03 ,,	for 12
6.	S. A. Coldham	Cooper	51.70 ,,	,, 11
7.	R. W. Phillips	Fairley	51.23	,, 11
8.	J. R. Stoop	Spink	50.24 ,,	,, 11

Next month, a review of the results and retirements.

J.O.H.S.

Driver.	*Retirements.*	*Cause.*
Saunders, G.	After No. laps	Broken down.
Underwood, A. A. D. ..	,, 1 ,,	Mechanical unknown.
Bosisto, J. F. J.	,, 1 ,,	Gearbox stripped.
Messenger, R. W.	,, 1 ,,	Stopped on Course.
Strang, C. H.	,, 2 ,,	Engine seizing.
Strathcarron, Lord	,, 2 ,,	Engine seized.
Gibbs, J. N.	,, 3 ,,	Mechanical unknown.
Clark, J. F.	,, 3 ,,	Mechanical unknown.
Fry, J. G.	,, 3 ,,	Engine seized.
Dryden, R. M.	,, 4 ,,	Engine bearing plates adrift.
Flather, D. G.	,, 4 ,,	Magneto broken.
Wharton, K.	,, 4 ,,	Mechanical unknown.
Moss, S.	,, 5 ,,	Sprocket adrift.
K. W. Smith	,, 6 ,,	Fuel Tank Split.
Grose, W.	,, 6 ,,	Brake severed by stone.
Smith, C. F.	,, 7 ,,	Stopped on Course.
Aikens, W/Cmdr. F.	,, 8 ,,	Engine seized.
Page, P. W. K.	,, 9 ,,	Unknown.

Casualty list—

This report is by no means comprehensive, accurate or complete. It would be greatly appreciated if those drivers who were unfortunate enough to be on this list, would give full particulars of their retirement so that the troubles may be analysed and an article written by a suitable person in the shape of a constructive criticism, which would be of considerable use to those enthusiasts who are still building.

Editor.

FREIKAISERWAGEN, 1936-48

By J. G. Fry

In the summer of 1936, a strange vehicle was entered for the Bristol Motor Club's Backwell hill climb. It consisted of a G.N. chassis with Morgan front suspension and a water cooled Anzani twin mounted behind the driver, surmounted by a Scott radiator. It was driven by Hugh Dunsterville, and rejoiced in the name of "Freikaiserwagen," having been built by David Fry, then aged 18½, after consultation with Dick Caesar, who suggested the rear engine layout from inspiration from the then successful Auto Unions designed by Dr. Porsche. From that time to the present the car has always been known as "Porsche" to those closely associated with it, and its official name, frequently a cause of conjecture and derision today, is obvious considering the German inspiration linked with the names of Fry and Caesar. At that Backwell meeting in 1936, the car had one run, clouting the bank hard on the top corner, and finishing more by momentum than cunning, in a cloud of steam with one back wheel looking like an egg whisk. "Porsche," however, had run and (just) finished.

During the autumn of 1936, David Fry went up to Cambridge, taking with him one G.N. chassis and a lot of ideas about making another and better "Porsche." There, during the autumn term, a lot of time was spent, both spare and otherwise, in building a new car, with the assistance of the writer and various long suffering bodies belonging to the kindly garage who had lent their somewhat sepulchral loft for the purpose. David had previously contacted Robin Jackson and procured from him an 1,100 c.c. 60° V. twin Blackburne engine of interesting origin and big potentialities. This engine was a modification of a design originated about 1928, and had been further modified in 1932 by Jackson in conjunction with the late Eric Fernihough with a view to three wheeler records, but had never been used. It was designed to run unblown and had very special connecting rods and crank. Running on a 10½—1 ratio with two Bowden carburetters and J.A.P. fuel, it was assumed the engine should give around 70 B.H.P., and subsequent results bore out that it probably did, although it was never put on the brake in unblown form.

This engine was installed amidships across the G.N. frame with a Morgan cone clutch and external flywheel with a short tail shaft leading direct to the bevel box. The transmission was suitably strengthened up to take the unaccustomed power, a 100 ton bevel shaft and axle being made. The latter was adapted to take M.G. hubs to which were fitted 16″ knock-on wire wheels and 16 × 600 tyres. The Morgan front was retained but adapted to take Rudge motorcycle wheels and brakes, and ⅓ strength springs replaced the original Morgan ones. The rear of the car was made as low as possible by tilting the spring mountings on the chassis and the springs were made more flexible than the standard G.N. A rack and pinion steering with Morris track rods and gravity fuel tank over the engine just about finished the recipe. The car was then fitted with an enclosed body similar in many ways to the present day 500 with—we thought—adequate provision for the air to go in and out, and towed triumphantly to Brooklands for its first trials. Alas and alack, Nemesis, in the form of chronic overheating soon overtook our youthful endeavours, but by the expedient of removing the body complete and throwing it away—we never liked the look of the thing anyway—and a lot of plug gazing and mixture adjustment by Robin Jackson, we eventually got the vehicle going really

J. Fry—Freikaiserwagen—in one of its early forms.
(By courtesy of " The Motor ")

well at the expense of a good deal of time and two wrecked barrels and pistons.

In this rather denuded and unfinished form the reborn Freikaiserwagen ran in its first speed trial at Whitchurch, near Bristol, in May, 1937, where it had only one run but put up second fastest time of the day to Hadley's Austin, beating several Alfas and Bugattis as well as Evans' blown Q type M.G. and Hartwell's rapid 1,200 c.c. of the same make. The cause for the single appearance on this occasion was the well known and disastrous trick of the G.N. transmission of getting into two gears at once, which as any G.N. owner will know, is not good for the back axle ! After Whitchurch the car was finished with an aerofoil section covering the fuel tank—a device which caused much ribaldry and talk of motor mowers. Actually, the function of this was to deflect air on to the cylinder heads and generally promote a flow of air over the engine, which it succeeded in doing quite well. It was not, as seemed to be generally supposed, full of fuel, but concealed a small 1-gallon fuel tank and even smaller oil tank only.

During the remainder of 1937, the car was run at Backwell, where it made second best time to Bloody Mary in 24.7 seconds, driven by David ; Poole, where it was the fastest unblown car ; Lewis, and Shelsley, where it was sixth fastest car in 42.58 seconds and again fastest unblown vehicle, this being the writer's first experience of the Worcestershire acclivity.

After the 1937 season, the quest for further speed was upon us and it was decided to fit a supercharger to the engine. A Marshall blower was procured and the work was carried out by Jackson, a task which involved a considerable amount of work and research into induction pipe length and shape. A single large size S.U. carburetter replaced the original Bowdens and the blower was driven by chain from a sprocket inboard of the flywheel. Finally the whole chassis, with installation, was put bodily on the test bed and given extensive running to achieve maximum results. Our hopes were fully justified, the engine giving off about 98 B.H.P. at 5,500 r.p.m. In this form the compression ratio was 6½—1 and the blower pressure 12 lbs. per sq. in., a figure which later proved to be an optimum with this particular supercharger. The fuel used was Pratts Esso R.

In this form the car was run throughout the 1938 season with practically no alteration to engine settings and no trouble whatever. The first event was Syston Park, where the car broke the course record but was finally just beaten by Ian Connel's 1½ litre E.R.A. Perhaps a brief summary of other 1938 results might be of interest.

Boness. Course record on demonstration run in 35 sec. dead, the official runs having been spoiled by some nonsense with the gear selection. Incidentally, this was a somewhat shorter course than that which has been used since the war.

Shelsley. 41.52 seconds in May and 41.93 seconds in September, giving 5th and 6th F.T.D. respectively. In each case the 1,100 c.c. class was won. The latter time was put up by David, this being the first and only time he has driven the car at Shelsley.

Prescott. Best time, 47.62 secs., achieved at the closed Vintage meeting. At the time this would have stood as a record but the official B.O.C. timing was not in operation so it did not count officially.

Wetherby. 28.82 seconds, which was a class record and compared favourably with the F.T.D. of 28.37 secs. put up by a 3.3 G.P. Bugatti.

Backwell. Second F.T.D. again to John Bolster conducted by David in 23.3 secs.—Mary getting down to 23 secs. dead.

Unfortunately, at the last meeting of the year—the International Prescott, where we much hoped to equal or improve on our previous time—the writer very stupidly drove into the woodwork on the inside of Orchard corner with a resounding smack on a practice run, doing no good to the front suspension and badly lozenging the chassis. So a successful season came (literally) to an abrupt end.

In its pre-war form the car weighed about 6¾ cwt., and the four speeds used give maxima of about 50, 65, 85 and 110 m.p.h. respectively. First and second gears only were used at Prescott and third at Shelsley. The car handled well but the brakes were never very good due, as we have since learned, to unsuitable linings. Most of the rear suspension was provided by the flexing of the G.N. chassis rather than by the springs.

During the winter of 1938 plans were thought out for building a four wheel drive vehicle by installing the second Blackburne which we had then secured (only the two were made) to drive the front wheels. After all, John Bolster by then was motoring about with four engines so we thought we at least should have two ! However, a lot of difficulties and snags to this scheme were quite logically put forward by the slide rule king, whom we consulted on the matter, and the project was never put in hand before the war came along and put paid to any further thoughts on the scheme.

During the war years the Blackburnes were carefully stripped and put away by David before departing into the R.A.F. and the fastnesses of the North Atlantic, but the remainder of the car did not fare so well, bits lying around here and there and the chassis complete with Morgan front being sent for scrap to help the salvage drive.

Eight years later, in 1947, David and I decided to resurrect " Porsche " after encouragement to this end by the writer's wife, Pat. A search of various sheds and garages revealed more than we had dared to hope of the essential bits. The aerofoil section and tanks, back axle and sprockets, bevel box and shaft, our precious rack and pinion steering, all came gradually to light. We had, however, no chassis or front suspension, but were lucky to procure the Watkins G.N. complete and out of the best bits of the assembled mass of components an almost exact replica of the pre-war " Porsche " was built up in the short space of one month. We now had better rear brakes than before, but owing to the impossibility of procuring Rudge wheels and brakes for the front in time we had to be content with the totally ineffective Morgan ones which we had. However, owing to this and various other detail alterations, the finished car was probably somewhat lighter than before.

The best parts of the two engines were assembled up by Robin Jackson into one unit and certain modifications were carried out to increase the power output which included enlarging the inlet ports considerably. When all was ready the car was taken to an aerodrome where, after running in the correct fuel settings were once more obtained and it was found that " Porsche " lacked none of her pre-war fire—in fact seemed to be going better than ever.

By now the 1947 season was well advanced and the car was only able to be entered for five events of which it ran in four. The month of September, 1947, however, was perhaps one of the most hectic from the point of view of hard work. Whereas before the car was never touched between events, now everything went wrong. Frequently it was necessary to strip out the entire transmission between the practice and the event proper, due to broken dogs on the layshaft. Chains broke in all directions, and worst of all, the engine started to give trouble. Pistons cracked across the crown and the internal flywheels would not stay put on the taper of the crank pin, despite every trick known to man, including copper plating to make them do so. The car was withdrawn from Prescott for this reason and actually ran at the Shelsley meeting with the flywheel $\frac{3}{8}''$ out of true, after yet a further crankpin, which had been machined up, failed to hold. Quite why the engine did not fly to pieces on this occasion nobody will ever know, as it was taken up to over 6,000 r.p.m. during ascent.

All these troubles, however, were attributable to definite causes, as all troubles are, and were tackled successfully by Robin Jackson in carrying out very considerable modification to the engine for 1948. Put briefly, the engine was giving too much power and had to be strengthened up " downstairs " to take it. Some details of the modifications are given later in the article.

Briefly summarised, the 1947 results were as follows :—
Brighton. S.S. Kilo, 29.52 secs. The car threw second gear chain on both runs.
Poole. 3rd F.T.D. to Poore and Hutchison in 37.15 secs., only ½ sec. outside the record. Unfortunately, the car was spun round on the second attempt and failed to complete the course.

Shelsley. Fastest Shelsley special in 40.61 secs.

Southsea. Fastest 1,100 c.c. racing class.

(To be continued.)

★ ★ ★

CAR BADGES

The position in regard to car badges has not really changed since the report in the October issue, as we got a big delivery from the manufacturers and they all had to be returned owing to some defect having developed in the manufacture. This completely set the makers back and they don't seem to have recovered yet. However, they have promised an early completion so let us hope that all those from " T " onwards will receive badges within the next week or two.

EDITOR.

★ ★ ★

500 c.c. RACING

Cdr. A. Yorke, R.N., has spent much time and money in producing films which he is prepared to hire out for a fee of 10/- per night, payable to the Club (free to members). The film consists of about 200 feet of 9.5 m.m. Pathé, obtainable from the Editor.

★ ★ ★

CHANGE OF ADDRESS

Strang, C. H., Burnham, Sudbury Hill, Harrow-on-the-Hill, Middlesex.
Austin, B., 51 West Lockinge, Wantage, Berks.
Chambers, P., 447 Gillott Road, Edgbaston, Birmingham.
Fillingham, W. P. I., Test Pilots' Office, De Haviland A/C Co., Hatfield, Herts.
Stevenson, Kenombo Farm, Post Restante, Salisbury, Southern Rhodesia.

IS STREAMLINING WORTH WHILE ?

By Capt. K. W. R. SMALE, M.C., Royal Marines.

This is written by a keen type, and will, I hope, promote healthy argument. I don't know the science of aerodynamics, but the situation as it strikes me is as follows.

Over the past years many articles have been written, and much time spent in discussing the value of streamlining. Many articles end with the frequently forgotten statement, " Streamlining is only really effective, and only pays good dividends at high speeds." By comparative values I feel that speeds of 100–150 m.p.h. may not be considered high. The difference in range of a streamlined 15″ shell over the ordinary " flat based " type travelling at 2,800 ft. per sec. is only in the neighbourhood of 5%.

A cube placed in a high speed wind tunnel would have turbulence fore and aft, but the final flow of high speed " air " forms a streamlined envelope of aerofoil shape.

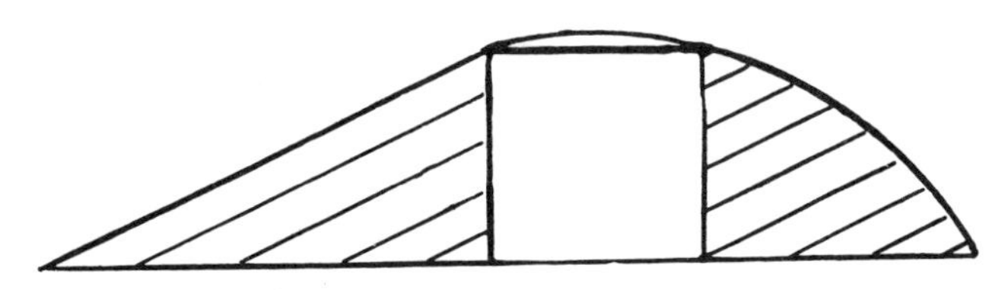

If speed reaches a sufficient height, a certain amount of power is lost in the effort to build up the aerofoil.

Why are modern production cars streamlined—for looks, cleanliness, or to reduce noise of windrush ? All three, but not really to increase speed. Surely it would be more beneficial to save weight and " skip " the " fancy body." Side wind has more effect on a car's performance than frontal wind, control governs the speed at which a car may be driven, surely side streamlining is more important ? This can be shown as follows :

Place a plank " edge-wise " in a tank of water and move it to hit a point on the tank side.

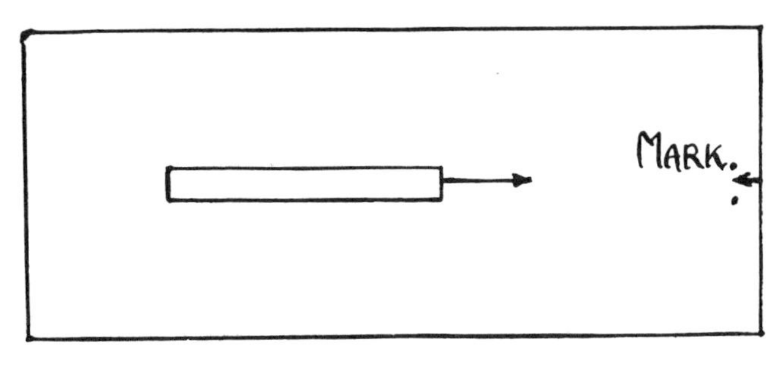

This can be done fairly easily. Now do the same *across* a stream.

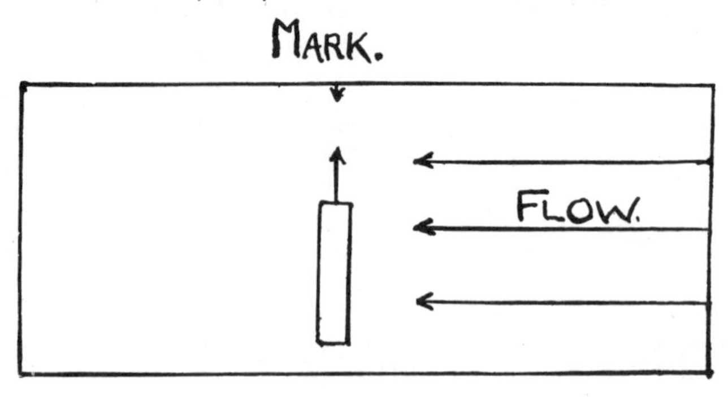

The speed at which you may move the plank to be certain of hitting the mark is reduced owing to having to compensate for the side force or cross flow—in other words, the speed depends on the plank's " linear " stability. Much effort is spent on reducing frontal areas, but very often the side area just has to fit in as best it can with the general frontal design. I feel that if more effort was concentrated on side areas, a special would be more stable and more consistent in performance.

I hope I have started a train of thought, and perhaps, except for comfort, streamlined " noses " are not all that they are supposed to be, except that they " finish " off the job nicely. I can foresee almost insurmountable difficulties in cutting side area, but it is worth special thought, or———— ? ! !

As I have been privileged to have a preview at the above, I feel I must have a smack at Captain Smale.

Firstly, I should like to attack the start of his thesis. I should prefer to see it put like this—the results of poor streamlining and consequent bad airflow round the vehicle which exist *at all speeds* are emphasised, owing to the application of the velocity cubed law, at very high speeds. They are clearly noticeable at speeds from 50 m.p.h. up, and reach values at 80 m.p.h. and over, which make their reduction a matter of high importance.

Of course in the ordinary go to town motor, the application of streamlining is most useful in reducing fuel consumption, enabling the designed speed of the car to be reached on the streamlined car more easily (i.e. with less throttle opening) than on the standard all bits and pieces condition exhibited by the traditional English sports car. Alternatively, the gear ratio may be raised; giving an increase in top speed at maximum power, owing to the lessened resistance.

A " streamlined " 15″ shell is not truly streamlined. It also has a flat base though admittedly this is of smaller diameter than the main bore. Also the shell has one (if not two) driving bands which make tiresome interference effects over the tail.

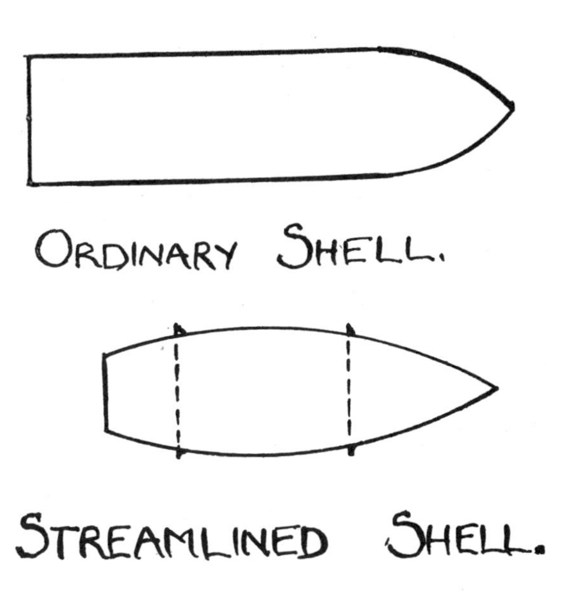

If the remark about the cube placed in a high speed wind tunnel was correct—then we should *never* need to put streamlined shapes or fairings on our cars or aeroplanes, since the air would form them for us.

I agree side wind effect is most important, and non-comprehension of it has resulted in the loss of more than one of the greatest of racing drivers, Bernd Rosemeyer (of Auto Union fame) among them.

I don't quite " get " the stream analogy. If the stream is flowing at all the plank will never hit the mark in the second picture—unless of course it is " aimed off " to the right !

Cdr. C. A. YORKE, R.N.

TWO YEARS HARD LABOUR

By W. T. Mackay

After reading the very persuasive circular distributed by Cdr. C. A. Yorke, I felt that it was time to put pen to paper in order to help "IOTA" by describing my hitherto unseen, unraced, unheard of special.

I have heard it said that it is advisable to draw the thing before you start to build. In my case I did draw the complete car before starting work on the chassis, which incidentally was made from $3\frac{1}{2}'' \times 1\frac{1}{4}'' \times$ 12G steel channel—ex M.G., boxed in at the bends, and braced with six tubes of 2″ O/D × 16 G.M.S. The channel was liberally motheaten with 2″ dia. holes to reduce avoirdupois. The 2″ tubes also served as engine and gearbox mountings. The inevitable Fiat front suspension was used front and rear, and the springs supported on platforms built up from rectangular tube and M.S. sheet, welded to form a bridge across the chassis. The front shock absorbers were Fiat type, but have been replaced by a pair of home brewed type, the rear are double acting Luvax. The front wheels are standard Fiat type, but have suffered the ravages of a $1\frac{1}{2}''$ dia. hole cutter. Standard 8 wheels have found favour at the rear, and are shod with 4.75 × 16 tyres. Brakes are hydraulic all round, front being as fitted to the 1939 Fiat, and rear as fitted to a 1934 Morris Minor G.P.O. van, with M type M.G. brake drums and hubs with cable operation for the hand-brake on rear wheels only.

The Fiat steering box has an adapted column and quickly detachable wheel fabricated from two layers of plywood with a core of duralumin to form the rim and spokes. The splined shaft from an Alvis Speed 25 fan spindle was pressed into service as a means of removing the wheel. This latter operation greatly facilitating the endeavours of the driver to come to grips with his machine. The track rods have been modified to suit the centrally mounted steering box, which has a lengthened arm which now gives $1\frac{1}{2}$ turns lock to lock. Back-rest and frames are constructed from $\frac{5}{8}''$ dural angle and 20 G. sheet stiffened with 20 G. angle section. The seat pan looks more like an egg tray, but has been stressed not to let its occupant down in times of need. The dashboard is burdened with three instruments, oil pressure gauge, rev. counter, magneto switch and numerous lightening holes.

The body is also home brewed with single curve panels, but the nose and tail cowlings were aircraft aluminium drop tanks suitably cut and bulged to fit, thereby relieving me of the necessity of obtaining the services of a professional tin basher. The oil tank is tinned steel and the fuel tank copper. A large capacity long range tank is now under construction.

A Triumph Twin of '39 vintage was chosen as motive power, and was purchased from Colin Strang. Considerable alterations have changed the outlook on life of this engine, the only original parts remaining being the modified crank and crankcase. The most noticeable alteration being the alloy head and barrel, two 15/16″ T.T. carbs., 14 to 1 pistons and the reversal of the head to avoid a tortuous exhaust system.

The Triumph gearbox has not been tampered with except for removal of the kick-starter mechanism, but the clutch has received a liberal peppering from my drill, and is now a mere shadow of its former self. The drive shaft is a cosmopolitan affair, being built up from M type axleshafts, Ford gearbox mainshafts, Ford universal joints and Ariel sprocket. The centre portion of this shaft runs in two 1″ dia. self aligning ballraces, and is adjustable for chain tension in conjunction with the gearbox which is also adjustable for primary chain tension. Gear selection is by the orthodox hand lever coupled to the sawn off foot change lever. I have a choice of seven top gear ratios from 6.6 to 5 to 1. Total weight is 524 lbs., wheel-base 6′ 8″, front track 3′ 8″, rear track 3′ 5½″.

W. T. Mackay's "500."

The car has taken me over two years to build single handed, in my garage equipped with a 3½″ Drummond lathe, and ½″ electric drill, plus a good set of tools. The only work done professionally was the welding. For the benefit of the poor and needy, like myself, the total cost has worked out at £150, although this figure is more than I really intended to spend, it has been distributed over the last two years and therefore did not come so hard on my pocket, or even relegate my family to the poor house as some people imagine special building does. I have driven the car about 30 miles with much verve and reckless abandon, and so far nothing has broken or come adrift, although the coming season may prove otherwise and find me either full of pride or deciding to give up motoring for good !

GOODWOOD MOTOR CIRCUIT

Although much work has been done at the Goodwood Road Racing Circuit since the inaugural Meeting in September last, the big response from the public at Easter demonstrated both the popularity of car racing at Goodwood, and the need for additional safeguards. This need is in some measure due to the incidence of unauthorised entry both to the Course and to Stands, which undoubtedly affected the comfort of legitimate spectators.

The new measures decided upon will be put into effect as soon as possible, but after consultations between the Goodwood Road Racing Company, Ltd., and the British Automobile Racing Club, it has been found impracticable to complete these in time for the advertised Whit Monday Meeting, having regard to the present-day difficulties in obtaining materials. It has been decided, therefore, to cancel the forthcoming Whit Monday Meeting.

The next car race meeting at the Goodwood Circuit will accordingly be held on 17th September, by which time the constructive criticism of some spectators who complained of an inadequate view of the racing will have been met, and everyone will be able to see the racing in comfort and security.

SILVERSTONE—May 14th, 1949

The weather, consistent with this year's motor racing weather, was lovely—it was a grand day. Car parking facilities were much improved, in fact the whole organisation outside the course appeared to work like a clock.

Inside the course the organisation appeared to be somewhat overdone. None of the 500 drivers or mechanics were allowed over the bridge even on Practice Day. Unfortunately I do not know the full story as Iota is not, if you please, allowed a Press Pass. This, therefore, is only a brief report, the full report will be published when more accurate details can be assembled.

The proceedings opened for the South Grand Stand with an amusing demonstration of how to run down an R.A.C. patrol by an official car; luckily no damage was done.

The 500s were started by Rolling Start. The method being to do one lap in formation, and as soon as the flag goes down, off they go. When the formation passed me it looked really grand. A mass of most attractive colours, pretty bodies and exhaust noise ! No words of mine can really describe the scene and do it justice.

Several blokes had trouble starting and spent this lap nipping round trying to catch up with the bunch. They were Jack Moor, in the Wasp 500, Watkins, in a Cooper, Rhiando, in a Cooper, Fry, in an Iota, and one or two others.

The following made fastest practice times and were therefore put in the front rank:—

			Non-Starters:
Dryden	..	Cooper	Cox
Moss	..	,,	Gladstone
Rhiando	..	,,	Rippon
Aston	..	,,	Wharton
Page	..	,,	

Very shortly after the start young Stirling Moss cantered off into the lead, where he remained. Both Dryden and Aston kept within striking distance, but Moss always appeared to be able to get away from them if they pressed too hard.

In the meantime Spike Rhiando, who was half a lap behind at the start, was diceing really hard. His speed through Stowe had to be seen to be believed. There was no doubt that had he not made that bad start, Moss would have had more competition.

Spike, however, must have been using too much loud pedal, as around the 12th lap, having worked up to 7th or 8th, retired with a burst motor.

Watkins, another of the bad starters, drove a magnificent race. He motored smoothly through the pack to 5th place. Most of the time he was lapping at the same speed as Moss.

The field started to thin out almost immediately. The M.A.C. being, I believe, the first. Poor old Gibbs—he watched the race sitting on his front wheel looking very unhappy. Weeks of work for a bitter disappointment. What a life !

By the time the chequered flag fell only about 50% were left running, the order of the first six being:—

1.	Stirling Moss	..	Cooper	23
2.	R. M. Dryden	..	,,	11
3.	W. S. Aston	..	,,	2
4.	M. A. H. Christie	..	,,	6
5.	K. Watkins	..	,,	38
6.	J. G. Reece ..	..	,,	28

One of the newest cars, the Parsenn, amateur-built by Keith Steadman and Jeremy Fry, was doing very well, having just got into 4th place, had to retire as the gear box started to part company with the rest of the outfit.

Grose, in his very " Merc " like motor looked good, but did not seem to be going as fast as it should.

Frank Aikens went like a comet as long as he lasted, and hung on to 4th place but something went wrong with the works and put him out.

Bond, in the Bond Type C, was disappointing; big things were expected of him, but it just did not seem to go. It is rumoured he was rather over-geared.

Next month I hope to be able to produce a complete report of the race with the list of finishers, casualties and faults. Please try and send me all this information before the 20th of the month. There must be a number of people reading these words who were watching the race, so try and put some of the incidents you saw on paper and send it along. In this way it will be possible to reconstruct the whole race and produce a description which is not possible any other way.

Personalities

VICE-PRESIDENT

(Photo by Charles Lytle)

LAURENCE POMEROY

Laurence Pomeroy is a person of remarkably wide interests, and this is reflected in the breadth of vision which he brings to bear upon problems of all kinds, both mechanical and human. With this is coupled a positively ruthless capacity for ignoring non essentials so that his opinions are generally constructive and often pungently unconventional.

In mechanical matters, both as the son of his father and in his own right, he has an immensely wide experience, and this, coupled with his other qualities and his remarkable literary gifts, has made him a world wide authority on his subject.

His driving technique is forceful, unconventional, and effective, and there can be few people who possess a keener critical faculty in assessing the handling qualities of a car, or who takes a keener pleasure in driving a car which handles well, whether it be his 1914 Vauxhall, or his 1949 Morris Minor.

In addition to being one of our Vice-Presidents, Pomeroy is the current President of the Vintage Sports Car Club.

For

with

CONFIDENCE

use

LODGE

RACING PLUGS

JERSEY
INTERNATIONAL
ROAD RACE

April 28th, 1949

AGAIN WON

by user of

LODGE PLUGS

F. R. GERARD – E.R.A.

(Subject to usual confirmation)

Lodge Plugs Ltd., Rugby, England

THE

RACING-TYPE COOPER

EFFICIENT & SUCCESSFUL PRODUCTION RACING CARS

500 c.c. £575 **1,000 c.c. £775**

LIST OF 1948 RACING SUCCESSES:

March 31 LUTON HOO SPEED TRIALS
1st & 2nd 500 c.c. Class RECORD

June 5 BRIGHTON INTER-NATIONAL HILL CLIMB
1st & 2nd 500 c.c. Class
1st 1,000 c.c. Class

June 12 SHELSLEY WALSH HILL CLIMB
1st 500 c.c. Class RECORD
1st 1,000 c.c. Class & Unblown Record RECORD

June 13 PRESCOTT HILL CLIMB
1st 500 c.c. Class RECORD
1st 1,500 c.c. Class & Second-fastest time of day
Unblown Record & Team Prize RECORD

June 27 BO'NESS, SCOTLAND
1st 500 c.c. Class
First 1,000 c.c. Class & Unblown Record RECORD

July 4 BROUGH, YORKSHIRE
1st, 2nd & 3rd 500 c.c. Class & fastest time of day

July 15 BOULEY BAY, JERSEY, HILL CLIMB
1st 500 c.c. Class RECORD

July 18 PRESCOTT HILL CLIMB
1st 500 c.c. Class RECORD

July 25 GREAT AUCLUM SPEED TRIALS
1st & 2nd 500 c.c. Class RECORD
(Second-fastest time of day)

Aug. 20 BOSCOMBE SPEED TRIALS
1st 500 c.c. Class RECORD
(Second-fastest time of day)

Sept. 4 BRIGHTON INTERNAT-IONAL SPEED TRIALS
2nd 1,000 c.c. Class, Fastest Unblown Time
Fastest foreign competitor, International Trophy (Spike Rhiando)

Sept. 12 PRESCOTT INTER-NATIONAL HILL CLIMB
1st 500 c.c. Class
1st 1,000 c.c. Class

Sept. 18 GOODWOOD CIRCUIT RACE
500 c.c. Class 3-Lap, 7-mile Race
1st, 2nd & 3rd

Sept. 25 SHELSLEY INTER-NATIONAL HILL CLIMB
1st 500 c.c. Class RECORD

Oct. 2 SILVERSTONE 500 c.c. GRAND PRIX 50-MILE RACE
1st, 2nd, 3rd & 4th and Fastest Lap

Oct. 9 DUNHOLME AERODROME 500 c.c. 30-MILE RACE
1st, 2nd, 3rd & 4th and Fastest Lap

★ **Order your Model now for next Season's Racing**

COOPER CAR CO., LTD., 243 EWELL ROAD, SURBITON : ELM 3346

ECONOMICAL "500"

By John Baldock

This is not the story of a car to climb Shelsley in 40 secs., or break any lap records, but just a very ordinary "500."

It all started with an advertisement in IOTA, "Austin 7 chassis and Velocette 500 engine, £25." Having long had ideas of making a special of some kind, this seemed a good start, wanting only a gearbox to make a car! It hasn't been quite as easy as that, but snags have been relatively few. A start was made first on the back

General chassis arrangement.

axle. The crown wheel was removed and a $\frac{5}{8}'' \times \frac{3}{8}''$ chain sprocket of the same diameter was bolted on in its place. The diff. housing was cut away sufficiently to allow exit of chain. The diff. was locked by the simple method of pouring in molten lead.

The rear chassis cross member was removed, and the side members were lengthened 4" with 3" × 4" angle iron. The missing cross member was replaced by two $1\frac{1}{2}''$ tubes, which carry the plates for mounting both engine and gearbox. This structure was welded into position by the local expert. The rear springs were inverted and fitted to the axle with rubber bushes to allow slight movement. The axle was located with combined shock absorbers and radius arms bolted to the ends of the extended chassis. The superstructure supporting petrol tank and back of seat was the framing of a Messerschmitt 109 cockpit cover. This fell from the sky on a Sunday afternoon in 1940 and has been waiting ever since for suitable employment.

Complete assembly less body.
A strong and rɛliable engine mounting.

This stage was reached last autumn, and being anxious to test engine aand trns-mission before bad weather started, the front end was completed very rapidly in a temporary design. The front suspension was utilized in exactly the same way as its maker intended, but the front of the chassis was much higher than the rear. The steering box was mounted centrally on a new cross member, and in this state the vehicle is shown as in the first photo. A number of test runs were made, and the questionable transmission stood up to its work with no trouble at all. The acceleration seemed very satisfactory, and maximum speed was left for a later date to decide.

Encouraged by results everything was stripped down and has since then been carefully rebuilt with an improved front end. The axle is now inverted with a layout similar to that tried by Clive Lones, and shown in an IOTA photo some months

An interesting front end arrangement.

ago. This gives a ground clearance of 5″, using 3.50 × 19 tyres. I know it has a number of disadvantages, but on test, it seems to work, and is very easily carried out, almost entirely with Standard Austin 7 parts with steering box from a Triumph 7 mounted at the front. The completed chassis layout is shown in later photos.

The Velocette engine is in no way a racing motor, and at this stage has been only slightly modified. It has been assembled with a good deal of care, and a Martlet H.C. piston has been fitted to allow use of alcohol fuel. A body is now in the course of construction, and we hope to be ready for the road in a few weeks. Which brings us to the point—what shall we do with it now ? I appreciate very much all that has been done by various clubs to give " 500 " owners an opportunity to try their cars, but the number of events, suitable for beginners still seems very small. Perhaps there will be more novices events—hill climbs or racing—in 1949.

The whole car has been almost entirely amateur home constructed, and only ordinary garage tools have been used throughout, with the exception of a good power-driven drill. Welding has been limited to the cross members previously mentioned, and one or two other minor parts. The only other outside engineering help was fitting the chain sprocket to the back axle.

500 CLUB NEWS

The Secretary's Column

BY JOHN F. GALE

Looking back on July 9th, it is easy to see quite a lot of improvements that could have been made — always provided the chap to execute them can be found — but there can be no doubt that the races were good fun and provided some extremely close finishes.

Poor publicity presumably was the main cause of the small attendance, and I feel the Motoring Press could have done a lot more for us.

Entries were also smaller than anticipated. Over eighty known drivers were circulated, but the late appearance of the June *Iota* with all the details of the meeting must have had some bearing on this.

The response to the appeal to members to act as marshals on race-day met with under ten offers of assistance, so it appears the Club member prefers to watch his racing from the public enclosure rather than round the course.

I am quite sure everyone will agree that the starting method produced better results than ever before obtained with that number of 500's. The starting problem is peculiar to this type of car. It needs a push-start, and, in some cases, a tow, but cannot be kept waiting on the line for fear of over-heating.

We were glad to welcome Sir Algernon Guinness, Bart., as the R.A.C. Steward, and Bob Gerard, who acted as the Club's Steward in conjunction with Colin Strang. Other personalities present were Mrs. Kay Petre and representatives from the Irish, French, and Dutch 500 Clubs.

That's all on our own Silverstone meeting, except I hope to produce a Balance Sheet by next month, to enable all members to appreciate the £ s. d. of such an affair.

I am becoming more convinced that motoring enthusiasts are very active in expecting things to be done for them, but not so active when it comes to doing things for themselves. And 500 enthusiasts are as bad as the rest.

This is not meant to be a thoroughly chiding monthly letter, but I would say that I have had a regretful note from Reg Trevellick to say that he is disappointed in his recent request to Midland men to contact him. If you are still wanting to do so, now is the time either to put pen to paper — his address is 84 Goodrest Avenue, Quinton, Birmingham 32 — or to telephone him at Woodgate 2837.

From A. B. Cambridge in Worcester comes more cheerful news, for they do meet on the last Thursday of each month at the Alma Inn, Lowesmoor, Worcester, at 7.30 p.m. This month's meeting will have as its feature a Talk and Demonstration on the Speedway J.A.P. engine by the Centre Chairman, Mr. R. Lambourne, who is a motor-cycle Speedway and Grass-track rider, and knows what he is talking about when it comes to tuning the J.A.P.

A. B. Cambridge is the Centre Secretary, and his address is 13 Ashcroft Road, Worcester. There is a Centre Committee, consisting of D. Kiteley, D. Soley, G. Stallard, and R. Skinner, with Miss Green as Treasurer.

BRANDON BRILLIANT AT PRESCOTT

Record Broken on Wet Road

If ever Eric Brandon has been able to claim Prescott as his speciality it was at the Open meeting on July 17th, when a showery day, which left the road damp throughout the afternoon, disorganised everyone except him.

He was favoured with no better road conditions than the rest of the 500 entrants, but, whereas no one else got below fifty seconds, he not only cracked this figure but proceeded to set a new 500 record for the hill in 48.67 seconds (the previous best, also by Brandon, was 48.80). Faultless, is the only way to describe what must be something of an epic drive.

A glance at all the other times recorded is the best way of appreciating just how good it was, on a day when the fastest of all was M. A. H. Christie, with the 1,000 c.c. engine in his Cooper. He made 46.76 seconds.

Brandon made a perfect start, and, aided by the Z.F. diff., flashed through the hairpin and the esses under immaculate control all the way.

P. J. Collins, running the Silverstone winning Cooper, now using its sprint J.A.P. motor, flashed into Orchard, but not out of it, for he neatly slid through a gap in the hedge, created by Wilkes' Rover during practising the previous day, and dropped smartly into the gully which faces the unwary at this point. Fortunately, the Rover had succeeded in depositing some straw bales in the gully, and these nicely cushioned the Cooper's fall.

Collins stepped out quite unhurt, and a cursory glance revealed no damage to the car, though by the time this had been retrieved and got back to the paddock the scrutineers reckoned their examination would not be over in time for him to have another try that day.

Fastest in practice had been D. F. Truman with the Bardon J.A.P. in 49.83 seconds, but this success seemed to encourage him too heartily, with the result that on his first run he spun round in the esses, and did not complete the climb.

Experiment Failed

Of fifteen 500 entries, J. Derrick (Cooper) and J. Rowe with his own Special failed to arrive. Colin Strang tried hard, making a number of experiments with gear ratios in practice, and now using Fiat wheels front and back, but to no purpose, and he did not appear completely happy during his runs. Even more unhappy was C. J. Tipper, who still seems to be unable to get the feel of the somewhat tricky Monanco, so that to him fell the doubtful merit of being the slowest of the 500's, and, indeed, of the 750's.

The latter class produced H. C. Lones' proposal to sidestep some of the fiercest 500 opposition by using an engine bored out to 526 c.c. This time, the experiment failed by one-hundredth of a second, as for once the Austin contingent were on form, and K. C. Jarvis managed a first run of 50.46 Lones was actually more consistent, for his times were 50.47 and 50.87 whereas Jarvis only made 52.61 on his second climb.

continued on page 2[illegible]

Rumours and Realities . . .

500 drivers who have had difficulty in getting their cars to the Continent at all, apart from the difficulty of finding a race there in which to run, will hardly be consoled, but may be interested, that 1949 bids fair to break all records for cross-Channel motoring. The various touring agencies all report a flood of applications for space on the overcrowded ships, and the R.A.C. alone had, by the end of July, arranged the shipment of 50 per cent more cars than during the whole of the 1948 season. Whilst not begrudging the holiday motorist the pleasures of unrationed petrol and service from hotel keepers, the serious motoring competitor comes off rather badly in this scramble, for such are the habits of Continental race promotors that drivers rarely know a reasonable time in advance whether they are to be among the select band of invitees or even just allowed to enter at all. Next season the problem may be even more acute for 500 drivers, for with the increasing success and popularity of the class on the Continent and rumours of impending extension of the scope of recognition, it is certain that there will be a widening number of events for Class D vehicles when next year's international calendar is framed.

* * * * *

By the time this issue of *Iota* is in readers' hands the great Lapwing mystery may be nearer solution. This is not a problem for ornithologists but something to tantalise the enthusiast as being either a supreme example of amateur car building or one of its biggest hoaxes. For those who are not yet pondering on the mystery it may be revealed that the Lapwing is alleged to be a hush-hush jet-propelled car designed to attack the world's land speed record. So far so good, except that no one seems to have actually seen the projected monster being assembled in the fastnesses of the Highlands, or being tested, as alleged, at 140 m.p.h. Strangest of all is that Dunlops state positively that they've not been approached as to the supply of tyres, and so far as is known the named driver has never appeared in a motoring event and does not possess a competition licence. At the time of writing, the Lapwing was still shrouded, or so the stories went, but this time in the substantial framework of a packing-case being borne through England on an eight-wheeled lorry. Quite why eight wheels no one seems to know, but at least the story has helped the provincial Press fill its columns.

500 enthusiasts would seem likely to find more substance in rumours of record attempts shortly in spheres nearer their hearts.

* * * * *

Latest force in the motor-cycle racing world, the Italian Gilera, a four-cylinder, twin overhead camshaft unit is claimed to develop more than 45 b.h.p. at 9,000 r.p.m. on the straight petrol fuels at present demanded by the two-wheeler racing rules. The whole bike only weighs 275 lb. Perhaps one day someone will go to Italy with enough lire and a persuasive enough personality.

MORE CONTINENTAL CHEERS

50,000 Thrilled at Zandvoort

Rain clouds and a traditional national phlegm did nothing to restrain 50,000 Dutchmen and Dutch women from cheering like a cup-tie crowd as British 500 drivers fought off the challenge of a lone Dutch competitor in a photo-finish to a ten-lap race over the winding circuit of Zandvoort on July 30th. And the cheers were not only for a magnificent effort by a compatriot as hearty-faced Lex Beels made his successful drive to force his way into the first three.

There were thrills in almost every yard of this ten-lap Class D event staged in conjunction with the annual Zandvoort Grand Prix run by the resoundingly named Koninklijke Nederlandsche Automobiel Club, which shall be shortened to K.N.A.C. hereafter. What must have given K.N.A.C. seriously to think was the fact that the 500 event was only introduced to the programme as somewhat of an afterthought and on pressure from some persistent Dutch enthusiasts.

Fortunately this enthusiasm prevailed to the extent of having this particular race staged between the Grand Prix heats and final, peak viewing hour as the televisers would say, and thereafter a good time was had by all, once near tragedy had been just avoided in a somewhat ragged start.

Lateness of the decision to stage the race at all left the actual composition of the field in doubt up to a late hour, later in fact than the printing of the programme, but eventually eleven cars were assembled, an absentee being John Cooper himself, still apparently sunning himself on holiday in England. Nine of the cars were his products, the remaining two coming from C. F. Smith's Clapham workshops in the shape of Smith's own C.F.S. and D. Parker's Special. Led by Stirling Moss, who had come on direct from his Bouley Bay exploits, the other Coopers were handled by Dryden, Aston, Sir Francis

Result

1. **Stirling Moss** (*Cooper*)
   23 mins. 21.2 secs.; 66.90 m.p.h.
2. **W. S. Aston** (*Cooper*)
   23 mins. 29.2 secs.; 66.52 m.p.h.
3. **Lex Beels** (*Cooper*)
   23 mins. 29.3 secs.; 66.50 m.p.h.
4. **E. Brandon** (*Cooper*)
   23 mins. 29.5 secs.
5. **C. Dryden** (*Cooper*)
   24 mins. 20.6 secs.
6. **S. A. Coldham** (*Cooper*)
   25 mins. 06.9 secs.

AWARDS: £50, £40, £30, £20 and £10 respectively.

Fastest Lap — **Beels,** 69.1 m.p.h

Samuelson, J. Habin, Coldham, Brandon, P. J. Collins and Beels.

Curly Dryden and Collins were sticking to their Norton power units, but all the rest had J.A.Ps. Beels' apparently having had some attention from the local mechanics, though he had only had the car a couple of weeks.

Practice took its toll, both Smith and Brandon coming to a standstill with engines which it would be flattering to call slightly shop-soiled. Brandon popped in the spare sprint unit which he had carted across the Channel for just such an emergency, and Smith, who was not so well provided for, was grateful for the loan of a unit from Samuelson. Equilibrium was restored when it was found that a few practice laps by Moss, in which he had beaten up the 1,500 c.c. Simca, were made with two pots on the crankcase with the object of persuading the authorities to let him have a run in the Grand Prix proper. The authorities were sympathetic, but declined, whereat the 1,000 c.c. crankcase, from which has been deleted one cylinder, was installed, having been fetched from England in the interval since Bouley Bay by Moss, Senior.

The general post, with engines and the other excitements normal to practice, resulted in Moss and Brandon, separated by Southampton Speedway star Jack Habin, taking the front row in the grid line-up for the race proper, with Moss in the pole position. Behind the leading trio were Parker and Dryden; then, in Row 3, Coldham, Collins and Aston; Row 4, Smith and Beels, with Samuelson all alone in Row 5.

Rain squalls which had earlier driven spectators under the shelter of umbrellas, and left the course liberally bespattered with puddles, held off during the race, though the road was wet enough to need treating with respect.

Near Tragedy at Start

Despite a few outbursts of officious officialdom earlier in the meeting, and despite a starting-grid mishap which had incapacitated the Clerk of the Course, no one seemed to attempt to restrain the enthusiasm of Habin's mechanic which led him to dash out at the last minute to help Habin restore his position after his car had crept forward on the grid.

And whether or not the Starter was too intent on watching the Assistant Timekeeper counting off the seconds to appreciate the situation will probably never be revealed, but the fact was that he brought down the flag with the hapless mechanic still in the midst of the pack. He stepped backwards as Habin shot away, and was struck and flung into the air by Moss's car, to land in the road and be avoided by Aston by, it seemed, a miracle.

Concussed and struggling, he had to be hauled off the course by officials and rushed to hospital, from whence, fortunately, reassuring reports were later received.

Moss checked, but was quite rightly waved on by officials, and managed to complete the lap in second place behind Brandon, where he stayed for one more lap, but on Lap 3 he had taken the lead, followed by Brandon, Aston, Beels, Dryden, Coldham, Samuelson, Habin and Collins. Habin had been third on the first two laps, but was now dogged by misfiring, whilst Parker had fallen out on Lap 2 with ignition trouble, and Smith had seized his borrowed engine on the same lap. Collins had lost a plug lead and then lost a lap replacing it.

The order remained unchanged from Lap 3 to Lap 8, except that Samuelson also fell out, with a dead engine, but all the time everyone except perhaps Moss, whose driving becomes more and more polished as the races go by, was trying all he knew, and the gaps between the cars were constantly changing, so that the crowd could not relax for a moment.

On the eighth lap Aston got past Brandon, and Brandon tried to repass along the straight in front of the pits, but failed and seemed to lose some of his speed (he later said he had, in fact, lost his gears, except top). Beels now chose to make a supreme effort with his orange car, and drew level with Brandon coming out of the corner at the back of the pits. He just managed to draw away, and at the end of the ninth lap was literally level with Aston.

The crowd was wild with excitement in cheering these three — Aston, Beels and Brandon—as they raced on in the last lap. From the last corner, they came into the straight abreast, and, crouched in cockpits, took the last half-mile in grim determination; to pass the finish in aforementioned order with not more than three-quarters of a length between each car. So determined was this scrap, that it continued for a full extra lap, after which the first four did one more lap in triumphant line abreast.

Habin and Collins were still motoring at the finish, but had both been lapped by the first six. Dryden reported to his helpers that his engine was some 1,000 revs. down on its normally available peak throughout the race, with no ready-to-hand explanation for the loss.

There was some junketting in the Town Hall later in the day, when competitors received their prizes and did their best to avoid speech-making, though Moss did not quite succeed. Once the first night in Holland, spent on army beds in the local barracks, had been negotiated, hospitality to the British contingent became pretty overwhelming.

MEMORIAL CIRCUIT

The Zandvoort circuit is literally based on the Nazi occupation of Holland. Rubble from demolitions made by the Germans in this popular seaside resort forms the foundation of the road, and salvaged bricks are the material of construction of the pits and other track buildings.

Tyre experts may think the road the most abrasive in Europe, but to the spectator it twines pleasantly for 2.7 miles through the sand dunes just outside the town of Zandvoort, and within sound of the North Sea. The dunes form natural grandstands, but for paying customers in the erected grandstand there is a double look at the races, as just past the pits the road doubles back on itself in a sweeping curve, and this back-leg returns only a few yards behind the pits.

It is not a fast circuit, the longest straight being only about three-quarters of a mile.

BRANDON IN FRONT ALL THE WAY AT RECORD 79 M.P.H. PACE

Huge crowds — official estimate said over 100,000 — at *Daily Express* boosted meeting organised by the B.R.D.C. on August 20th, saw a magnificent race won by Eric Brandon from Stirling Moss by a length.

Both were driving Coopers, Brandon's, as usual, spotless polished aluminium, and, by virtue of practice times, started in the front row of the massed start along with J. Reece and R. M. Dryden, also Cooper mounted. Brandon treated the ten laps of the 2 mile 1,710 yards circuit as though it were a sprint, and for the first two laps led from Dryden, with Moss third.

Moss by then saw that there was no time for finesse, and moved up to second on the third lap, 2½ seconds in arrears. From then on he drove with everything he knew and kept the crowd spellbound by his efforts to pass Brandon. For the first time, the full perimeter track with no obstacles was used.

Reports came in that he was cornering on two wheels, and by the fourth lap he was right on Brandon's tail, near enough to make use of his slipstream, and was crouching low in the cockpit to try and get the last ounce of speed. The Moss Cooper, as usual in its recent appearances as a 500, was using one cylinder barrel on a big twin crankcase, and just had not the knots necessary to pass the Brandon machine, which had the more normal sprint J.A.P. motor. The only hope seemed to be for Brandon to make a mistake, but he was driving the race of his life and seemed unable to do wrong.

Brandon and Moss take the last corner together *Photo by Guy Griffiths*

As the leaders began to lap some of the slower men from the sixth lap onwards, it was, in fact, Moss who fell back through being forced out of the leader's slipstream. Onlookers reported that Brandon's speed on the run down Hangar straight was phenomenal, and flag marshals were kept busy as he overhauled more and more of the stragglers.

Dryden, who had suffered a momentary seizure of his Norton engine on the fourth lap, made a come-back and by the seventh time round had re-passed Reece to take third place. Here he stayed to the end, after a battle with Reece which very much parallelled that being fought out by the leaders. At the end fifteen were running of the twenty-four which started, and eleven were officially placed at hitherto unapproached speeds.

Result

1. E. Brandon (*Cooper*), 22 mins. 22.4 secs.=79.61 m.p.h.
2. S. Moss (*Cooper*), 22 mins. 22.6 secs.=79.59 m.p.h.
3. R. M. Dryden (*Cooper*), 22 mins. 38.6 secs.=78.77 m.p.h.

4. J. G. Reece (*Cooper*), 22 mins. 45 secs.; 5. K Watkins (*Cooper*), 23 mins. 23 secs.; 6. J. N. Cooper (*Cooper*), 23 mins. 24.8 secs.; 7. D. Parker (*Parker Special*), 24 mins. 0.2 secs.; 8. P. J. Collins (*Cooper*), 24 mins. 1.2 secs.; 9. G. Saunders (*Cooper*), 24 mins. 1.6 secs.; 10. E. J. Moor (*Wasp*), 24 mins. 3 secs.; 11. P. W. K. Page (*Cooper*), 24 mins. 30 secs.

LIVE LETTERS

26, Mansfield Avenue,
Weston-Super-Mare.

Dear Sir,

I am herewith forwarding some suggestions which I think would help the club :—

1. **Meetings.**

I suggest that meetings should be held every alternate month at, perhaps Bristol, where the Club was founded. The purpose of these meetings would be to discuss the progress of the Club and of members' racing cars. For example, if a builder had a technical handicap, he could put his case or difficulty before other members who may be able to help him. This atmosphere of suggestions and criticisms would be to the benefit of all.

2. **Mechanics.**

At a meeting such as a hill-climb, I think that it would be a good idea for the Club to have five or six mechanics to help any member in difficulties. A team of mechanics to represent the Club would help the movement as a whole. It would be ideal to see the mechanics in blue or white overalls bearing the club badge.

These suggestions are from a young builder and I would be only too pleased to hear the " pro's and con's " from members.

Yours faithfully,
M. F. Matthews.

* * *

37, Nurstead Road,
Erith, Kent.

Dear Sir,

I would like to take this opportunity to say a few words about " D " wagon frames and the apparent trend in design.

It would appear, from descriptions and photographs already published and the nomograph in the current issue, that the popular idea for frame construction is large diameter tubes suitably cross braced etc.; may I, at the risk of stirring up a hornets' nest, express the opinion that this type of construction is not so efficient regarding strength for weight as the more conventional channel section frame. Taking as an example the IOTA Chassis. The main members of which are $2\frac{1}{2}''$ o/o 12 SWG tubes, weighing 2.67 lb./ft., the main loads on a frame of this type are static loads due to weight of engine, driver, etc., which put the side members into a pure bend, the side loads due to cornering, and shock loads due to the road surface, added to which we get braking and acceleration loads, but as these essentially only alter the direction of the static loads, which mean that they can be covered by increasing the factor of safety of the frame in bending. The side load, due to centrifugal effect, is limited by the frictional resistance of the tyres on the road—in other words, this load is at a maximum when the car is in a broadside skid and is not more than the static load. The loads due to the road shocks tend to twist the whole frame and are at a maximum when wheels diagonally opposite are riding a bump and the remaining two wheels in a pothole, in a straightforward rectangular frame with parallel cross bracing, this twisting of the frame puts each side member into torsion, but as this torsion is a secondary load, and dependent on the stiffness of the whole frame, and particularly the joints, it can be reduced by stiffening up the whole frame.

From the above it is apparent that the highest loading will be the vertical loading on the frame—with due allowance for braking, etc., and the side members should be designed to take these loads, and bracing is placed as to render these members strong enough to take the side loads.

The tubular side members are equally strong in all directions, so that with cross bracing the frame is made many more times stronger sideways than vertically, whereas a channel member is much stronger vertically than sideways, depending on the depth; now a channel of equal strength to a tube in vertical bending need only be three quarters the weight of the tube, or alternatively a channel of equal weight to the tube can be designed to be more than twice as strong vertically, so we can now make our choice between a lighter and equally strong frame, or a stronger frame of the same weight.

I could carry on from here, but as space is vital I will finish by saying that I am all for tubular construction when used as in the Cisitalia, or as a single tubular backbone.

I might add that I am not connected with the Automobile industry but am a structural and engineering draughtsman.

Yours faithfully,
H. WHITELEY.

* * *

Red Roofs,
Uxbridge Road,
Stanmore.

Dear Sir,

As one who is engaged in the study and development of small high efficiency I.C. engines and a prospective special builder, your "IOTA" technical articles are of special interest to me.

There have been many points I should like to query, but my main objection is to Mr. Harding's list of "alleged" suitable Power Units which is in my opinion very misleading. In fact, it gives the special builder the idea that any old engine will give the required power if it has overhead valves !

My own experience of motor cycle engines is only small so I discussed the list with a development engineer who has spent much time working on these engines and has owned many famous machines.

We found that apart from five very well known power units—all of comparatively recent design and manufacture the list comprised of obsolete, unobtainable and touring or otherwise low powered engines.

For instance, the O.H.V. Panther is a touring engine which without radical modification would not deliver the power. For the purpose for which it was designed it is admirable. Also in this class are the Flying Squirrel Scott and the D.K.W. which sound *very* powerful, but are again touring engines.

I think I am right in saying there are no 500 c.c. Velocette racing engines in the hands of the public.

Mr. Grant has done much to dispel the theory that B.H.P.'s grow on rubbish heaps in breakers' yards, and what he has said about the D.T. "Douggie" also applies to a very large percentage of the power units mentioned in the list. Am I right, Mr. Harding ?

Yours truly,
B. T. PRITCHARD LOVELL.

Heard through the megaphone

A rear view of an array of the latest 500s suggests that a megaphone is becoming a fashionable conclusion for the exhaust pipe. In addition to those who are adpoting it for the first time, a longer pipe has brought the megaphone on the Parker Special into more prominence. Parker was a pioneer in using this device with the J.A.P. engine, and the niftiness of his special would seem to be full justification for its use. The facility with which an exhaust pipe can be " tuned " with a megaphone has tended to enhance its popularity, despite the fact that the now familiar cone was first thought up by the motorcycle people merely as a means of extending an exhaust pipe in length without affecting its extractor effect.

★ ★ ★

Stirling Moss celebrated his twentieth birthday with his fine win at Goodwood. His polished driving seems to have become even more assured following on his taste of Continental experience this season. The question now in his mind is whether the new 1,100 c.c. J.A.P. will give him the horsepower he deserves next year.

★ ★ ★

Brighton and Weston are the two sprints of the year where a driver's quickness of reaction pays special dividends. The Loughborough-Hayes timing apparatus and signal lights were used at both meetings, and the timing starts from the moment the green light shows to indicate to a driver that he may sart. Many who should know better think that the familiar " hockey sticks " record the starting time, but in fact they merely record the fact that a driver has started before the green light came on.

★ ★ ★

A pity that Lex Beels was not able to get an entry to Brighton in time. He could not have failed to win the magnificent " foreigners' cup " which stood disconsolately unclaimed at this year's prize presentation. To judge by his performances he would have deserved it too, apart from receiving it as the only foreigner present.

★ ★ ★

Dryden's winning speed at Blandford was 73.65 m.p.h. Kenneth McAlpine won the 2-litre sports car race at 73.74 m.p.h. with the Connaught, scoring a rare point off the 500. Honours were reversed in the matter of fastest laps, for Carter attained 76.60 with his Cooper, McAlpine, who also made fastest lap, stuck at 75.17.

★ ★ ★

It was very nice for John Cooper of the *Autocar* to be congratulated in error at Zandvoort on the excellence of the cars produced by John Cooper of Surbiton, but it was possibly carrying things a little too far when the Blandford programme mistakenly credited him with the other John's initials. To put the record straight, car-maker John is J. N. Cooper, writer John is J. A. Cooper, A.M.I.Mech.E., M.S.A.E.

GOODWOOD

Moss keeps two hands on the wheel nowadays. *Photo by Guy Griffiths*

With an organisation rechecked in the privacy of August's members meeting B.A.R.C. elected to use their last available date in the 1949 race calendar to once again attract a paying gate to Goodwood on September 17th. Either the unruly considered new spectator arrangements gave them their money's worth, or they had forgotten to bring wire cutters. This time all the customers were well behaved, and around the circuit the police had shepherded cars off the roads into new car parks so that late arrivals had an uninterrupted run right up to course reception points.

As well as the public present in numbers varying from a pessimistic estimate of 15,000 to the B.B.C.'s repeated insistence on 40,000, the actors were there in strength too, 83 in all, including every name which is a name in British driving.

Unashamedly ignoring members who think the B.A.R.C. neglect the sports car owner all eight events were for racing cars only, but the programme conceded to modern fashion to the extent of a 500 c.c. race elevated from curtain raiser to full viewing time of 2.50 p.m. As some reward for the effort and enthusiasm which has gone into the Goodwood circuit project, this September meeting which marked the anniversary of the first-ever race meeting at Goodwood, really gave the first rate sport which had been expected of it, and the *Daily Graphic* again came forward with a money bag for the prizes which, whatever one thinks of the ordinary attitude of the Daily Press to motor sport, must be regarded as a splendid bit of encouragement.

As the autumn sun shone strongly enough to give excuse for the flowered shirts of some of the males as well as females, and cars were manœuvred in and out of new covered stalls around a paddock in Brooklands style, the whole scene suggested full justification for the Junior Car Club's decision to adopt the time-honoured title of B.A.R.C. It needed concentration on the extreme casualness of the timekeeper's " box," the scaffold pole stands, the tents housing officials as well as the different contours of the circuit as a reminder that one really wasn't near Weybridge. So many of the people were the same, though they did look that much older. Sir Algernon Guinness paced up and down by the start line, Earl Howe conducted the Duke of Kent to a vantage point. Bunny Dyer even wore a pre-war B.A.R.C. members' badge, a reminder of the time when he headed H. J. Morgan as secretary of the J.C.C.

Happy man again seeing a dream come true, and with biggest stake in the venture was the Duke of Richmond and Gordon, always desirous that four wheels should outdo four legs in presenting speed at Goodwood.

To the relief of competitors and the stewards the controversial white line was eliminated from Woodcote, and drivers left to their own initiative and good sense in the matter of obstruction of the faster cars in the handicaps. The initiative of certain people led them far off the beaten track, to the accompaniment of clouds of dust and the considerable detriment of the cabbages adorning areas of the " in-field."

Drive it and See

The 500 race was third on the programme, and had attracted 19 entries including three reserves necessitated by an official limit of 16 starters imposed through lack of road width in starting area. Actually six drivers failed to get to the line, including E. S. Limpus with the still unveiled Emeryson. Only Jeremy Fry (*Parsenn*), J. Sparrowe (*Marwyn*) and D. Parker (*Parker*) broke the Cooper ranks, which included G. Saunders, K. E. Carter, S. A. Coldham, K. Watkins, P. Collins, C. A. N. May, P. W. K. Page, R. M. Dryden, J. D. Habin, and L. Beels, the latter, though from Holland, piloting Holtrusts's beautifully turned out orange machine.

Parker got a front row place at the start, in company with Coldham, Habin and Dryden, but the knowing had recorded their faith in Collins with the bookmakers as soon as the rumour was confirmed that he had installed a genuine twin overhead-camshaft Norton engine straight from the works and with an alleged power output of 48 b.h.p. Alleged, because the power curve supplied to the proud owner stopped short at 43 b.h.p. he being instructed to drive it and see upon being inquisitive enough to enquire what happened above that point.

From the drop of the flag Coldham took the lead, but by the end of the first lap Collins was in front and there he stayed till the end. Poor Jeremy Fry was left on the line with a dud plug, result of untoward clearance between piston and barrel following a seizure in practice, and Carter went out with a defunct piston in the first lap, whilst Parker was a bit over-eager on the back stretch, spun and dropped to tenth.

By the second lap Beels had displaced Dryden for second place, and Coldham was fourth, and this order was maintained to the fifth and final round until Coldham nipped past Dryden, now suffering from over-heating, coming round to Woodcote. No one carried out freely muttered threats to protest against the presence of a Dutchman in a purely national race, so that the question of Beel's eligibility now awaits "higher authority."

Collins 74.95 m.p.h. is a 500 c.c. race record, and Beels set a new one-lap figure of 76.8. The finishing order behind Dryden was Habin, May, Parker, Saunders, Page, Watkins and Sparrowe.

Erstwhile 500 drivers, Stirling Moss, Eric Brandon, W. S. Aston, W. J. Whitehouse, M. A. H. Christie, G. Hartwell, R. Merrick, J. P. Fergusson, and even John Cooper himself elected to join Eric Winterbottom in concentrating on the 1,000 c.c. job. After Moss had won the first race at 73.05, including a lap at over 82 m.p.h., his luck was out, and consequent upon bearing trouble in his own engine he borrowed John Cooper's car for the Goodwood Trophy, only again to fall by the wayside.

BEND BUT NOT BREAK

After its retirement from the public eye since mid-August the Parsenn was re-presented by K. B. Steadman and Jeremy Fry with a much altered back end. There is a quite new chassis section aft of the bulkhead behind the driver's seat, and the engine, gearbox and final drive sprocket and brake assembly are now mounted as a unit between a pair of light alloy engine plates, and the whole lot very flexibly suspended on rubber blocks.

Co-designers Steadman and Fry claim thereby to have eliminated the vibration which has dogged them since this exceptionally interesting machine first appeared, and which previously has caused all sorts of odd chassis breakages whenever any distance has been attempted.

As an arrangement which gave K. McAlpine 16 seconds over Moss and Brandon in the fourth race was typical of the peculiarities of the handicapping it could not be expected that the big twin Coopers would get many awards. Probably purely apocryphal was the story that the reason poor C. Heath with his home-made Standard 8 suspended J.A.P. engined Heath Special was expected to concede one whole minute to Dunham's 2-litre Alvis in five laps was because the handicapper did not know the difference between him and John Heath.

The ever-enthusiastic Archie Butterworth had a poor reward for the midnight oil he had burned on Friday in order to replace a con-rod and cylinder barrel in his Steyr engine, when another rod chose to seek daylight via the crankcase wall.

John Bolster fulfilled his first public engagement since his Silverstone mishap, his date being with the course microphone from a perch in the top storey of the control tower in company with a B.B.C. party who are reported as being neither as well informed nor as successful at race reading as John.

A New Year Message.

"NO TIME TO REST ON OUR LARELS"

Those who remember the earliest days of the 500 movement must feel that at long last the class has reached its target. You may remember, that when all this began an astounding amount of uninformed, rather nasty, criticism appeared. People made fun of the idea behind a 500, alleging that you might as well race perambulators, and anyhow this was only a motorcycle on four wheels.

Inevitably there was a long delay before the first machines of what we hoped would be a new class appeared on wheels. Another period when the equally inevitable teething troubles drove most people nearly frantic. But then things began to change. Strang and Lones made history, the little machines promised well, and though there was a whale of a lot of work to get organisers to see the possibilities of a special class at a meeting, even this came along in due course.

Then Coopers put the 500 c.c. really on the map, and now we reach the stage where the owners of large, expensive and exciting racing machines are never very sure that they are going to get fastest time of the day if many of the 500 c.c.'s are anywhere about, and the annals of every hill-climb are records of success for the class.

Mind you, a great deal happened behind the scenes, but a 500 c.c. movement was created by fervid enthusiasts and, moreover, enthusiasts with very definite ideas of what should be done on each and every occasion. But couple this to a slightly sketchy idea of the administration and organisation necessary to run a club, and you will see quite easily why there were moments when more experienced members of the various committees were wont to tear their hair under the impression that divine power only would straighten out the tangle. And the tangle was at times serious, because the more enthusiasm there is in a project, the less likely there is to be a sound financial basis for that project.

But—and this is the great thing—we have come through all that to success fighting every inch of the way, and the success has been so marked as to leave one a little dazed, a little worried lest the thing may not be quite so good as it appears.

The curtain-raiser to Silverstone that put the 500 c.c. on the map as a road-racing machine marked one period. Recognition of the 500 c.c., to the Formula evolved years ago, as the third type of machine for which international Grands Prix can be organised is, practically, the zenith of everyone's hopes. And the 500 c.c. doctrine has spread abroad in no uncertain fashion until in every country where there are races, there are

Mr. S. C. H. DAVIS, 500 Club President, pauses for refreshment in the kind of scene with which he has been so long identified—in this case Prescott, where he chats to Robin Jackson.

Now, "Sammy" Davis, arch-enthusiast, racing driver, and for thirty years Sports Editor of the "Autocar," has decided on what he calls "semi-retirement." All good wishes will go with him and it is hoped that it will be many years before he finally deserts the scenes of motor sport.

Photo by Guy Griffiths

also machines of this class, some extraordinarily odd, some obviously capable, all of them interesting. And a 500 c.c. racing car attracted a great deal of attention at the recent show in Paris.

Moreover, the Club, as a club, has reached the calmer waters of efficiency and method, even though much yet remains to be done. The administration is at least in hand and, I believe that the financial results for this year emphasise that point. So at last we can all say that the critics have been confounded, that the 500 c.c. class is a complete success.

Now, just this word of warning; this is no time to rest on our laurels, however hardly those laurels may have been won, for now that the type is international, obviously more expensive versions of the simple car we had in mind will appear, and expense is to be avoided like the plague if the original conception of the car is to remain.

Now and then come suggestions involving four-cylinder supercharged machines with normal gearboxes and transmissions, excellent enough in every way, but liable to be outside the price range of the very people for whom the 500 was created. Then again, the tendency to convert the car to 1,000 c.c. or more, needs watching, for though it opens up a wider field where general racing takes place, that again may not benefit the 500 c.c. class and its special machines. And we have yet to face a really nice long race, to see whether the Formula 3 cars can really survive the sort of test which Formula 1 and 2 has had to face for very many years.

Anyhow 1949 ends in success: 1950 begins with full promise of greater things, and that is sufficient reward, I think, for all the work done by all the people who began the movement, so that there is every prospect of the merry Christmas and the successful new year which I, for one, would like to have wished everybody interested in the 500.

S. C. H. DAVIS, *President*, 500 *Club*.

POSTBAG

Something to say? We'd like to hear about it, and so would your fellow readers. Address your letters to: "Iota," 51 Cranley Mews, London, S.W.7.

Dull chronicle of success.

Mr. P. W. DAVEY; of Plymouth, writes:

I would like to take this opportunity to express my enthusiasm for the 500 movement, and also to offer a couple of suggestions which in my opinion would improve the value of *Iota.*

The magazine for the amateur car-builder is in danger of becoming a dull chronicle of successes gained by a few fortunate owners of Coopers and similar " off the peg " machinery. Perhaps these accounts could be pruned in order to leave more space for articles dealing with the technical side of the sport.

Allied with the foregoing is the question of illustrations, for I think that " stills," whether of complete cars or components, would be of far more use than the " action " pictures which seem to predominate.

Most people know what a small car looks like at speed, but want to see some of the genuine amateur productions with the lid off.

Perhaps when my present task, the rebuild of an M.G. Magna, is finished, I shall be able to think seriously about a 500. If Formula III has not put the home builder right out of business by then.

Cooper rival needed.

Mr. R. MARTIN, of London, writes:

I would like to wish *Iota* continued success in 1950, and to hope that the 500 c.c. movement reaps full reward from its new internation-status.

As a potential constructor of a 500 c.c. device the advent of Formula III has really crystallised my ideas, and provoked me to make a start at last. I hope that the introduction of the Formula will have the same effect upon others as upon myself, who doubted whether the class was worth bothering with.

From what I hear it seems that a lot of people who might have drifted away into other categories will be kept in the ranks, and there should be a real incentive to the construction of a worthy rival to the Cooper.

No sport can be at its best if dominated by one name, and what have been so disappointing are the ineffective efforts made by various amateur constructors. Most people seem to have forgotten that the Coopers were only amateurs a short time ago.

I am glad that " Iota " has avoided giving publicity to some of the

more dreadful creations which I have seen, for however poor a builder may be there seems no excuse for spending one's time on fundamentally unsound design or for merely bad workmanship.

May I congratulate "Iota" on producing such excellent descriptions of some cars which were well worth the space given to them, and also for the photographs, mostly by Guy Griffiths, which really bring the spirit of motor racing to life?

What hope for the amateur?

Mr. H. E. N. PEARS, of Pembridge, writes:

As the 500 c.c. movement was started as a means for the poor man to join in motor racing, I naturally wonder upon what basis drivers will be chosen to appear in the various Continental events which will be on the new Formula III International Calendar.

One can only assume that there will be some financial assistance to starters, as there already is in the case of other races, and surely this could be just the opportunity needed by the impecunious amateur to enable him to get—figuratively speaking—on to his racing feet.

Unfortunately, if established practice is anything to go by the poor amateur will never get a chance to go abroad, for all the invitations will go to those who can afford to race and make a name for themselves in this country.

Regarding motor racing as a commercial venture rather than as an amateur sport, I suppose promoters can do little else than choose the successful. Just one more instance of "to him that hath shall be given."

I have always regarded it as being the object of the 500 Club to bring racing to him who hath not, or not much at any rate, and I am hoping that the Club has some ideas for giving the ordinary driver at least an occasional chance.

VARIATIONS ON A THEME

Below, Marwyn. Right, Cooper.

500 c.c. car constructors are becoming unanimous in their decision to use independent rear suspension, and the simple layout of pre-war specials as exemplified by the Marwyn does not appear to give the wheel adhesion required by modern performers.

Having chosen independent suspension there is nevertheless no lack of variety of thought as to how to achieve this end. As a pioneer of simplicity it is natural that R. D. Caesar should choose a swing axle for the Iota, and this is constructed without benefit of a spline or even a taper, and a total of four ball-races.

The Monaco layout of trailing arms has given excellent wheel adhesion in straightaway sprints, whilst the C. F. Smith full De Dion axle also includes a Z.F. differential.

Coopers have also added a Z.F. on some cars but have not departed from their original geometry of a parallel wishbone effect.

Above — 1st. Left, C.F.S. Special. 2nd. Left, Monaco. Above, Iota.

The clutch sprocket was of 44 teeth, and output of 18 teeth driving to a 46 tooth rear sprocket.

The wheelbase is 7 ft. and track 3 ft. 6 in.

The three-piece body comprises undershield, nose and tail cowlings; the tail being held in position by two straps, and having a small flap to give quick access to plug and carburetter. The undershield serves a double function, being of sandwich construction, and by means of a scoop taking cooling air into the engine compartment.

The main body bulkhead is a structure of sheet and angle Dural, giving great strength for a weight of only 3 lb.

The car not having been used in long-distance event, it was possible to keep the fuel tank down to a capacity of one and a half gallons, and accommodate it at the front of the car, where it is suspended on rubber mountings. The downhill start at Blandford Hill Climb found a weakness in this arrangement, the " head " not being sufficient to prevent fuel starvation, and later a bicycle pump was fitted to provide a slight air pressure.

One other failure experienced was that of the gear lever, which was an Elecktron aircraft throttle lever of imperceptible weight, and apparently sufficient strength . . . until it broke on the Esses at Prescott. It was then replaced by a steel tube.

A minor fitting which proved of great value in a push start was a gear position indicator on the dashboard, linked to the gearbox by a bowden cable.

No real records were kept of the time taken to build the car, and any record would have been somewhat confused by the amount of experimenting which was undertaken. Mr. Adams reports that his loft seems to be full of parts which were not finally used, but he guesses that in its finished form the car took up evenings and week-ends for at least nine months.

His usual insurance brokers granted cover without too much fuss when he wanted to license it for road use, and the taxation people were co-operative when he had signed a declaration as to the origin of the various parts.

Apart from the use of the Rudge engine, the road equipment mainly comprised a small bulb horn, a strap to hold the handbrake in the on position, mirror, and light mudguards.

The mudguards could be attached or removed, complete with their stays in a matter of a few minutes. Lacking the necessary instruments, it was diffiicult to make any records of the performance achieved on the road, but it appeared to be somewhat undergeared, and was sold before any really serious trials were made.

* * * *

Getting on to the Megaphone

The clamour in Bracebridge Street continues, in a very polite way of course, as the queue of hopefuls await a chance to acquire a Norton engine of the coveted twin overhead-camshaft variety. Most hopeful of success are Peter Collins, C. A. N. May and J. W. Cox. No doubt Dryden and Moor will continue to use Norton power units, though so far they have had only the single-cam design, whilst a car has been under construction in a Bournemouth bedroom for a long time which was to be endowed with a Manx Norton unit.

* * * *

Gerald Spink has also chosen a Norton for his G.S.2, and Alf Bottoms recently acquired the Cowlan chiefly because of its Norton engine. As well as revamping the rear axle layout, the Bottoms' plans include some more urge from the " works," in which project he has the invaluable asset of ownership of a Heenan and Froude brake.

K. W. Smith hopes to be back in the fray this coming season with his special, which follows closely the layout of the original Cooper, and performed to some purpose prior to a temporary lay-up following the 1948 season.

* * * *

First in the field in bargaining for British drivers are the Norwegians, who hope to stage an international Formula Three event in early June. Preliminary talks suggest that they will be generous to the fortunate few who can make the trip, and that they have hopes of getting at least one of their drivers into some races in this country. Chief brake on the 500 movement in Norway is at present political, import restrictions frustrating efforts to import cars, including Coopers. Any hopes of building cars locally are faced with the complete lack of a suitable power unit, and acquisition of J.A.P. engines is equally subject to currency restrictions.

* * * *

Press date for " Iota " has again come round prior to official release of a Formula Three international calendar, but espionage suggests some twelve French races to supplement at least one apiece in Italy, Belgium, Switzerland, Holland, Sweden, and Germany.

Blame Detonation when 'mice' get at the piston crown

*Fuel Facts from *Bob Ginn*

Urge being the main requirement, and as far as most '500s' are concerned, urge from an air-cooled engine without much air-cooling, a methanol-based fuel is the obvious choice.

In a motorcycle the engine obviously has a better chance of keeping cool than in the average 500 car; and it is not just a question of this state of affairs being satisfactory for sprints and a necessary evil in long distance racing, for if the engine is operated at peak, a few seconds can be as injurious as several laps of Silverstone. Only Major Clot is likely to hurtle off the line at Shelsey with a cold engine.

That the fuel should be required to compensate for cooling deficiencies is not very satisfactory—but that it is required to do so is borne out by the relative jet sizes for the same engine in a motorcycle (1,100 jet) and in a car (1,400 jet).

Consider the average owner with a four or five-stud J.A.P. with the standard iron barrel. Piston burning is a particular problem with the five-stud engine, and, without decrying the excellence of this power unit, this burning is, in the writer's opinion due to two things : one, the oil system, the other the iron barrel. This engine was designed to operate for very short bursts, and the excellent performance obtainable under adverse conditions in a car is proof enough of the basic worth of the engine. So do not construe these remarks as carping criticism of an excellent power unit.

The oil system is on the total-loss principle, therefore the oil is used for its true purpose, lubrication, and little or no heat transference is effected by it ; a dry-sump engine, on the other hand, circulates oil at a considerable rate, and significant quantities of heat are removed and dissipated.

The iron barrel does not give sufficient cooling in the close confines of a car.

Now piston burning, if the mixture strength is satisfactory, indicates detonation, the same occurrence that leads to the tinkling noise in the family barouche when the loud pedal is depressed on Pool. No racing single in full cry will allow such a noise to offend its driver's ear, chiefly due to the fact that the machinery in general is all vibrating at or about the same frequency.

**R. J. Ginn, M.B.E., A.M.I.Mech.E., A.F.Inst., Pet. is a member of the technical staff of the Anglo American Oil Co. He offers advice to competitors who write to him at 83 Albert Embankment, London, S.E.11.*

The driver's first clue is a departure of urge accompanied by a woffling noise and nothing else. The cause is a phenomenon occrring in the unburnt portion of the mixture before the normal flame front has proceeded from A to B, and the effect is a hold in the piston. Hot debate ensues when anyone attempts to account for this phenomenon, but the fact remains that local temperatures are apt to be more than somewhat and if pressing on regardless is the order of the day, the aforesaid woffle will duly appear.

A general reduction of engine temperatures may or may not be a remedy; this can be done in a limited way by increasing jet sizes and using the excess fuel as a combustion space coolant. Another way is to reduce the compression ratio; but this has the penalty of reduced power attached to it.

Take some water with it

If neither of these is attractive, 5 per cent water in the methanol will often be extremely effective. Water will affect power, but not to the same extent as a reduction in comp. ratio.

For car use therefore the writer believes that an iron barrelled, total-loss oil system engine must be modified to an alloy barrel and the installation of a dry-sump oil system.

Now why only an alloy barrel? Apart from the fact that an alloy barrel is a much simpler (and cheaper) proposition than an alloy head, heat dissipation from the piston is a function of the ability of the barrel to get rid of heat—remember the heat from the piston crown travels via the ring belt and the lubricating oil (if any) to the bore and thence to the cooling fins.

Again, with a dry-sump oil system, there is a much greater quantity of oil brought into intimate contact with the underside of the piston crown and with the bottom end generally, so considerable heat is transferred by this means.

Another useful modification would be to turn the cylinder head through 180° bringing the exhaust port to the rear where the writer is convinced most of the cooling breezes blow in the average type of 500 car.

An all alloy engine would be very nice, but the head is an expensive item justified only when the regulations insist on Pool, which the God of speed forbid for 500 racing.

By and large, methanol is a very kind fuel to an engine; the rate of pressure rise is a comparatively slow and dignified affair and considerable cooling benefit results from the high latent heat, as has been already discussed. Allied to this is a liking for rich mixtures; weak mixtures are a bad thing causing afterburning, which can result in exactly the same effect as detonation.

So far, we have only considered methanol fuels generally; now for something a little more specific. Neat Methanol is a possible fuel, but it can be greatly improved with other constituents. Some of these will depend on the engine, but acetone is always a good bet, if only from the starting angle.

Methanol, due to its comparatively high boiling point (64.7° C.) and high latent heat is difficult to vaporise, and can cause difficult starting from cold. Pool petrol and any normal motor fuel has a low initial boiling point around 35—40° C. The factor most affecting cold starting is the 10 per cent distillation point, that is, the temperature at which 10 per cent of the fuel has boiled away ; an average figure for Pool is 60° C. whilst pre-war petrols averaged around 55° C. It is easy to see that Methanol misses out, as its initial (and only) boiling point is some 5° C. higher. The addition of small amounts of acetone, which has very similar properties to Methanol allied with a boiling point around 45° C., successfully overcomes this difficulty, and may also help the vaporisation under running conditions. Anything from 2 per cent to 10 per cent is beneficial.

Another constituent is benzole; this is generally used when the engine is over-cooled—a rare state of affairs—and in the order of 5 per cent to 15 per cent. Benzole will increase the quantity of heat being put through the engine.

Water has already been considered—and here might be mentioned the fact that 5 per cent of 1 gallon is 8 fluid ounces (the baby's bottle should come in handy), but there are other and more exotic constituents. Quite popular is nitro-benzene which gives the distinctive boot-polish smell at the exhaust pipe, but the writer has never seen an automatic gain from the addition of nitro-benzene whereas he has experienced the

The layout of the light alloy chassis frame of the Adams Special which was described in full in February's " Iota ".

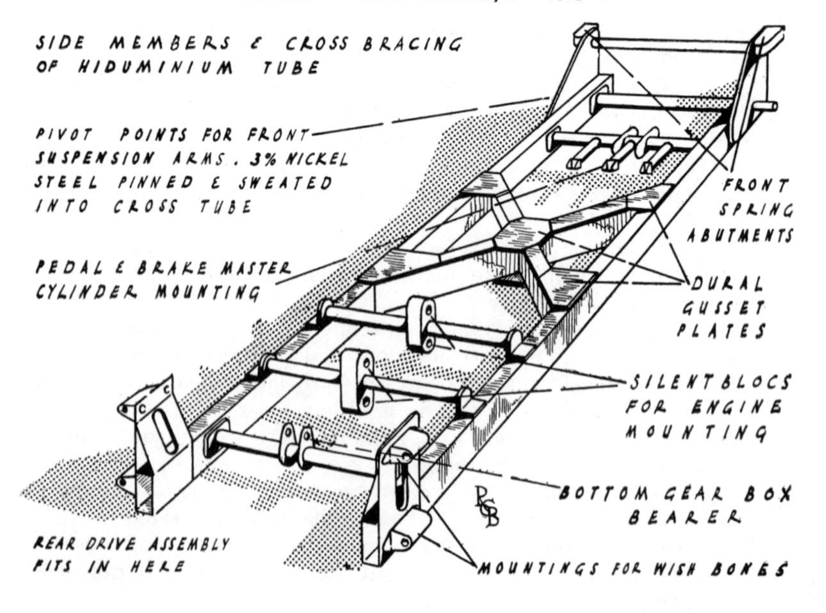

formation of nitric acid from the same source. Never add water to a fuel containing nitro-benzene.

The use of a nitro-compound is presumably to supply nascent or atomic oxygen which will be in very intimate contact with the base fuel. Oxidation (combustion) should therefore be quicker and more complete. Considered solely as pro-knocking agents (ignition promoters), the following figures were obtained in the C.F.R. engine on 80 octane petrol. 5 per cent nitro-benzene reduced the octane value to 78; 5 per cent nitro-methana gave 70 octane; 5 per cent nitro-propane 68 octane. It is impossible to assess these substances' relative effects on methanol in the same test engine, so we have to rely on intuition and bench tests of racing engine when anyone has the time to make them.

No amount of an exotic dope will ever take the place of careful and painstaking preparation of an engine.

Protect from vibration

This may be the point where grandmother is introduced to the gentle art of egg-sucking, but another point, unconnected with the fuel, but intimately concerned with the fuel dispensing device, is the trouble experienced with undue vibration of the carburetter float chamber; this can lead to very puzzling symptoms of over-richness at speed with disastrous consequences when the jets are reduced. Nearly all road-racing motor-cycles have rubber insulated float chambers.

Whilst still in the hints and tips corner watch out for the diaphragms of fuel pumps; methanol does not treat them kindly.

Standard methanol racing fuels are :—

(i). 2% Acetone, 98% Methanol.
(ii). 10% Pool, 10% Benzole, 80% Methanol.
(iii). 10% Acetone, 5% Benzole, 85% Methanol.

So much for the fuel, now let's take a look at the lubricant angle. The castor oil brigade still look like the Bisto advert. when a motor using it (castor, not Bisto) passes by, but really the chemists have learned something in the last fifteen years, and now the only argument is about the viscosity (thickness) of the oil.

Without looking under any stones, the prediction is made that the must-have-body-in-the-oil types are due to be somewhat shaken in the near future.

A query that pops up regularly is the one concerning methanol and the lubricant. The idea is that, as mineral oil won't mix with Methanol, the fuel is less likely to remove the oil from the cylinder walls. Now, experiment has shown that Methanol has a very great washing action on all oil-coated surfaces, whether the oil be castor or mineral. To the author's mind, from the fuel angle, the type of lubricant is immaterial. If neat methanol is getting past the piston the results with either oil are likely to be equally unhappy. If castor, then the engine will be lubricated with a thin liquid composed of castor and methanol; if a mineral oil, then presumably slugs of methanol will be chasing slugs of oil through the system. In either case, bore wear will be very high.

Availability of power units may be deciding factor in international 500 c.c. racing.

At present Britain and Italy are supreme, but Germany has the 'know-how" with the B.M.W., and also suitable chassis parts such as the Volkswagen components which are used as the basis for the special shown here.

SOON WE SHALL KNOW WHAT THE CONTINENT CAN PUT UP AS A CHALLENGE

By the time that the next issue of IOTA appears it will have been possible to make a more accurate assessment as to the strength of the initial Continental challenge to present British supremacy in 500 c.c. class racing. Writing now the picture is one of rumour and conjecture, not helped by the rapid cancellation of races which France had optimistically inscribed on the International Calendar for Formul 3.

Some facts must emerge soon as replies are given to the Royal Automobile Club in answer to invitations now being issued to cover foreign representation at Silverstone on May 13.

The official procedure in such circumstances is to ask each national club to nominate drivers, and no doubt invitations will have been sent to all countries subscribing to the Formul 3 International Calendar. These are, France, Italy, Holland, Switzerland, Belgium, Sweden and Norway.

In most of these countries the scene appears to parallel that in Great Britain a few years ago, with lots of people frantically building cars, but it being practically impossible, even for the natives, to distinguish between the complete and ready to race, nearly complete, . mere pipe dreams or drawing board doodles.

Acting as IOTA'S No. 1 espionage agent Spike Rhiando recently returned from Paris with tales of having seen a prototype car nearly completed by Bernardet, whereas the magazine of the Belgium 500 Club records Bernardet as building nine cars. The same magazine lists 14 finished cars, some of which are two seaters, for the Continentals seem to be taking quite seriously the idea of 500 c.c. sports car racing, this is perhaps not so remarkable as it may seem at first considering some of the tiny vehicles which have in the past completed the Bol d'Or. Chaix is given as having three single seaters, and Colle, Constantin, Dalmaze,

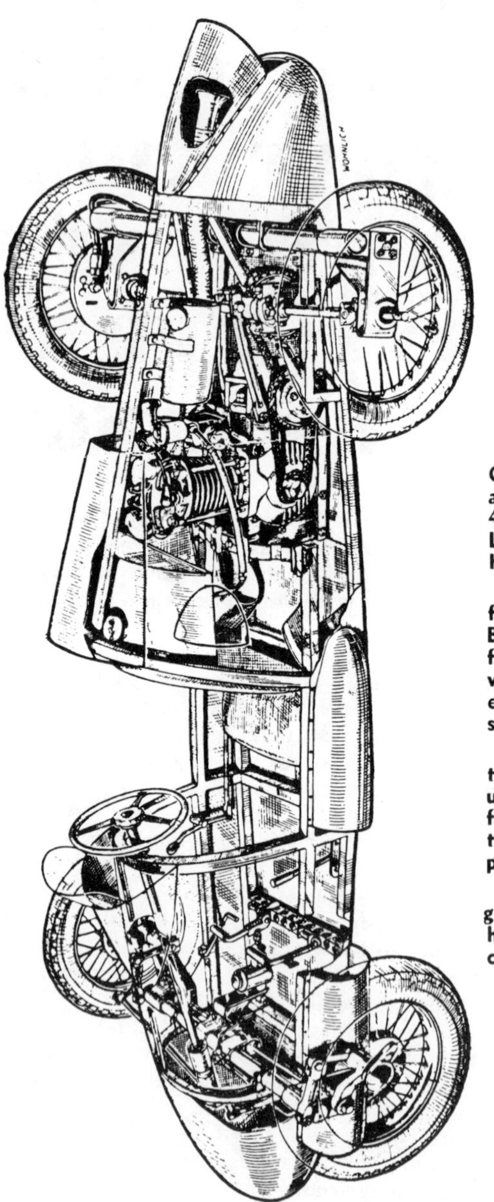

The Kaspar is one of the few Continental designs which has already raced, having achieved 4th place in the 1,100 class at Lucerne last year, driven by Hubert Pattaey.

The adjacent illustration from the "Automobil Revue Bern" shows the chassis formed from welded square tubing, with circular cross tubes at each end carrying the suspension units.

The actual springing is by torsion bars which lie just under the cross tubes, running from a central anchorage to the swinging arms of the suspension system.

The engine is a J.A.P., the gearbox Norton, brakes Lockheed, and the wire wheels carry 4.00 by 19 tyres.

Denis, Freiss, Masse, Pages, Rouge, and Otterbein as having one car apiece.

It is also said that three D.B. have been completed and delivered, and Spike brings reports of a special engine being produced by Panhard with a good deal more urge than the souped up standard model.

The car which Bernardet has nearly finished has a tubular chassis, with wishbone suspension fore and aft. There are pairs of superimposed wishbones at each corner of the chassis, and they seem to be of nearly equal length.

The actual springing is carried out by coil springs which lie horizontally across the top of the chassis, and are operated by the top wishbones via bell cranks.

The whole car looks reasonably light, though being fitted with Fiat wheels when seen. These wheels are due to be replaced by light alloy ones as soon as supplies arrive. At the moment there is one Norton and one Rudge engine available.

Less news has filtered through from Italy, perhaps because they have not yet got around to publishing a "500" magazine, but rumours persist as to the activities of M. Enrico Nardi, who appears to have lost his partner Danese, but who advertises chassis for sale in America, or complete cars if you desire them.

It is said that one of these chassis has been tried out fitted with one of the genuine works Gilera four cylinder motorcycle engine units, and is quite a vehicle : as it rightly should be. The question in doubt is whether or not Gilera have now retrieved the engine for their motorcycle racing programme.

From Rome a certain Taraschi announces that he has a car which he would like to bring to England, but he gives no details of the vehicle.

The foreign amateur constructors seem reasonably able to obtain Fiat parts, and using these and a J.A.P. engine Jakob Keller assembled a neat looking car in Zurich, from whence has just appeared Der Motor Sport. In addition to the Kaspar, this magazine describes a machine constructed by R. Deslandes, and powered by a Triumph Tiger 100 engine.

With a very svelte exterior to its light alloy bodywork, this machine has four wheel independent suspension by means of wishbones and torsional rubber bushes at the wishbone anchorages. The wishbones are fabricated by welding.

Brakes are Lockheed, and detachable wheels carry 5.00 by 15 tyres. An electric pump supplies fuel from longeron tanks with a total capacity of 20 litres.

Using the usual chain drive, it seems that a differential is also fitted.

The Geneva show produced two cars, one of which can be safely ignored it would seem, for despite a good exterior, it is based on the two stroke Aero Minor, which is hardly in the 40 b.h.p. class.

The other, the Este claims 45 b.h.p. from an American Crosmobile engine linered to bring it from 750 to 500 c.c. A five bearing crank, and overhead camshaft may make this possible. Shaft drive includes a 5 speed gearbox. The rest of this car is basically Fiat, the transmission putting the driver's seat rather high up, and the weight is also probably fairly high.

BRILLIANT BRANDS HATCH OPENING

Whitehouse and Carter share star honours

It is recorded on another page that Brands Hatch offers the spectator a superlative view. Not only was there a view, but there was also sunshine on April 16th, when the 500 Club promoted the first of four meetings scheduled there this season. The attendance should have pleased owner Joe Francis, and if the enthusiasm of the crowd is anything to go by there will be a lot more people present on June 25th.

As for the racing itself, it would not be extravagant to claim that rarely before has any meeting seen such battles. At some time in every race a mighty struggle was fought out, and though in some instances the eventual winner came home by a comfortable margin, this was only because of some mechanical frailty on the part of the opposition.

On the mechanical side, this meeting added another character to the writing on the wall which must soon state plainly the fact that the power unit position is becoming critical. It appears that the J.A.P. can still just hold its own, but now some serious-minded people are beginning to ask for how long, as the Norton starts to invade what might almost be regarded as sprint preserves. A Norton carried " Big Bill " Whitehouse to victory in the final championship race of the day, sounding as crisp and unperturbed as when starting a race schedule involving a total mileage of seventy-seven.

Ken Carter was responsible for the fact that Whitehouse failed to make a clean sweep, for Carter beat him for first place in both the heats and final of the Open Challenge Race, the result being that Whitehouse collected a purse of £65 10s. instead of a possible £70. By the luck of the draw Carter and Whitehouse met again in a heat of the Professionally-built Car Race, but this time Carter had to take second position.

Minus shock-absorbers

Commenting upon the apparent lack of stability of Carter's Cooper seen from the height of the announcer's box, John Bolster had evidently failed to spot that Carter was bereft of both rear shock-absorbers in the latter race, the result being a not unnatural liveliness at the rear end. Indeed, what was really remarkable was that he managed to stay where he did among the leaders.

If Whitehouse's engine gets the laurels for the afternoon, then Carter should perhaps take those for driving, only one incident marring his display. Perhaps thinking that he was going so fast that no-one could possibly attempt to pass him on the uphill paddock bend he pulled across the track just as Alf Bottoms did try to pass. Bottoms had no option but to go off into the rough, and got himself tangled with the anti-motorcycle trip wire,

Carter (Cooper) and Bottoms (J.B.S.) lead the pack coming out of the Clearways curves at Brands Hatch.

fortunately doing no real damage, but effectively eliminating himself from the Open race final.

An easy victory previously in the third heat, which he won at 61.95 m.p.h., compared with Carter's 61.97 m.p.h. in the second heat, got Bottoms into the Championship of the Meeting for the ten fastest cars of the day, and he was a very nice third behind Whitehouse and Brandon when the fuel tank of his J.B.S., which was described in last month's "Iota," decided that the stress of a pressurised fuel system was too much for it by the eighteenth lap. There was never any chance of anyone effectively challenging the two leaders of this race during the remaining twelve laps.

It seemed to be Bottoms' unlucky day, for he should easily have won the first race of the afternoon, reserved for non-production motorcars, if it had not been that the very much production motorcar towing him to the course shed the teeth from its crown-wheel. Thus, by the time Bottoms arrived, the race was over.

The non-production cars which raced were in almost as much trouble, and perhaps it was as well that Clerk of the Course John Gale inadvertently stopped the race at ten laps instead of the scheduled twenty. At that time Parker was cruising along easily in the lead, Paul Emery was nurturing a sick Emeryson thirteen seconds behind, and Gerald Spink in his new and beautifully-turned-out special was a whole two laps behind.

Meanwhile Spike Rhiando was busy in the paddock with the engine of the glistening Trimax which he had entered in the Professionally-built Car Race. Just to tantalise everyone it did go well for a few laps, and showed remarkable cornering qualities.

Results on page 14

Personalities

OUR PRESIDENT

S. C. H. DAVIS

(By courtesy of the " Autocar ")

S. C. H. Davis, " Casque " of *The Autocar*, grew up with motor racing, having first ridden a Werner motor cycle in 1900 and been apprenticed to Daimlers in their racing days.

He has driven successfully everything from Austin Sevens to a Sunbeam. Land Speed Record holder in every kind of event, but is perhaps best known as a leading member of the Bentley team during that grand firm's period of triumph.

His book " Motor Racing " is probably the finest expression of motoring enthusiasm ever written and overflows with humorous delight in the human as well as the mechanical aspects of the sport.

The sport is the thing with him ; to anyone who thinks likewise and is all for doing something about it he is a friend indeed.

Proving a Theory

NEW EMERYSON HAS FRONT DRIVE AND 'TWIN' ENGINE

" I wish I had got interested in 500s earlier on," confesses Paul Emery, which statement will arouse thoughts of what might have been. To judge from the results of his now acquired interest, given longer to exercise, it should have had a profound effect upon the development of car design within the class.

In one sudden swoop he appears to have vindicated the front-wheel-drive supporters, and to have confounded those armchair doubters, among whom it must be confessed was the Editor of " Iota." Maybe it is because accepted theories get a little ragged at the edges when it comes to 500s, and maybe it is because one can get away with a lot of things with a 500 which would not be possible on a vehicle of higher power to weight.

Maybe it is either of these things, but undoubtedly on the showing of the new Emeryson 500 at Goodwood and Brands Hatch its design has got away with it. Emery himself will be the first to say that he would not have used front-wheel-drive if he had been building a Grand Prix car—and he should know, for he's one of the few people who have. But, he wasn't! He was building a car with a power output of around 50 b.h.p., and a laden weight of 600 to 700 lbs. Within these limits there is no doubt that the recipe works. Observation of one lap at Brands will confirm as much.

Not only does the car go right, it looks right by conventional big car standards, with the driver seated well back and a long bonnet ahead of him to assist in " sighting " when indulging in some of the on-the-limit cornering of which the vehicle is capable.

The protagonists of f.w.d. have long put forward claims for improved weight distribution, improved engine cooling, improved handling, and improved driver response in that the whole feel of the car will be more normal than for a rear-engined machine.

In examining the way that these objectives have been sought in actuality, the first matter for comment is that though the whole car looks so well balanced and designed for the job a more detailed examination shows that some important parts of it make use of standard components. As it happens, this is not the first time a product of the little Emery workshop at Twickenham, where Ted Landon sometimes assists in the tasks at hand, has exhibited this flair. In part, this explains too, why the idea which was first born in the early months of 1949 did not motor in earnest for some twelve months. Wherever stock parts have been chosen they have been selected with some care, so as to blend in with other components almost as if designed for the job.

The chassis frame is a very simple " ladder " affair made of $2\frac{1}{2}$in. outside diameter by 16 s.w.g. steel tubing, welded into a structure which tapers in plan towards the rear, and is horizontal in elevation. There are main cross-tubes at each end, and also one about amidships, as well as a pair of subsidiary cross-tubes of one inch outside diameter which serve to carry the brake master cylinders and the front of the seat.

The suspension units are attached to pillars built up from light steel sheet, and which stand up at the four corners of the chassis. Again fabrication is by welding. Each pillar carries on its top a double cylinder Girling shock-absorber of standard pattern, as fitted to production independent suspension layouts, the arms, of which there are a pair, forming the upper wishbone. The bottom wishbone carried on bearing projecting from either side of the bottom end of the pillars, is fabricated from steel tubing, whereas the two sides of the top wishbones are made of forgings. These forgings are liberally drilled for lightening purposes, and a pretty painstaking drill attack has been made on most suitable bits of the chassis,

such items as control pedals being almost drilled out of existence.

The wishbones are arranged to give a geometry, the effect of which is that the track remains substantially constant, and even on full bump, which is over three inches, there is little perceptible departure from this aim. The aim has been so thoroughly carried out that fully reversible steering has so far proved quite acceptable, the actual steering gear being of the rack and pinion variety. The rack is cut from a rectangular Dural bar, which is carried on widely-spaced plain bearings, and the pinion is a hardened steel spur-wheel of Rolls-Royce ancestry.

The upper wishbone is of eight inches effective length, and the lower ten inches, the steering rack being arranged to operate on the mean axis of these wishbones, and in the straight-ahead position the points of attachment of the track-rod ends are located at a compromise centre in the vertical plane. Care as to the rigidity of the steering and the correctness of its geometrical layout over the useful operating range seems to be the main factor in overcoming any theoretical weakness, and what is more interesting providing most satisfactory operation without a differential gear in the drive, or constant velocity universal joints.

In this picture taken in the paddock at Goodwood, by Guy Griffiths, Paul Emery is at the wheel of the Emeryson and Ted Landon (in cap) helps to push.

The cylinder heads can be seen of the 50 degree V-twin J.A.P. engine from which great things were, and indeed are, hoped, though when it next appears it will be a 60-degree unit, utilising the latest big-twin crankcase assembly. The engine was built up by Emery from ex-Fernihough and Worters parts, and consists of two complete racing 250 c.c. cylinders mounted on a common crankcase. Steel connecting-rods are used, one rod being forked, and the rods bear on a plain sleeve, which in turn is carried on roller bearings. A good deal of speedway J.A.P. parts are used in the valve gear.

At Goodwood the fuel system was not right, and a piston went, but in later trials a steady 7,000 r.p.m. was achieved with exceptional smoothness. The speedway crankpin did not like the power developed, hence the coming change to the latest crankcase assembly.

If Emery's hopes are realised, vibration which has so long been a bugbear of the single cylinder engined cars may be defeated, for the twin accepts a rubber engine mounting, and is as smooth as the proverbial nut.

Among the Palm Trees.

Monte Carlo Circuit suits Moss and the new J.A.P.

Monte Carlo! The very name has glamour associated with it, and on the round-the-houses circuit of the Monaco Grand Prix many an epic struggle has been fought. And on May 20th, 1950, 500 c.c. cars were to take the stage on these hallowed roads, beneath palm trees and Mediterranean sunshine, to race for the Prix de Monte Carlo, the very first formula 3 prize to be contested in the principality.

Of twenty-one entries nine had been offered £60 starting money to represent Great Britain, all with Coopers except Donald Parker and Spike Rhiando, and as Spike failed to appear it was left to Parker to uphold the prestige of individuality, something he proceeded to do with considerable gusto. In practice on the Friday evening Nigel Rowland was rather too enthusiastic on the left-handed lower Ste Dévote corner on the sea front, and crashed into the stone-built tobacco kiosk where two days later ten cars were to pile-up in the Grand Prix.

An inspection by C. N. Cooper, who had arrived by 'plane in company with a new J.A.P. engine for Stirling Moss, confirmed that there was no chance of straightening out Rowland's car in time for the race.

Before fitting the new engine, the first of the special car type 500s to be released from the Tottenham factory, Moss put in a lap at 57 m.p.h., a speed somewhat faster than a good many of the Grand Prix cars. His engines were then changed, and he trustingly went on to the starting line without any trial of the new unit, but forswearing himself to a maximum rev. limit of 6,000.

The race was arranged to take place in two heats and a final, but by the time Saturday came the field had been reduced to fifteen and the organisers let it be known that anyone who could get his car to run could take part in the final. Stan Coldham went even farther, as he started in both heats as well, having lost his ignition ascending the steep hill from the start in the first heat.

In addition to Coldham, the first heat brought out the Coopers of Moss, K. E. Carter and Swiss L. Noverraz, Parker's Parker, Pagnibon's D.B., Otterbein's Simca Surva, and Lex Beels' new J.A.P.-engined special. Moss did not have to hurry to win, but Parker and Beels had quite a good scrap for second place, Parker eventually making it. For some reason or other Alan Brown decided it was necessary to hurry in heat two, in which his Cooper faced those of Coldham, C. A. N. May, W. S. Aston and Harry Schell, the

D.B. of E. Bayol, J. Tergi's amateur-built and Triumph-engined J.R., and another Swiss entrant in the form of P. De Toledo's Este.

Thus, Brown took the lead from the start, and promptly pranged at the same corner as Rowland, to his considerable mortification as the car was Bilton's, being borrowed whilst his own was undergoing a post-Silverstone straightening. This left Schell and Aston to make a fight of it, and possibly Schell's lack of respect for engine rev. limits allowed him to win by 4.8 secs.

Twelve cars survived for the final, the absentees, in addition to Brown, being the two four-cylinder engined cars, the Simca Surva and the Este. Both had been somewhat slow, and the latter only just surmounted the hill up to the Casino.

Run over 31.6 miles, the final produced a splendid rolling start in which Aston took the lead, to lose it to Schell before the end of the first round. Moss stayed close behind Schell until the fourth round, when he slipped through and was not headed again. Schell's blithe anticipation of disaster in the engine compartment did not materialise, and he was able to chase Moss all the way. Aston disappeared with geabox trouble on lap five, thus letting Parker into third place. He was strongly challenged by Beels, but Beels spun round on lap twelve, and became a victim of the curious Monaco rule that if you do a tail to nose you are excluded from the race.

Carter became a sufferer from a clutch which didn't clutch hard enough and was eventually forced to run alongside the car going up the hill, keeping the engine going by a dextrous twitching of the throttle cable. Coldham was also in trouble with his engine, and May stopped with a disconnected plug lead, but managed to restart though meantime letting Bayol, whose D.B. was the more potent of the two up into fourth place.

His contretemps Beels was going well with his new car, which has a very stiff tubular chassis, Fiat front suspension parts, hydraulic brakes operated from two master cylinders, a transverse spring at both front and rear. Though the suspension arrangements are somewhat similar to the Cooper, the springing is softer, and by moving together the rear sprocket mountings it has been possible to extend the length of the drive shafts sufficiently to permit the use of fabric universal joints as a weight-saving item. The chassis frame is built up on a series of triangularations.

Results were: (Heat distance, 12 laps, total 23.7 miles. Final distance, 16 laps, total 31.6 miles. 1 lap = 1.976 miles.)

Heat One: 1, Moss (*Cooper J.A.P.*), 26m. 10.5s., 54.36 m.p.h.; 2, Parker (*Parker J.A.P.*), 26m. 28.3s.; 3, Beels (*Beels J.A.P.*), 26m. 35.1s.; 4, Carter (*Cooper J.A.P.*), 26m. 41.9s.

Heat Two: 1, Schell (*Cooper J.A.P.*), 25m. 57.8s., 54.80 m.p.h.; 2, Aston (*Cooper J.A.P.*), 26m. 2.6s.; 3, May (*Cooper Norton*), 26m. 44.5s.; 4, Coldham (*Cooper J.A.P.*) 27m. 3.7s.

Final: 1, Moss, 34m. 3.6s., 55.70 m.p.h.; 2, Schell, 34m. 10.4s.; 3, Parker, 35m. 26.5s.; 4, Bayol (*D.B.*), 15 laps; 5, May, 14 laps; 6, Carter, 14 laps.

POSTBAG

Something to say? We'd like to hear about it, and so would your fellow readers. Address your letters to: "Iota," 51 Cranley Mews, London, S.W.7.

A. C. Rippon writes from Chelmsford:

Firstly, many thanks to all concerned for a grand day at Silverstone. I could not ask for a better day's sport, having taken delivery of my Cooper five days previously. Thinking discretion to be desirable in consequence, I did not exceed 5,500 r.p.m.

Now, may I perhaps utter a heresy. The rolling start is a spectacle that has come to stay it seems, but cannot we have starting positions by ballot? If one cares to "dice" during practice good times can be made, but engines do not grow on trees, and it is possible that the driver may care to spare his engine.

No one would suggest a handicap start, but this is what happens at present—the faster drivers do start before the slower. A ballot start would seem fair to all, and would not depend on how much one dare risk in practice.

My suggestion does not mean that the keen (if not so experienced) home-builder will balk or stop Frank Aiken or Stirling Moss, but it would give him a little encouragement not to be in the back row.

(*Rather you than I, Mr. Rippon. See opposite page for views on the present danger of the rolling start. Many will shudder to think of the fast drivers being forced to thread their way through the slow. An increased safety factor is main reason for allocating positions on a speed basis.*—ED.)

T. U. Ewen, of Westlake, writes:

Now that we have successful front-wheel drive as well as rear-wheel drive 500s, I wonder when one will appear with four-wheel drive?

Remembering the exploits of Robert Waddy's Fuzzi in pre-war sprints, this would seem a comparatively easy way of employing a pair of the potent 250 c.c. engines, such as mentioned in last month's editorial, and at the same time gaining the benefit of maximum traction.

For the benefit of those with a short memory, may I recall that Fuzzi had all the "modern" appurtenances such as a tubular chassis frame, torsion-bar springing, all independent wheel suspension, and one engine drove the front wheels and another the back. For anyone in search of the hill climb championship a similar car equipped with a pair of 1100 c.c. J.A.P.s would seem a very likely vehicle.

The four-wheel-drive car should gain most in wet conditions, and it is a fact that it is not always fine during an English summer. I could not help thinking of Fuzzi when watching Eric Brandon dealing with the mud on the starting line at the Opening Prescott meeting.

500 CLUB NEWS

The Secretary's Column

by John F. Gale

If a prophet of disaster is at all a responsibly minded individual, there is no consolation in saying " I told you so " after the anticipated disaster has come about.

So, I can see little consolation in the fact that the 500 Club has consistently deplored the present type of rolling start when the major pile-up occurs, and occur it is bound to do sooner or later. It may be a thrilling spectacle for the onlookers. Such of them as have not the imagination to consider the possible consequences, but for everyone else 30 cars plunging together into a corner at a near three-figure velocity, as was the case at Silverstone, is nothing but infernally dangerous.

Considering the care taken to avoid danger in other directions, I just cannot imagine why the R.A.C., of all people, encourage this sort of thing. It has always been something of a mystery to me as to how this form of start became adopted internationally as part of the requirments for an international formula 3 race. The Club has never advocated it, and certainly the drivers don't like it. Indeed, you may recall that at our last A.G.M. there was a unanimous vote dominated by drivers condemning the whole thing.

I have seen pictures of the Silverstone start indicating that there was an almost miraculous avoidance of a major smash. Perhaps miraculous is the wrong term, for the credit must go to the skill of the various drivers taking part. But, they should not be put to this supreme test.

As a practical example of the Club's disapproval, we propose to skate around the rolling start arrangements for our own international race at Brands Hatch on August 7th, and to take advantage of the fact that any start in which the car moves more than 10 centimetres is recognised by the International Sporting Code as a rolling start. All we shall do, therefore, is to have the starting line a yard or two in front of the starting grid, and drop the flag when the front cars go over the starting line.

This is purely a subterfuge to obey the letter of the rules, but should result in there being no more danger than from the normal type of standing start which we practice. We may stage a try-out of this idea at the next Brands Hatch meeting on June 25th.

* * * *

The Secretary's address is—"Forest View," Clewer Hill, Windsor, Berks. The full Club Subscription, including " Iota," is two guineas per year, and membership application forms may be obtained from the Hon. Secretary, who will be pleased to answer any queries as to the Club.

IN A FEW WORDS...

AS a regular performer at Silverstone right from the beginning of racing there, W. L. Grose has had little luck with his well-turned-out Grose Special. Too often has he needed the attention of the breakdown lorry supplied from the Grose garage business in nearby Northampton which stands by at all Silverstone events.

A welcome change of fortune came at the S.U.N.B.A.C. meeting on September 2nd, when Grose found a one-minute start in a mixed handicap well within the capabilities of his Special, now using a J.A.P. motor in place of its original Norton power unit.

With such potent machinery as Mrs. Binn's Riley and Oscar Moore's O.B.M. behind him, Grose proceeded competently to stave off this challenge whilst overhauling such vehicles as an Allard and some speedy Ford Ten-engined specials to which he had given up to 50 seconds start. His winning speed was 69.50 m.p.h., and R. C. B. Chapman, in his Lotus, followed him over the line. The programme also featured a 500 c.c. race proper which drew an entry of 23 cars and was consequently divided into two heats. There was no final, the result being determined by the better time in the heats.

Some starting casualties.

Norman Pugh was beset by a dragging clutch whilst awaiting the start of the second heat, and the Pugh Special, now with a J.A.P. instead of a Scott engine, slowly rolled forward from its appointed place in the back row almost to the front row. By this time the starting flag had fallen and when Pugh let his clutch in, the rear chain promptly snapped.

Grose was another who failed to leave the line when the flag fell; he stalled at the start of the first heat, and could not get going until the rest of the field had covered nearly three-quarters of a lap.

The race eventually went to D. A. Clarke (*Cooper*), who won the first heat at 70.51 m.p.h.

Fast times at Brighton.

In sunshine and a stiff breeze at Brighton, Don Parker succeeded in cornering the 500 c.c. class reward for the straight line kilometre sprint which annually entertains seaside visitors there.

The racing car classes included an entry of eight 500s, and Parker again found himself challenged by that outstanding sprint performer, C. J. Tipper's Monaco.

At Brighton cars are started in pairs, and Tipper came to the line in company with R. M. Dryden's Cooper, both using Norton engines. The light weight of the Monaco soon showed to advantage as Tipper gained a commanding lead on his heavier rival. Peter Collin arrived equipped with two Coopers, using the Norton-engined machine which had its first outing at Silverstone in the 500 c.c. class, and his earlier car with specially built 750 c.c. J.A.P. twin to win the 750 c.c. class in 28.20 secs.

D. Parker (Parker Special) starting off to break his own class record at Brighton Speed Trials. He covered the standing kilometre in 30.20 seconds, and reached 98.4 m.p.h. over a timed 88 yards, at the end of the section.

Cooper hillclimbing success .

If Ken Wharton had nominated Bo'ness as one of the hills to count towards the R.A.C. Hillclimb championship, he would almost certainly have become reigning hillclimb as well as trials champion. Ken made fastest time with his Copper " 1000," but because he had not nominated this run, he did not score any points, whereas a runner-up, R. D. Poore, did. Wharton again beat Poore at Bouley Bay, Jersey, but again Poore scored from a second f.t.d. and made certain of the championship.

International Formula III meeting in Spain.

RACING at San Sebastian on September 3rd consisted of two 60-lap finals for the same drivers. Aggregate times decided the winner.

In the first race, Coldham left the bumpy road but suffered little damage, and Wicken did the same thing in the second race but damaged his car rather more. John Cooper lost a rear wheel in the second race, but was placed third in the aggregate results as there were so many other non-finishers. Ken Carter collected altogether nine trophies. English entrants were: K. Carter *Jap*), J. Cooper (*Cooper-Jap*), E. Frost (*Cooper-Norton*), S. Coldham (*Cooper-Jap*).

RESULTS

Race One	1, K. Carter; 2, G. Wicken; 3, J. Cooper.
Race Two	1, K. Carter; 2, E. Frost; 3, S. Coldham.
Aggregate	1, K. Carter; 2, A Belgian driver; 3, J. Cooper.

ADVICE FROM DEAN DELAMONT.

You must scheme if the cost is to be cut

IN last December's "Iota" I wrote upon the problems faced by the enthusiast seeking to build a Formula III car. The conclusions reached in terms of time and money remain if anything on the optimistic side, gloomy as they were, but the difficulties should have been surmountable by at least a proportion of those who seek to enter the racing field.

That they are not being successfully tackled, is giving concern to many who pioneered the 500 movement. Not only is the trend towards complete domination by series-built cars a matter for regret, in regard to potential builders of the future, it would seem that apart from Bottoms and Parker, even those who have been operating individually-built cars are losing some of their zest for the fray.

With the winter "recess" again in sight, I am encouraged to write a few more words in the hope that some of the many correspondents who still announce their desire to build a car will have a machine ready to unveil next spring.

Self-confidence needed.

Before considering the car itself, I propose to give some time to the matter of morale, it being evident that just at the moment the troops are far from being in good spirits.

When approaching motoring, a great many, indeed perhaps the majority of enthusiasts, seem to discard powers of criticism and logic which they would apply to other realms of sport. The average club cricketer would hardly expect to be chosen to play in a Test match, and he will undoubtedly listen with respect to a County coach.

If our supposed cricketer did by some miracle find himself representing England at Lords, it is fairly safe to assume that he would make certain that he had a bat with a comfortable grip, and that there were some laces in his boots. It is also likely that his primary aim would be to stay in, rather than exhibit flashing strokes.

But not our potential speed ace. At least, not the average one seen so far. His seat and driving position would undoubtedly handicap even Stirling Moss, assuming that our enthusiast's car is capable of finishing the race anyway, which is unlikely. The odds are that the car will fall out because of a fuel or oil failure, a nut slackening off, or a chain breaking.

Preparation must be thorough.

Which is one reason why I am a little unsympathetic when people complain about the cost of racing, for any one of these things can be avoided by a little thought and the expenditure of no more than a few shillings.

The most prevalent single cause of failure of 500 c.c. engines is fuel starvation, and this is followed closely by poor preparation in the way of locking nuts, and generally fitting the chassis together properly. If enough fuel and oil are getting to the engine, and every nut and bolt on the chassis is properly locked, then you stand a very good chance of finishing any race.

And, should you not be capable of seeing that at least these things are done, then you shouldn't be racing anyway.

If you believe you can pass this test, then we may consider the car on which you will operate. In December, I suggested that an average season's expenses excluding the car will be between £120 and £200, and the materials from which to construct a car will cost over £200.

How much over will depend upon whom you know, for that governs what can be obtained via the back door for a packet of cigarettes, or what will result in a bill to make your bank manager whistle.

People who can help.

Fortunately, it is not difficult to get to know people who will help you either by advice or in kind, if you set about it in the right way. The opening phases of the campaign will involve tracking down a metal merchant and a tool merchant who will allow you trade terms, and here the odd ten shilling note to a storekeeper will be well repaid. A further few shillings can be spent on having some order forms printed with a business title on top. While the type is set up it will not most much to have some notepaper as well, for the occasions when you want to write to any big supplier.

Motor-cycle repairers are used to dealing with customers with rather less money than car owners, and you should find out who supports the local grass track riders. In fact, it is a good idea to spend some time studying the

A beautiful example of a home-made 500. W.T. Mackay's Special.
Photo by Guy Griffiths

motor-cyclists, because you are going to use one of their engines anyway. So, join a club which promotes plenty of events, and put your name down for a job as an official. A conscientious and intelligent official will be welcomed by any club secretary, including John Gale, who more than once has appealed for more helpers at Brands Hatch.

If you are really going to build this car at home for the minimum cost, then you must know at least two other people, and preferably three. One will either lend you a lathe, or do a job for you for the price of his tobacco, one will weld, and the third will be a panel " basher " anxious to earn a pound or two at the week-end. You may find them all among the motor-cyclists, but, if not there, one immediate spot to investigate is the local technical college. In the days when I attended such an establishment, the instructors were delighted if one brought along a piece of genuinely constructive work to be done, but if this no longer holds good, there will certainly be some apprentices there who will be able to get a job done for you, or introduce you to someone who can.

Many enlightened firms allow their staff to buy material and have work put through the shops at cost, and it is amazing how people will get enthusiastic over the idea of building a car.

Another important link in the chain is a co-operative car breaker's yard, though these places are not what they used to be.

Instructive search.

Above are the foundations of economic special building. The people concerned will not be found queueing up on your door step, but they do exist, and even should you take six months to find them, it will be a very instructive search, and certainly a profitable one when completed.

We are still not quite ready to get down to building this car, unless you have a garage equipped with electricity and some form of heating. In it should be a stout bench, at least 4ft. by 2ft., equipped with a 4in. vice, plenty of shelves, a $\frac{3}{8}$th electric drill, grindstone, and plenty of hand tools.

Some people would have said firstly, but I am saying finally, you need a drawing board and its etceteras. Providing that you were certain of getting all the other things before losing enthusiasm, a drawing board is the sensible starting point, but personally I like to confine my drawing to the things I know I can make.

Perhaps that last sentence should be underlined. It is not the slightest good designing something which you cannot make yourself, or which will practically ruin you to have made unless you can be absolutely certain that every penny you spend will be more than repaid by improved speed and road-holding.

The other day I received a letter from an overseas enthusiast, who incidentally is very short of facilities and materials, in which he says, " I can, of course, copy Mr. Cooper, but I prefer designing my own." It all depends upon how much money you have, and how soon you want to race, but as this article is aimed at those with the leaner type of bank account, my advice is copy like mad.

By copying, you at least let other people do the paying for development, and as it happens no one seems as yet to have produced a car which handles better than the Cooper.

There is no need to copy nut for nut, but the basic layout of four wheels independently suspended on parallel wishbones, or wishbones plus a transverse spring, with approximately a 50/50 weight distribution fore and aft, with a track around 4ft. and wheelbase around 7ft., seems from all the evidence displayed to date to be a formula which will at least provide a reasonable motorcar at the first shot.

Try copying another design.

Fortunately, for the newcomer, there are some very pleasant people engaged in 500 c.c. racing, and if you can speak at all knowledgably there is no difficulty in getting them to talk. Perhaps it is not fitting that I should explain here ways of getting into the paddock without the necessary passes, but if you carry out the previous suggestion of acting as an official you will get to know the ropes.

There is an old saying that time is money. Just as true, indeed truer as far as the potential enthusiast is concerned, for he must have time to give that does not cost money, is the axiom that knowledge costs money. Plan to get your knowledge at the minimum cost to yourself and you will be able to race in the least expensive way.

A car which set out to be different, the Bond was the first exponent of front wheel drive for a racing 500. So far, plans to put the car into production have not materialised.

Photo by Guy Griffiths

Results on Page 28

Brands Hatch Successes.

Most Exciting Racing In England

" C'est ci Bon " Wicken, Stirling Moss and Bill Whitehouse kept up this duel for five miles, until Whitehouse " ran out of road."

Photo by Guy Griffiths

" The most exciting racing in England, without doubt, is to be seen at Brands Hatch, and it really can be seen, because cars are in full view all round the twisty tarmacadam circuit."

If " Iota " had made this statement perhaps there would have been suspicions of prejudice, but fortunately it was made for us by " The Motor " following the International Meeting at Brands Hatch on August Bank Holiday.

The meeting brought out the finest field of Formula III cars yet assembled, the most regretted absentee being Raymond Sommer, who was detained to deal with the fact that his house had been burned down in a French forest fire. On the other hand, the doctors had allowed Stirling Moss to discard the plaster cast over his left kneecap, cracked in his Naples Grand Prix pile-up, and he was out to follow up his appearance at Brands Hatch on June 25th, when he won every race for which he was entered. At that meeting he had been able to repair a faulty carburettor between races, this time he could not cope with a gearbox which lost its gears, though he upped the lap record to 67.54 m.p.h. for the mile circut in trying to catch George Wicken in the final of the first race of the afternoon.

It would be belittling Chelmsford dairy-owner Wicken to say that this was his lucky day. He drove superbly throughout the meeting, and the J.A.P. engine of his Cooper, prepared by his own hands, a task completed at only 3 a.m. on the day of the meeting, did not miss a beat. The only part that might be called luck was crossing the finishing line after thirty-five miles to win the £100 prize and " Daily Telegraph " Trophy for the grand finale of the meeting with nothing more than the smell of alcohol in the three-gallon fuel tank which distinguishes the tail of his car from other Coopers.

Unlucky was Alf Bottoms, fastest heat winner of the day except for Wicken, who found Parker in his way when trying to retrieve a poor start and had to take to the grass, breaking up his offside wheels in the process.

The foreigners who did take part, Americans Harry and Philip Schell, and Johnny Claes (*Cooper*), and Dutchmen Lex Beels and J. Richardson (*Beels-J.A.P.*), never provided any serious opposition.

Results, August 7th

RACE 1. Three 7-lap heats; 15-lap final (One lap equals one mile)

Heat 1. 1, G. H. Wicken (*Cooper-J.A.P.*), 64.27 m.p.h.; 2, W. J. Whitehouse (*Cooper-Norton*); 3, I. Burgess (*Cooper-J.A.P.*).

Heat 2. 1, S. Moss (*Cooper-J.A.P.*), 62.32 m.p.h.; 2, D. Parker (*Parker Special-J.A.P.*); 3, S. A. Coldham (*Cooper-J.A.P.*).

Heat 3. 1, A. Bottoms (*Cooper-Norton*), 63.83 m.p.h.; 2, E. Brandon (*Cooper-Norton*); 3, J. N. Cooper (*Cooper-Norton*).

Final. 1, G. H. Wicken (*Cooper-J.A.P.*), 13 mins. 56 secs., 64.59 m.p.h.; 2, S. Moss (*Cooper-J.A.P.*); 3, I. Burgess (*Cooper-J.A.P.*).

RACE 2. Non-production cars (10 laps)

1, D. Parker (*Parker Special-J.A.P.*), 9 mins. 45 secs., 61.54 m.p.h.; 2, K. W. Smith (*Smith* 500-*J.A.P.*); 3, D. F. Truman (*Bardon-Turner-J.A.P.*).

"DAILY TELEGRAPH" INTERNATIONAL CHALLENGE TROPHY RACE (Four 7-lap heats; 35-lap final)

Heat 1. 1, W. J. Whitehouse (*Cooper-Norton*), 63.16 m.p.h.; 2, E. Brandon (*Cooper-Norton*); 3, J. N. Cooper (*Cooper-J.A.P.*).

Heat 2. 1, S. Moss (*Cooper-J.A.P.*), 63.49 m.p.h.; 2, S. A. Coldham (*Cooper-J.A.P.*); 3, K. Wharton (*Cooper-J.A.P.*).

How strong are these challengers?

The EDITOR on Italian and German cars

THE coming season is all set to witness the crystallisation of half-litre success into a matter of weight and b.h.p., and for a long time the unsolved query in the minds of British contructors has been "What will Italy do?"

There is not likely to be much sleep lost at Surbiton or Feltham following the publication of some details of the first Nardi 500, which is now undergoing trials. Despite the fact that Nardi and Co. advertise for sale in the United States a car complete with the coveted Gilera four-cylinder engine for 2,750 dollars. This first machine has been fitted with the Swiss made Universal twin, a 360 degree air-cooled twin much on the lines of the Triumph, except that it has twin overhead camshafts.

M. Nardi appears to have disregarded John Cooper's view that a successful racing five hundred should be considered as a motor-cycle with four wheels and, instead, has followed the lines of the Nardi 750c.c. sports car in the use of Fiat components and shaft drive, though he has transferred the engine to the rear.

Front suspension is practically standard Fiat "Mouse," somewhat disguised by the use of large light alloy hubs incorporating the brake drums into the wire-spoked wheels. English constructors, frustrated by the unwillingness of Dunlops to produce lightweight wheels, will envy the duralumin wheel-rims but, apart from this feature, there appears no reason why any of the components should weigh less than those of English rivals. The shaft-driven back axle, which uses a Fiat axle-casing with strengthened internals, is likely to depress the scales more, besides introducing adverse torque reaction. The chassis frame is a very pleasingly designed structure of light-gauge tubing adequately triangularated in a pattern of which Nardi have considerable experience.

Short wheelbase and light weight

Primary drive is by chain to a motorcycle-type gearbox, and the final drive gives a ratio of 11/39. A large air scoop on the near side directs cooling air on to the exhaust side of the engine, which is fitted with dual carburettors.

Quarter elliptic rear springs are anchored at their rear ends on the Bugatti pattern, brake reaction being attended to by torque arms. Fuel is contained in a large header tank, the height of which causes the car to look

There is plenty of room for the Cobra's fuel tank alongside the driver's legs

over in fact that the cylinder barrel is not obstructed by the driver and there is a direct flow of air past the side of the driver on to the cylinder and head, which project above the bodywork.

From the engine the drive is taken forward by chain to a Norton close-ratio gearbox, and then to a split countershaft, which spans the car and has its ends carried in self-aligning ball-races mounted on light alloy plates bolted to the side-members. The countershaft is composed of one long and one short shaft, the inner ends being joined in a female-splined sleeve running in two ball-races. The ball-races are carried in a light alloy housing mounted on an extension of the gearbox mounting plates. The countershaft has a sprocket at each end, and the sprocket mountings incorporate spring-type cush drive. As the countershaft is fixed, the final chains (of which there is one on each side of the car) are adjusted by means of slots in the lugs which carry the suspension guides. Primary chain adjustment is by movement of the gearbox mounting plates.

Engine set far back

Both engine and gearbox are mounted on plates of light alloy and, as an indication of how far back the engine is set, the magneto platform is behind the centre-line of the rear wheels. A tubular aluminium oil tank holding 1¼ gallons is mounted in straps alongside the engine, and there is a small fuel header tank, also of light alloy, mounted on the bulkhead behind the driver's seat feeding the twin pressure-type float-chambers of the Amal carburettor. Fuel is transferred to this tank by means of a mechanical pump driven by a cam on the countershaft. This pump draws its fuel supply from a 7½-gallon aluminium tank carried in the nose alongside the driver's legs. Both fuel and oil are carried by flexible pipe-lines to the engine compartment.

In order to make absolutely certain of engine cooling, a scoop behind the simple grille in the nose of the car guides air into an air duct which passes along the bottom of the main fuel tanks, and is continued under the driver's right arm so as to direct air over the crankcase and clutch. The floor of the driving compartment is liberally perforated, and when the driver presses the brake pedal he operates two Girling master cylinders. The brakes, also Girling, measure 8in. by 1¼in. and operate in well-finned light alloy drums with an inserted cast-iron liner. Friction-type dampers are fitted, and the wheels are steel disc-type of Fiat manufacture, shod with 4.25 x 15 Dunlop tyres. The cockpit has the usual items, including a rev. counter, ignition cut-out switch and advance-and-retard lever.

Not as short as it looks

The bodywork fits closely around the chassis frame-tubes, so closely in fact that the side diagonal bracing-tubes are outside the body, and the general outline is very much governed by the chassis shape. The general " stubbiness " of appearance gives the impression of a very short car, but the actual measurements are: wheelbase 6ft. 6in., front track 4ft. 5in., rear track 3ft. 6in. The approximate weight is 575lb.

One dimension which the constructors of the Cobra will no longer have to consider is the now deleted minimum ground clearance. The original design gave a clearance of 3in. and to comply with the 4in. minimum rule in force last season, light alloy spacing pieces had to be fitted above the coil springs, reducing somewhat the available amount of wheel travel on the suspension guides.

If the doctors have made as workmanlike a job of Tom Bryant as he and Corbin have made of the Cobra car, both are hoping for better things in 1951.

NEW CARS AND STAR DRIVERS

Above: Stirling Moss looks non-committal as he is pushed to the line at Goodwood in the new prototype Kieft. This front view of the new car fails to indicate the extreme forward-seating position of the driver, but it does show the negative camber of the rear wheels in the static position, and the care taken to lighten the car wherever possible. Note also that the front brakes are without backplates except for supporting the brake - operating cylinders.

Right: Spike Rhiando is the muffled figure in the Flather Steel Special as it plunges through the murk at Silverstone on May 5th. Similar in many respects to a Cooper, this new car employs an H.R.D. engine and Spike reports that its handling is good, though more speed has yet to be found.

Several
nteresting
ew cars
nd drivers
hotographed by
uy Griffiths.

Above: Motorcyclists have always taken to half-litre car racing with great elan, and Brands Hatch two-wheeler star D. H. R. Gray confirmed his skill on four wheels by his International Trophy win at the Kentish track on May 12th.

Below: Bedtime story at Brands Hatch. Perhaps Spike Rhiando is reading from "The Rocket" to sleeper Harry Schell, the new lap-record holder at Brands Hatch.

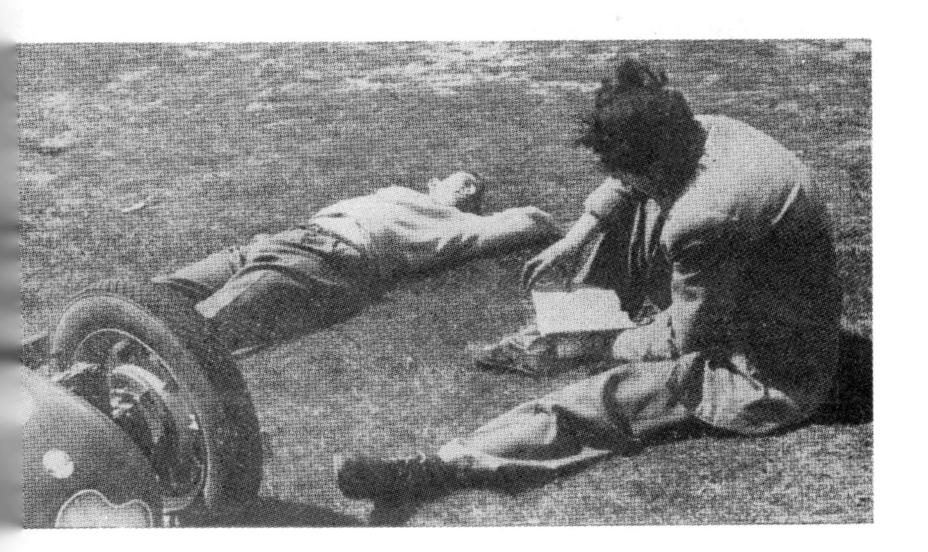

May 1951

HALF-LITRE CLUB NEWS

by the Secretary

AT the end of May the contest for the new Club car badge closed. Designs have been received during the last six weeks and I should like to record the thanks of the committee for the hard work put into the various and excellent entries submitted so far. Response to the Club tie and silk square idea was good enough to warrant a decision to place an order for both. We may now expect to see the field brightened by headscarves patterned with speeding 500's.

Club members, I'm sure, will join me in wishing our new assistant secretary, Ron Smith, every success, not only in his job as administrator of 500c.c. affairs but also personally, as Ron plans to get married early in July. Needless to say, the honeymoon has been arranged with due regard for the Club calendar, so entry forms and letters will still go out on time.

To all who voluntarily gave their services as marshals at Silverstone for the "Daily Express" Trophy Race, B.R.D.C. Secretary Desmond Scannell sends his thanks for a fine job of work done, under conditions generally considered to be far from good. The next meeting at Silverstone is the British Grand Prix and, once again, I should like any member who wishes to act as marshal to write to me on a plain postcard, marked *Silverstone Marshal.* Twenty-five volunteers are needed.

Finally, the Club is arranging a series of social meetings at the Albert Hotel, Kingston, on the following dates: July 2nd, August 13th, September 3rd, October 1st, November 5th and December 3rd. Further details will be sent individually to every member in the near future, but make a note of the dates now.

K. A. GREGORY.

J. Gregory takes to the plough at Brands Hatch. *Photo by Guy Griffiths*

'500' International

Foreign drivers unsuccessful at Brands Hatch

THE season's first international race meeting at Brands Hatch, organised by the Half-Litre Car Club on May 12th, again showed that Continental opposition as yet provides no match for British cars. A brace of Swedish Effyhs in the hands of I. Pepperson and K. Ericsson went steadily, though, as has been apparent before when these machines have raced on British circuits, their short wheelbase seemed to be a disadvantage.

France's sole representative was a D.B. in the hands of F. Liagre, and he was eliminated by a valve dropping into one of the cylinders of the forward-mounted flat twin engine, which meant that most of the afternoon was spent in repairing the resultant damage.

Lex Beels and P. Richardson, both in Beels cars, drove the remaining foreign machines, and it was left to foreign drivers in Coopers to provide the strongest international challenge. Piero Taruffi had been lent a Norton-engined Cooper by Charles Cooper himself, and, though he showed his Grand Prix-acquired skill in cornering, he was obviously unfamiliar with the car and particularly puzzled by the motorcycle-like gear change. Americans Harry and Philip Schell had brought over their Coopers, which still retained J.A.P. engines, and they appeared to be at some disadvantage compared with British-tuned units. It was with some surprise that the big crowd heard that the timekeepers had recorded a new lap record to the credit of Harry Schell in Heat 1 of the Open Challenge Race.

Lap records apart, the feature of the meeting was the emergence of another motorcyclist as a four-wheeled star—Don Gray returning to the scene of so many of his motorcycle triumphs at the wheel of a J.A.P.-engined Cooper, and walking off with the big race of the day.

Gray won the final of the 40-lap *Daily Telegraph* International Trophy, after a ding-dong battle with the two Ecurie Richmond drivers, Brandon and Brown. Brandon led in the early stages but was closely pursued by the motorcyclist who passed him on Clearways and began to draw away. As the race reached the half-way mark Alan Brown also passed his team-mate and took up the chase of the flying Gray; Brandon shed a primary chain, and Loens lost interest in the race when his car motored clean off the course following a stub axle breakage. Although Brown was driving superbly and gaining a second per lap on the leader, he failed to catch Gray.

HALF-LITRE CLUB **BRANDS HATCH (May 12th)**

Open Challenge Race (10-lap heats, 15-lap final)

Heat 1: 1, B. C. Ecclestone (Cooper-J.A.P.), 66.50 m.p.h.; 2, Alan Brown (Cooper-Norton); 3, D. Parker (J.B.S.-J.A.P.).

Heat 2: 1, D. N. Brake (Cooper-Norton), 65.08 m.p.h.; 2, R. W. A. Frost (J.B.S.-Norton); 3, A. J. D. Brown (Kieft-J.A.P.).

Heat 3: 1, J. F. Westcott (J.B.S.-Norton), 63.69 m.p.h.; 2, A. M. Beardshaw (Cooper-J.A.P.); 3, P. Taruffi (Cooper-Norton).

Heat 4: 1, E. Brandon (Cooper-Norton), 65.57 m.p.h.; 2, D. H. R. Gray (Cooper-J.A.P.); 3, P. K. Braid (Cooper-Norton).

Final: 1. E. Brandon (Coper-Norton), 66.08 m.p.h.; 2, D. H. R. Gray (Cooper-J.A.P.); 3, D. N. Brake (Cooper-Norton); 4, P. K. Braid (Cooper-Norton).

" Daily Telegraph " International Trophy Race (10-lap heats, 40-lap final)

Heat 1: 1, B. C. Ecclestone (Cooper-J.A.P.), 66.03 m.p.h.; 2, D. Parker (J.B.S.-J.A.P.); 3, P. Emery (Emeryson-Norton).

Heat 2: 1, E. Brandon (Cooper-Norton). 65.93 m.p.h.; 2, D. N. Brake (Cooper-Norton); 3, D. Powell-Richards (Kieft-J.A.P.).

Heat 3: 1, Alan Brown (Cooper-Norton), 66.23 m.p.h.; 2, J. F. Westcott (J.B.S.-Norton); 3, A. C. Rippon (Cooper-J.A.P.).

Heat 4: 1, D. H. R. Gray (Cooper-J.A.P.), 64.93 m.p.h.; 2, A. Loens (J.B.S.-Norton); 3, R. W. A. Frost (J.B.S.-Norton).

Final: 1, D. H. R. Gray (Cooper-J.A.P.), 65.43 m.p.h.; 2, Alan Brown (Cooper-Norton); 3, P. Emery (Emeryson-Norton); 4, H. L. Daniell (Emeryson-Norton).

CLASSIFIED ADVERTISEMENTS

Those readers who wish to put in Classified Advertisements in Sales and Wants Columns may do so for a minimum of 5s. for four lines, and a shilling a line for each extra line.

Members of the Club, however, may advertise their " Wants " only, free of charge, up to four lines.

Send to " Iota," 2-3Norfolk Street, Strand, W.C.2.

WANTED. *Iota,* January, 1949 and January, 1950. Andrew, 27 Littlegreen Rd., Woodthorpe, Nottingham.

WANTED URGENTLY by American constructors anxious to develop the 500c.c. Movement: *Iota*—1947. All issues except July, 1950; all issues up to and including Aug./Sept. Box No. P.C.142.

DON SLATE for specialised engine tuning, flywheel balancing and assembly, crankcase aligning, H.C. pistons, K.E.965 valves, J.A.P. fuel. Let us find that extra urge necessary for you to remain in front. Don Slate, 130 Kirkdale, Sydenham, London, S.E.26.

BACK NUMBERS of " Iota." The following are available—1947, July; also the whole of 1948, with the exception of February, July and August. On application with remittance, to the Ex-Editor, c/o Allen, Davies & Co., Ltd., Nelson Street, Bristol 1.

CLUB BADGES are now available from the Assistant Secretary, Flat D, 6 Kidderpore Avenue, Hampstead, N.W.3. Price £1 each.

Constructor and driver Frank Bacon sitting in his new car for the benefit of photographer Guy Griffiths. The car is painted a pleasant shade of green but final touches still to be added when this picture was taken were hub caps and a name plate.

The Bacon car

Details of the car built by a pioneer of 500c.c. racing

WHILST so many of the original band of 500c.c. enthusiasts have deviated from the primary purpose of the movement (to stimulate low-cost racing between amateur constructors of cars) it is encouraging to note the tenacity of a pioneer such as Frank Bacon, who is still confident enough to pit his own skill and ingenuity against the best that series manufacturers can produce. Whether or not he achieves any success and whether or not it would be a good thing if there were more home-made and fewer factory-produced machines is immaterial. It would seem that the present con-census of opinion favours the factory-produced car. But we must not forget that half-litre racing would not occupy the leading place it does to-day without the optimism and hard work put into the movement by half a dozen or so enthusiasts among whom Bacon has taken a leading place.

His first car was conceived way back in 1947 soon after Colin Strang had produced the Strang Special, and as they lived not too far from each other in North London it was natural that the Bacon machine should have incoroporated some parts produced in the Strang workshop. This original car of Bacon's was based upon an Austin 7 chassis and even included the Austin gearbox and shaft-drive, to which was coupled a Rudge engine. This engine met its doom when the car's owner one day omitted to turn on the oil tap. That may have seemed a disaster at the time but it did encourage Bacon to change to a J.A.P. power unit, with which he obtained more consistent, if not spectacular, results.

He was quick to realise the limitations of the original car, and the first big task was to modify it and take the engine from the front and mount it at the rear in conjunction with a motorcycle gearbox and chain drive. In this guise the Bacon Special appeared consistently at all sorts of suitable events, until its owner had to face up to the fact that its solid front axle (and consequent road-holding qualities) coupled with an Austin braking system would never give him the chance to do full justice to himself in the company of more modern machines.

This decision to declare his car redundant was not delayed by any self-deceptive optimism, but rather because an effective change would involve Bacon in far more problems than any other half-litre owner. He is not in any way connected with the motor trade, and his garage will only just about accommodate the racing car. He does not even possess an electric drill, so that the prospect of settling down to months of hard work conceiving a new car could have justifiably daunted anyone with less enthusiasm than Frank. He is fully aware of the limitations of his own equipment, and most sensibly in designing the new car he has, one might say, exploited these limitations to the full. The other main consideration has been cost, and again equally remarkable results have been obtained.

The original estimates have been reasonably adhered to, and even including the major items of engine and gearbox—the former is a carry-over from the previous car—the total cost will be less than £200. It is signifi-

This view provides some idea of the bracing added to the tubular chassis side-members. The extra fuel tank for long-distance events nestles snugly beneath the driver's legs. The box-like structure carrying the front spring is detachable to give access to the steering box.

Photo by Guy Griffiths

cant that, at current prices, nuts and bolts alone will account for just about £7 of this total and, apart from the engine, the biggest item is tyres and, of course, tubes.

Bacon has the use of a lathe providing he can fit his needs into the machine's normal function. Those who have tried such a procedure will realise how difficult it is, and how much time is taken to turn even the smallest item if work has to be planned in advance. Whilst Frank operates the lathe himself he has not aspired to welding, and this part of the job has all been contracted out to a suitably co-operative small firm. Despite their willingness to be as helpful as possible, this also has entailed certain pre-planning and the correct preparation and assembly of all parts before they could be handed over for welding.

Basis of the car is a " ladder "-type tubular chassis frame of ¼in. and ⅜in. by 16 s.w.g. side-tubes and 1¾in. cross-tubes, the latter being passed through the side-tibes. The side-members are braced by a " truss " of ⅞in. by 14 s.w.g. tube welded above them. Sheet steel boxes are mounted on top of this frame at each end to carry the front and rear axles, and these boxes are framed up in angle-iron to give added rigidity. For ease of construction extensive use is made of stock angle-iron and strip, of thicknesses varying between ⅛in. and ¼in., 3/16in. being the most commonly used section.

A glance at some of the bends achieved with this material and the workshop's somewhat diminutive vice must cause surprise even allowing for the fact that most of them were made " hot." Frank could probably give an Olympic sprint champion points when it comes to getting from his living-room fire to his workshop.

The wishbones are made from flat strip, jointed by a tube at the base, and one side is deliberately kept straight as a base from which to develop the shape. The suspension system is conventional—a traverse leaf-spring at the top, both front and rear, and wishbones at the bottom. Fabricated members link the spring and wishbones. At the front these vertical members are in the shape of a Y, with a steel block welded between the sides where the top of the Y joins the tail. This block carries the king-pin to which are attached Morris Eight stub-axles, complete with their hubs, brakes and wheels.

Rear axle assembly

Morris Eight axle-ends, hubs, brakes and wheels are also used at the rear. The ends of a rear axle have been cut off and pressed and pinned into a steel block (again carried by the vertical link-members) the inner face of which is bored to carry a ball-race, thus providing the inner support to the outer axle sections. The centre section of the axle, which carries the sprocket and fuel pump cam, is a one-inch diameter shaft carried on self-aligning races and driving the outer axles by a pair of Hardy Spicer universal joints—actually the self-same assembly as used on a Cooper.

The suspension geometry is similar front and rear with wishbones 7½in. between centres and vertical members 10½in., but the front spring has four leaves and the rear spring five. Each spring is clipped to three inverted U-section bridge pieces spanning the top of the suspension boxes. At the rear this box is welded to the chassis, but the front box is detachable

Only a few minutes are required to unbolt and remove all the body panelling. This photograph was taken within 5 minutes of the one showing Bacon in the car. The oil is carried in the small cylindrical tank below the main fuel tank. Note the neatness of the general layout and the excellent accessibility. *Photo by Guy Griffiths*

to permit assembly of the steering mechanism inside it, the actual steering box being of Fiat origin.

Front track measures 3ft. 10in. and rear track 3ft. 7½in. Wheelbase is 6ft. 9in. An unusual feature nowadays are the 17in. Morris wheels. The engine and gearbox are carried in a cradle of light alloy plates mounted on U-channel members spanning the frame. The engine is J.A.P., whilst the gearbox is Norton.

The body is readily detachable and avoids double curvatures, whilst making use of Cooper nose and tail panels for the very good reason that they were donated to the job by " Bill " Aston, another contribution from him being an ex-Cooper combined fuel-and-oil tank which is mounted above the engine. This tank carries 1¾ gallons of oil and 3½ gallons of fuel and for longer events extra fuel is provided in an additional tank slung beneath the driver's legs. In scheming the body, special care has been devoted to engine cooling, and an undertray scoop carries air into a duct which directs it straight on to the cylinder head and barrel in contrast to the somewhat hit and miss air circulation so often seen.

Another unusual feature is the substantial handbrake arrangement. A cross-shaft carried within one of the frame cross-tubes is connected by cables to the mechanical operating cams of the rear brakes, the actual operating lever being fixed directly to one end of the brake shaft.

Frank Bacon is now concentrating on a programme of testing to ensure that everything is in order for the R.A.C.'s Grand Prix meeting on July 14th. As a tribute to his long association with the half-litre movement he is one of the very few driver-builders invited to pit his car against the massed ranks of present-day production machines. D.H.D.

August 1951

Nurburgring

Coopers sweep the board in Germany

IT has proved impossible to avoid featuring Stirling Moss in almost every major race report of the past few weeks. Not that Stirling's driving does not deserve praise on every page, but it is good to record that there are other drivers and cars. Nevertheless, it must be admitted that on current form they are completely outstripped by the new Kieft in Stirling's hands so long as it is running.

Perhaps it was particularly hard on the Germans to export the Kieft to Nürburgring on July 29th, for they were beginning to feel that there was some chance of taking the measure of the Cooper, known to them up till then as the outstanding British car. Stirling's first effort on arrival was to lop 40-odd seconds from the lap record in practice—yes, *forty* seconds, averaging more than 73 m.p.h. over this famous circuit, the contortions of which can only be described as fantastic.

With some 140 corners to its lap of just over 14 miles, the Nürburgring is sited on the side of a mountain, and was basically constructed to be one of the world's most gruelling motor race circuits. Apart from its corners, which include the celebrated Karussell (where the experts make use of the drainage ditch on the inside of the corner), many of the gradients are considerable; the road width appears to be constantly varying so that some of the more desperate sections have the least width of road.

The Kieft's practice lap excelled several by Formula I cars, and while scribe John Cooper was busy in the Kieft camp it was driver John Cooper who, perhaps with more current practice in spotting such things, pointed out to the already harassed Alfa team that one of the type 159s had a crack in its chassis frame. It was only meet therefore, that Ecurie Richmonds' mechanic Ronald Beddings should be called in to effect a welded repair. Which goes to show that anything may happen in motor racing on the Continent. Unfortunately Beddings was not handily placed with his welding torch when, during the next day's racing, the Kieft skidded to a standstill with drunkenly splayed front wheels following a steering arm fracture. But to relate this incident is jumping ahead rather too rapidly; other matters must be related first.

The Formula III race served as a curtain raiser to the first post-war German Grand Prix, and a crowd of anything between two and three hundred thousand eager spectators lined the forests and fields in which the Ring is set.

The Germans have done a good deal of 500c.c. racing while they have been awaiting re-entry into the fold of official international motor sport. Evidently they had no qualms about the reliability of half-litre cars, for the race was to be over six laps, i.e. 85 miles. The programme gave a list of no less than 67 entries, of which 49 eventually faced the starter. Some of these may have faced him, but one or two did no more. When the front ranks of the enormous starting grid roared away, feverish work was still going on in the background on the cars of the less fortunate.

The entry divided itself into a few reasonably recognisable types despite the variety of names given to the cars. First there were the Coopers and their derivatives, such as the Monopelettas (there were only two examples of this, the most successful of the native cars). In the Cooper class came also the Beels and the F.N. brought by Lambert Delhaes from Belgium, and powered by a twin o.h.c. F.N. single. This unit would appear to have potentialities for development beyond the 8 to 1 compression ratio used on this occasion. The French J.Bs. have wishbone suspension at both front and rear. The wishbones are of light alloy castings, and rubber bands form the springing medium. Of the four cars entered, two had J.A.P. engines, one a B.M.W. and the other a Zundapp.

Ted Frost's Emeryson, which has been barnstorming around the Continent for some time, was supported as a representative of front-wheel drive by a trio of D.Bs. A pair of Effyhs represented Sweden, and Hollmig had arrived from Finland with a Cooper, said to be the ex-Headland car. It was difficult to see why Frisch had called his home-built car a Cooper. Possibly because Gottfreid Vollmer had renamed his machine—a genuine Cooper—the Atlas.

Then there were the Scampolas of various types, all based on D.K.W. and Volkswagen parts. When they have a B.M.W. engine they appear under the name of Condor. This change of engine reduces the phon effect but improves the speed. By contrast the D.K.W.-powered cars

The magnificent scene at the Nürburgring on July 29th as nearly 50 cars got away. Brandon is already up in front. John Cooper is lying second, with the Kieft (driven by Moss) on the pits side. Fourth away is Alan Brown.

exemplify perhaps the production of minimum result with maximum noise.

Of the rest perhaps only the two varieties of Kieft (the new car of Moss, and the ex-record car owned by Alan Bruce and driven by Oscar Frank) ranked among the potential contenders. Though Bobby Kohlrausch will be welcomed back to racing, because everybody likes him, the beautifully constructed G.V.B. carried far too much of the equipment of a Formula I car. Weight alone will keep it from the front rank. The B.M.W. engine is mounted at the front, and, with shaft drive, the car looks like a beautifully prepared miniature of a full-scale Grand Prix machine. In the same category is Jacob Keller's special, from Switzerland, powered by a front-mounted Triumph engine driving through a car-type gearbox.

It still seems that the British engine units, even the J.A.Ps., have a reasonable " edge " on their continental rivals. But B.M.W. are now beginning to show something of the form which might be expected of the famous name. Walter Schluter's B.M.W.-powered Monopoletta would have been the fastest German car if it had finished, or rather, would have taken the prize for the fastest German. While it was running it was certainly the fastest, and held fourth place for the third and fourth laps.

Moss was a sick man, from food poisoning, when the race started, and perhaps that is why he was headed for the first few hundred yards. But by the time the cars had doubled back behind the pits, he had the nose of the Kieft in front—and was obviously interested only in getting back to bed quickly. At the end of the first lap, the Kieft was 22 seconds ahead of Brandon. Next time round he was 58 seconds ahead and still pressing on, but five minutes later, the loudspeakers announced that he was out with a broken front axle. When Ray Martin found out what really happened, he promptly cabled to hustle up deliveries of the new forged steering arms which they had hoped to fit before leaving England.

Ecurie Richmond leading

Eric Brandon was now left firmly in the lead, with team mate Alan Brown backing him up. At that Ecurie Richmond could well look cheerful. Nothing happened to disturb their smiles, but behind them some good battles were raging.

Bill Whitehouse had got behind Brown when Ken Carter's engine seized in the second lap, and there Whitehouse stayed, though threatened for two laps by Schluter, who had disposed of his team mate John Cooper. When Schluter fell out Cooper was left in fourth place. Storming along behind came Svensson (*Effyh*) and Montgomerie-Charrington (*Cooper*), the latter driving the race of his life and praying that his J.A.P. would stand the pace for 85 miles. He had stalled at the start and had to wait until everyone who would go had gone—Len Beels, for instance, went straight back to his pit—but was 16th at the end of lap one, 11th a lap later, 7th at beginning of lap four. Charrington automatically gained a place when Ted Frost retired from 6th position with a broken axle on the Emeryson, and then set out to come to grips with the Swedish car, passing Svensson on the last lap to finish 5th, the first J.A.P.-engined machine home.

NURBURGRING (July 29th)

6 Laps (85 miles): 1, E. Brandon (Cooper-Norton), 69.87 m.p.h., 1 hr. 12 min. 55.5 sec.; 2, E. Brown (Cooper-Norton); 3, W. J. Whitehouse (Cooper-Norton); 4, J. Cooper (Cooper-Norton); 5, R. Montgomerie-Charrington (Cooper-J.A.P.).

COOPERS WIN AT GENOA

STIRLING MOSS "lost" the rear suspension on the new Kieft when comfortably in the lead at Genoa on May 20th. An untried component did not do its job as well as theory would suggest. Moss's retirement let Coopers dominate the race, since the new Italian cars which started, some with M.V. four-cylinder engines, although extremely well turned out, were not a match for the British machines (Taraschi did manage to retain the lead for a few laps). The race marked a change in the fortunes of the official Cooper team, for Ken Carter went on to win from team-mate Bill Whitehouse, setting up a lap record in doing so. Ken Wharton was short of a few horses, but managed to finish the 75 miles through the streets of Genoa ahead of John Cooper.

GENOA (May 20th, 1951)

1, Ken Carter (Cooper), 68.83 m.p.h.; 2, Bill Whitehouse (Cooper); 3, Ken Wharton (Cooper); 4, John Cooper (Cooper); 5, B. Taraschi (Giaur); 6, Ted Frost (Emeryson); 7, A. Jacquiert-Bret (Cooper).

FORTHCOMING EVENTS

Saturday, July 14th: R.A.C. Grand Prix 500c.c. International Race at Silverstone.
Saturday, July 21st: Sheffield and Hall M.C. 500c.c. Race at Gamston.
Saturday, July 21st: Lothian C.C. and Berwick D.M.C. 500c.c. Race at Winfield.
Saturday, July 28th: Darlington and D.M.C. 500c.c. Race at Croft.
Saturday, July 28th: Great Auclum Speed Trials, near Reading (500c.c. Class).
Saturday, Aug. 4th: West Hants & Dorset C.C. 500c.c. Race at Ibsley.
Monday, Aug. 6th: Half-Litre Club International Race Meeting at Brands Hatch.

NOTE.—Races at Croft and Gamston on July 7th and 14th respectively have been cancelled, and the meeting at Ibsley on August 4th (closed invitation) replaces the International Race at Thruxton formerly arranged on that date.

Portrait of a Racing Partnership—

The partners: Eric Brandon, Jimmy Richmond and Alan Brown.

IT is perhaps dangerous to make categorical comparisons from memory, but it would be safe to say that rarely has success been achieved so consistently as that by Ecurie Richmond in half-litre races so far in 1951. Whereas the drivers, Eric Brandon and Alan Brown, are familiar figures in half-litre racing, Jimmy Richmond, although physically large enough to take a more prominent part, is not perhaps so well known. His enthusiasm urges him to attend as often as possible the meetings in which the team's cars are competing, so that he is not an unfamiliar figure in the paddock. Moreover, he can always be relied upon for cheery encouragement in the face of a contrétemps, large or small, which occurs even in such well-organised camps as the Richmond.

If you asked Eric Brandon how the team came into being he would refer you to Alan Brown as the prime mover, but Alan Brown would in turn deny such ingenuity. "I just talked to a few people and the idea seemed to grow," he would say. In fact, it seems that towards the end of last season Richmond and Brown discussed the possibility of the former sponsoring the latter's 1951 programme, but it was Alan who appreciated the extra strength which a team could give to an organisation, and who put the idea to Eric Brandon.

The 1950 season had not been outstandingly successful for either Eric or Alan and both would agree that lack of success was as much the result of mental as of material failure. That is certainly consistent with the belief that no driver can give of his best unless he goes to the starting line completely untroubled by external problems. A proper team organisation could relieve the drivers of such anxieties. Fulfilment of that belief accounts for much of the consistent showing by this pair since they joined forces. For instance, Eric Brandon has always been a competent driver, but he will admit that on many occasions he has failed to succeed through lack of the incentive to battle through to the front. Brown often held back in an effort to spare his machine, knowing that if anything went wrong the repair work would fall upon his shoulders.

It is wise to dwell upon this "peace of mind" because there are other drivers, probably as well equipped as Ecurie Richmond, who have in the past appeared equal in ability but who are now regularly outpaced by the fleet Brandon and Brown.

Three cars, five engines

The basis of the Richmond organisation is an agreed three-way partnership, and at the time of writing the partnership has at its disposal three Mark V Coopers (one of the larger chassis 1,100c.c. type), five double-knocker Norton engine, and a half-dozen-or-so gearboxes, in addition to an adequate supply of other minor spares. The whole of this impressive list of equipment will pack into the team's Bedford van which is specially equipped to carry three cars, the spares and a full range of tools including a welding outfit. It is small wonder that both drivers say they never spare their machines and that if the opposition warrants it they will drive until either they or their opponents blow up. On occasions when victory seems certain they are obviously not silly enough to blow each other up and sometimes an amicable settlement is reached before the race which thereafter is run to team orders, though care is taken to ensure that the public gets full value for its money.

The idea is to run in as many races as possible, but the team have a minor complaint that so far they have not had their entries accepted for Continental events as often as they would wish. They envy the drivers who are able to race every week-end of the season, not so much for the possible financial return accruing, but because of the increased skill and track-craft to be gained by regular racing, and both believe that their planned programme to date has greatly improved their skill.

The clerical work of arranging entries is handled by Mrs. Brandon and the main responsibility for preparing the cars rests on the shoulders of Michael (Ginger) Devlin, who is nominally employed by Brandon, but the engines for the outfit are in the hands of Beart and Lancefield, the former preparing Brown's units and the latter Brandon's.

The financial side

One remarkable factor in the beginning was the formation of the team organisation without any additional expenditure. Some quantity of the equipment was already in the possession of the partners and the cash outlay required to get things going was forthcoming from advertising returns. Since then, there has been no shortage of funds since starting money and prize money have brought the team's resources to a point where they cannot possibly lose on the season's operations. However, having kept detailed accounts, it has even surprised the team to find that, excluding transport and personal expenses, it costs £30 to start a car in a race.

Looking back, in the light of their smooth working organisation of to-day, it seems strange that the first race in which the entry of Ecurie Richmond figured (Goodwood, March 26th) was a most inauspicious beginning. Neither of the cars were properly ready and the drivers had not got used to their mutual understanding. Since then the team have gained

(Continued on page 16)

(*Continued from page 13*)

first place in all but two races in which they have appeared—at Brands Hatch on May 12th, when both cars were plagued by small mechanical trouble, and at Goodwood on May 14th, when Brandon suffered from gearbox trouble, and even then Brown was second to the new Kieft. The list of successes is impressive.*

As for the people who have achieved such success, Eric Brandon has been longest in the 500c.c. public eye, for it was he who helped John Cooper to create the original Cooper 500 way back in 1946. Since then he has driven Coopers consistently in all sorts of races with only one exception —a misplaced venture into the 750c.c. classe with a supercharged pre-war machine. Brandon is thirty-one years of age, lives at Surbiton and is the director of an electrical company.

Alan Brown's greying hair belies the fact that he is the same age as Brandon. He first came into prominence in 1949 when, having watched 500c.c. events, he announced that he could do as well as most drivers, and acquired a Cooper to prove it. He is technical representative for a firm of heavy vehicle manufacturers and is fortunate to have directors who view his racing activities with sympathy. Both drivers believe in colourful motor-racing and Brandon is noted for his addiction to red overalls, whilst Brown is equally consistent in his choice of blue. Not only do they believe in a smart personal appearance, but the Ecurie Richmond cars are also always presented at the starting line in an immaculate condition.

Jimmy Richmond is an enthusiast of the first order, but he believes (with some justification) that he could not satisfactorily be third driver because his weight of 22 stone is not really suited to half-litre car racing. He lives near Retford and will willingly drive two or three hundred miles in a day to see his partners race. When not engaged in motor racing he is a civil engineering contractor. At the end of this season we hope Jimmy will divulge for publication some of the inside secrets of the success of Ecurie Richmond.

ECURIE RICHMOND SUCCESSES 1951

Date	Event	Result
March 26th ...	Goodwood, International ...	2,000 class : Brandon 2nd with 1,000 c.c. Fastest lap.
April 8th ...	Brands Hatch	Race 1 : Brandon 2nd (1st in heat); Race 2 : Brown 2nd (3rd in heat); Championship Race : Brandon 1st (lap record); Brown 3rd; Fastest lap—Brandon.
April 21st ...	Brands Hatch	Race 1 : Brown 2nd (1st in heat); Brandon 3rd (1st in heat). Championship Race : Brandon 1st, Brown 3rd. Both drivers broke lap record.
May 3rd ...	Luxembourg, Grand Prix ...	Brown 1st (3rd in heat).
May 5th ...	Silverstone, International ...	Brandon 1st (also fastest lap); Brown 2nd.
May 12th ...	Brands Hatch, International	Race 1 : Brandon 1st (1st in heat); Brown (2nd in heat). Championship Race : Brown 2nd.
May 14th ...	Goodwood, International ...	Brown 2nd (1st in heat); Brandon 5th (1st in heat).
May 26th. ...	Boreham ...	Brandon 1st (1st in heat). Lap record.
June 24th ...	Draguignan, International	Brown 1st (1st in heat); Brandon 2nd (1st in heat). Lap record : Brandon.
June 29th ...	Boreham ...	Brandon 1st (4th in heat); Brown 2nd (1st in heat).

* *On July 14th, at Silverstone, Brandon gained fifth place and Brown sixth. But they avenged this defeat by achieving first and second places at Nürnburg on July 29th.*

Ecurie Richmond...

Photographs by G. R. Goddard

(Above left) The start of a day's racing with Ecurie Richmond: preparation inside the travelling workshop which also carries the two Coopers and spare engines.

(Above) Last-minute scene: Michael Develin lifts the engine cowl to watch the double-knocker working while Steve Lancefield and Eric Brandon look for results. Bernard Patrick (in dark glasses) and Alan Brown (sitting in his car) both look worried. In the centre, behind Develin's elbow, is Gordon Benson, who has put the puff into Alan's car for many of his wins.

According to plan: Brandon and Brown take up familiar positions, first and second—this time at Boreham on June 30th.

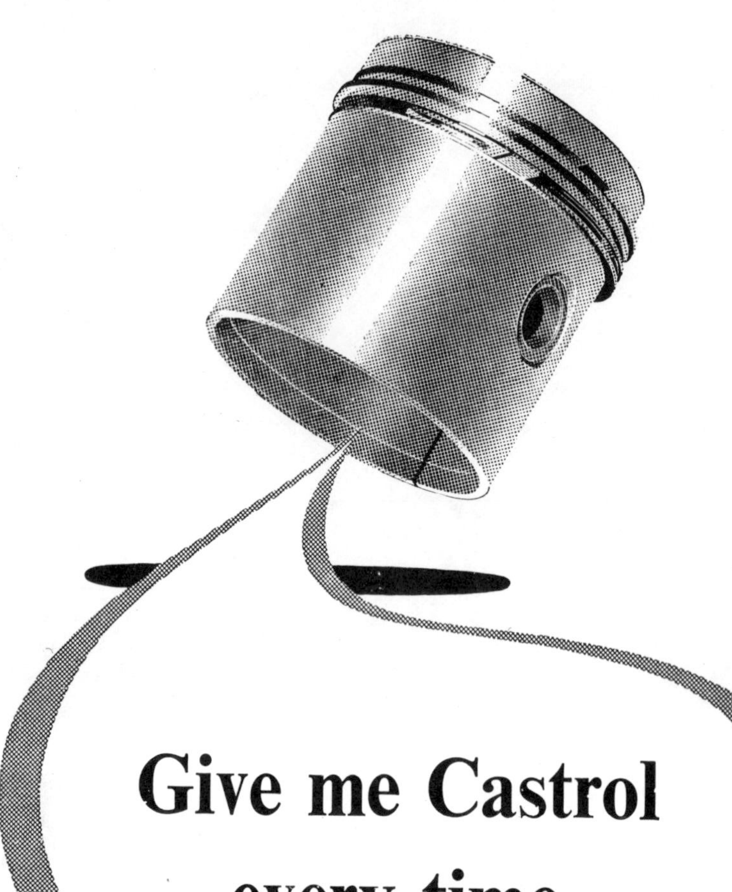

The Masterpiece in Oils—approved by every British car and motor cycle maker

Brighton Speed Trials

THE bright sun shining overhead suggested that for once the drivers would be blessed with fine weather, as they assembled for the Brighton Kilometre Speed Trials on Sunday, September 1st. But the weather again changed its mind; the rain began an hour and a half before the racing cars began their attempts, and continued to fall throughout the rest of the meeting. Formula III was well represented, and the fixed axles of the half-litre cars helped them to make some of the best starts of the day. The low gearing of D. H. Philips's Marwin-J.A.P. caused the car to start in a series of slides. His first run began with a series of pirouettes, but the second was completed without incident. Powell Richards also tended to slide somewhat. B. Lissa followed with a class-record Parker Special, but faded out only a hundred yards from the start. Honours finally went to Don Parker (*J.B.S.*), who completed his first run in 32.82, only 1.4 seconds slower than his record—a fine effort indeed in such conditions. B. C. Ecclestone (*Cooper*) took second place with 33.33, and Curly Dryden (*J.B.S.*) was third with 33.99. For the second run conditions were considerably worse, and the times were proportionately longer.

Bearing in mind the difficult weather one feels that the B.H.M.C. is to be congratulated for coping so well. However, the second pair from the 500 brigade were doubtless mortified at being left "cooking" on the line for so long. And it was remarked, not without justification, that the actual fastest time of the day might well have been achieved in the paddock.

R. S.

BRIGHTON KILOMETRE SPEED TRIALS (September 1st)

		1st run	2nd run
1.	D. Parker (J.B.S.)	32.82 secs.	35.16 secs.
2.	B. C. Ecclestone (Cooper)	33.33 secs.	34.97 secs.
3.	R. M. Dryden (J.B.S.)	33.99 secs.	—

CLASSIFIED ADVERTISEMENTS

Those readers who wish to put in Classified Advertisements in Sales and Wants columns may do so for a minimum of 5s. for four lines, and a shilling a line for each extra line.

Members of the Club, however, may advertise their "Wants" only, free of charge, up to four lines.

Send to "Iota," 2-3 Norfolk Street, Strand, W.C.2.

SLEEK SHAPE FROM SURBITON

Photographs by N. W. Norman

AS these words were written, existing speed records in Classes I (up to 350 c.c.) and J (up to 500 c.c.) were already being successfully attacked by this compact new Cooper. Its owner-drivers (pictured below with some of the Surbiton builders of the car) are Bill Aston and John Cooper, who began their attempts at Montlhèry on October 8th. The flowing lines of the new car, seen to good advantage in the three-quarter rear view above, belie the fact that construction is based on the standard Mk. V. Cooper chassis. Features peculiar to the record car include the aerodynamic body, installation of a special twin-cylinder J.A.P. engine (for 500 records), the "tailored" cockpit with practically horizontal steering-wheel and Perspex screen. The word "aerodynamic" is not lightly used in connection with the body work : an accurate scale model was constructed and given complete wind-tunnel treatment by Gordon Bedson, full-time aircraft designer and (as described elsewhere in this issue) a part-time "500" designer.

The two views at the top of this page show details of the front suspension and the cockpit of the record Cooper. Panels have been removed (an 8-minute operation) in the view above to reveal "airframe," engine, and position of the two $10\frac{1}{2}$-gall. fuel tanks. Owner-drivers Bill Aston and John Cooper are seen (right) with the car, which has an especially neat frontal aspect; the area is only $6\frac{1}{4}$ sq. ft. Gordon Bedson's wind-tunnel model is pictured below.

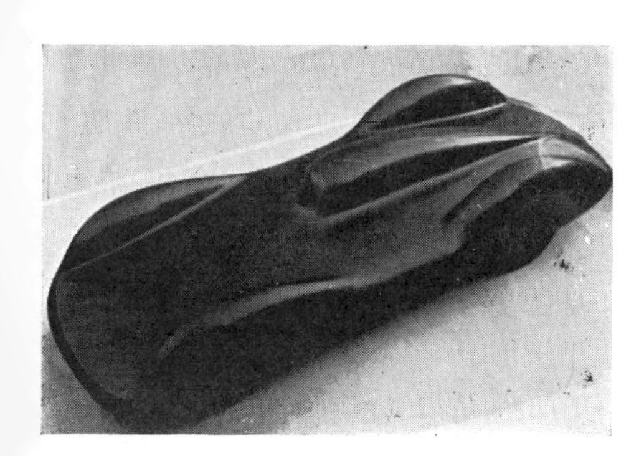

FASHIONS IN FRONT-WHEEL DRIVE

Front wheel-drive 500s appeal to the eye even if only because they look more like the traditional conception of a racing car

Ex-motorcyclist Harold Daniel driving a Norton-powered Emeryson at Silverstone. Simplicity is the keynote of the Emeryson front-end layout, seen right. Differential and constant-velocity joints are spurned. The motorcycle engine (J.A.P. in this picture) and chain drive are, of course, usual with British 500s. The single brake is mounted inboard and rubber bands provide the suspension medium.

The French D.B. (below) which is developed from the popular Dyna Panhard saloon by Deutsch and Bonnet has so far been somewhat handicapped by the comparatively modest power output of the horizontally-opposed engine.

On the left is a view of the power unit, which is mounted well forward of the front-axle. There are, of course, two cylinders but, when this picture was taken at Brands Hatch, M. Liagre was busy dealing with the result of a valve hitting the piston. This latest version has a wishbone as the bottom component of the front suspension instead of a leaf-spring as at the top. A differential is retained and there are constant velocity joints at the outboard ends of the axle shafts.

Photos by Guy Griffiths

Close-ups by photographer G. Goddard

of Stirling Moss driving the new Kieft.

Kieft Shape and Stirling Fashion

Monthly Round-up

Although bias against drivers is apparent in many of the plans put forward to reduce accidents, no one will object to the ideas behind the current vigorous campaign to reduce casualties on the roads. According to Dunlop's test-drivers, out daily in all areas and all weathers, bad manners are the main cause of accidents. As examples, they cite over-taking at any cost, leaving vehicles in such positions that they restrict traffic flow at dangerous places, following another car by night with headlights full on, and plodding slowly along in the centre of the road. Also blamed is incompetence—in such cases as reluctance to use the gearbox and taking a dangerously long time to pass the vehicle ahead.

Other theories on accident-prevention were put forward recently by the Duke of Edinburgh at a meeting of the Institute of Highway Engineers. He suggested that reflector studs should be placed on the sides of roads. Drivers could follow them better in bad or foggy weather, and would be given an idea of the width of the road. White lines, however, should be retained in the middle.

Starring Brands Hatch

A new Castrol colour film entitled "European Motor Racing," will soon be available for distribution to clubs throughout the country. Six international events are depicted in the film : the Grand Prix d'Europe; the British Grand Prix; the very wet August Bank Holiday meeting at Brands Hatch; the R.A.C. Tourist Trophy Race; a Prestcott hill-climb; and the German Grand Prix. Sounds of the cars were recorded on the spot, adding complete realism to a 40-minute feast of colourful spectacle. Castrol have also produced another 40-minute colour film on the eight classic motorcycle races in 1951. Enquiries regarding the films should be addressed to C. C. Wakefield and Co., Ltd., 46 Grosvenor Street, London, W.1.

Talk about tracks

Circuit managers from several European countries held their first international conference in Paris early last month. This country's sole representative was Mr. John Hall (Brands Hatch), who met counterparts from Monza, Chimay, the Nürburgring, Grenzlandring and Hocken-heimring, Montlhéry and Zandvoort. He tells us that, despite language difficulties, the conference was most interesting and highly successful.

Various aspects of circuit management were discussed, and after the reports of each representative have been studied, recommendations will be put forward to the bodies controlling motor sport, with a view to enforcing certain minimum safety measures. Subjects on the agenda included safety measures—fire and police services, first aid and crowd protection—accommodation for competitors and visitors, road surfaces, public address systems, time keeping and facilities for the Press.

Following the success of this first meeting, further conferences of circuit managers will be held annually.

GRANVILLE GRENFELL SPECIAL

Weybridge designer creates a light and compact half-litre car

Granville Grenfell's car is of trim and distinctive appearance—as this three-quarter front view shows. Workmanship throughout is of an unusually high standard

JOHN GRANVILLE GRENFELL cannot be classed as a newcomer to the half-litre field, for the machine illustrated on these pages is the second 500 c.c. car which he has built. The first was made in 1913 and used an ash frame, tubular axles and Norton engine. Nearly forty years later the second car resembles it in one vital factor—minimum weight; though the wooden frame has been replaced by steel, tubular axles are again used, and it is likely that a Norton engine will be fitted.

The re-entry to "500" construction of so experienced an engineer as Granville Grenfell would be an event worthy of note in itself, but the car he has created in his Weybridge workshops also compels attention. It is constructed to a standard not excelled by any half-litre machine of to-day, and the design is based on a number of ingenious features (some of which are the subject of patent application).

Novel front suspension

Of late, attention has been focused on swing-axle type of independent suspension at the rear, but this car employs a swing-axle at the front. The effective radius of each half of the axle is increased by overlapping the axle sections in the plan view, thus limiting the gyroscopic effect which is one of the major drawbacks of such a layout when applied to steerable wheels. Added to the novelty of the actual design is the fect that suspension is effected by pneumatic struts specially manufactured by Granville Grenfell. Whereas the front suspension is a novel advance, at first glance it may be thought that the rear end of the car exhibits a retrograde. A second look, however, reveals that all the desirable characteristics of the de Dion rear end have been achieved by careful design of a " solid " axle.

Tubular chassis

The two axles are linked by a simple tubular chassis based upon bottom tubes of 2in. diameter by 18 s.w.g. with a reinforcing 1in. by 16 s.w.g. tube lying 7in. above each bottom side tube. The resultant side members are linked by tubular bridges at front and rear of the main chassis frame. The length of the main section of the frame is kept to a minimum by the employment of outward-splayed, quarter-elliptic springs for the rear suspension.

Each half of the front axle consists in effect of a broad Y, the open end of the Y being pivoted to the chassis frame. It will be seen from the

A Triumph twin, which provided power for the first outing at Brands Hatch last October, is seen installed in the prototype Granville Grenfell car.

Details of the unconventional front suspension system are clearly visible in this view. The pneumatic suspension struts were specially built up by the designer.

illustrations how these pivots are arranged one on either side of the car so that the pivot axis lies at an angle of 45 deg. to the centre-line of the car.

The axles are built up from $1\frac{3}{4}$in. by 16 gauge 45-ton steel tubing; the kingpin is carried by a steel end-piece bronze-welded and pinned into the axle tube. Stub axles are of Austin origin, as are the hub and brakes. A good deal of machining has been done with the object of weight reduction. This has been so effectively carried out that the weight of each brake drum, for example, is reduced from $7\frac{1}{2}$ to $2\frac{1}{2}$ lb.

Strut attachment

The suspension struts are attached to the axle beams at the junction of the Y. The upper end of each strut is linked to a bracket on a superstructure (lying under the scuttle) to the chassis frame. Only plain fork-ends and pins are needed to mount the pneumatic strut because the axis of these pins is parallel to the axis of the axle centre. The superstructure also forms a convenient mounting for the steering gear, the dashboard, and the air reservoir serving both struts. The steering gear of the prototype car utilizes a Model " T " Ford reduction-box and a somewhat complicated linkage to a slave arm. It is proposed to modify this layout in the interests of simplicity. The modification will also include a re-positioning of the steering wheel to enable a complete wheel to be used without impeding the driver's access to the cockpit.

In the manufacture of his pneumatic suspension struts Granville Grenfell utilizes parts of ex-aircraft units. It has been found experi-

With Granville Grenfell (in car) are helpers "Clare" Sinclair and Don Lincoln. Grenfell's explanation for producing so light a car is not the use of light alloy but "plain work at the old slide-rule and a lot of years staring at good motor cars."

mentally that they will operate best on an inflation pressure of 30 lb., compared with a maximum testing pressure of 350 lb. per sq. in.

The control pedals are hung from a pedal bar which lies just ahead of the top of the front chassis bridge. Their construction is symptomatic of the careful attention paid to every detail of this car with the object of reducing weight without sacrificing strength or efficiency. The rear axle—outwardly so simple in design—is schemed to meet all the requirements of rigidity plus minimum weight, torque from the final drive chain being looked after by a radius arm adjacent to the sprocket in the centre of the axle. This radius arm serves as backplate for the single rear brake, the drum of which is mounted alongside the sprocket. The axle shaft is a piece of $1\frac{3}{4}$in. by 8 gauge high-tensile steel tube; apart from the central support bearing it is carried in a pair of self-aligning ball races at each end of the shaft. These races are in light alloy housings which also serve as the attachment points for the rear springs and the radius arms (which lie parallel to and beneath each spring). The suspension damping at the rear is catered for by small friction-type shock absorbers.

Compound brake

Brake operation is mainly by Lockheed, but the rear brakes also carry a Girling wedge-type expander connected to the handbrake lever. The wheels are specially built up from Dunlop rims and hubs fabricated by Granville Grenfell; front wheels are spoked so as to place the brake drums in the main air stream.

When the car was tried out at the end of last season a Triumph engine (an ex-generator plant for aircraft) was employed, together with an Albion gearbox. Unusual was the use of Bowden carburettors fed by S.U. electric pumps from a tank mounted beneath the driver's legs. The engine was run on petrol Benzol with a 6.75 : 1 compression ratio, so that the car's constructor had every reason to be pleased with a consistent 60 secs. lap at Brands Hatch. This was the first time its constructor had driven a racing car since 1936.

SPECIFICATION—GRANVILLE GRENFELL SPECIAL

Frame: Tubular steel; bottom members, 2in. by 18 s.w.g.; lower members, 1in. by 16 s.w.g.; hoops, 1in. by 18 s.w.g.
Steering (prototype): Model "T" Ford reduction box.
Suspension: Front—swing-axle with pneumatic struts; rear—solid axle with quarter-eliptic springs.
Brakes: Lockheed with Girling expander connected to handbrake at rear. Austin 10 drums and shoes.
Wheels: Dunlop rims and spokes; special hubs.
Tyres: Dunlop, 5in. rear, 4.25in. front.
Body: 20-gauge panel; construction by Wakefield and Sons, Byfleet.
Engine (prototype): Triumph.
Carburettors (prototype): Bowden.
Fuel system: 2½ gallon tank amidships; pressure feed by S.U. pumps.
Gearbox: Albion.
Weight (with 1½ galls. fuel): 451lb.
Wheelbase: 6ft. 6in.
Front track: 4ft. 5½in.
Rear track: 3ft. 11in.

Granville Grenfell started racing motorcycles in 1907, won several Swiss circuit events, and beat Nuvolari for second place on the Varez circuit in Italy in 1924. Superchargers have occupied a good deal of his attention since he left the Lancia company, where he was production engineer during the late 'twenties; the installations he has prepared include that on the late Eric Fernihough's record-breaking "Big Twin."

He was assisted in building his car by Don Lincoln, who works for him at Weybridge, but whose normal hobby is a formula Austin 7. Further help and inspiration were given by "Clare" Sinclair, whose enthusiasm for 500s was really the motivation for the machine, and ex-motorcyclist Rex Heatley.

The Granville Grenfell workshop is perhaps lacking in space, but certainly not in equipment. No praise can be too high for the standard of workmanship to which this car is constructed, and which reflects the methods of a team normally accustomed to the precision required by racing machinery.

U.S. Half-Litre Race

Palm Beach, Florida, was the scene of a 500 c.c. race organised by the Sports-car Club of America late last month. There were only four entries, of which two finished. First place was taken by Canadian Peter Dillunt in a 1950 Cooper; A. Dupont, also in a Cooper, finished two laps behind. At the time of going to press no other details of the event were available.

More News from South Africa

P. C. HARRINGTON-JOHNSTON resumes his racy commentary on "500" construction in the Union

MY last contribution to *Iota* [March, 1951] contained but scanty mention of Orlando Fregona and his achievements. This omission, caused by shortage of space, is now to be rectified. "Freg" started when he came back from the S.A. Forces with "eigenbau" products. There was a very rare 1½-litre Singer cam-four housed in an old Salmson chassis. When the con-rods on this "ran away from home," Fregona began experimenting with a pre-war Aprilia unit, but this shed a timing chain which could not be replaced anywhere. His proverbial bad luck gained him the nickname of "Unlucky Fregona."

The Tiger Cub

Then he and ex-I.O.M. rider Don Hall decided to "play 500's." The famous Tiger Cub they produced in mid-'48 had a '37-type Fiat 500 chassis. The base of the frame of a pre-war Tiger 100 motorcycle housing the engine and gearbox was mounted inside the back of the car chassis, the tubes bolted to ears welded to the Fiat back axle casing and the front swinging on a link resembling an Austin 7 shock-absorber aluminium-rubber-bush link. The top bush of this was mounted on the last chassis thwart, allowing for the unequal arcs created by the axle swinging on (a) the original back springs and (b) the engine "torque-arm."

(This cunningly got over a trouble on the Fidget, where I had merely a vertical truck steering-knuckle welded to the thwart, taking swivelling and "double-arc" movement. The ball joint used to try to come out of its hole, but never quite managed it. . . .)

Fuel and oil systems

The Tiger Cub's fuel feed was from an American Autopulse electric pump, bolted in the driving compartment and fed from a motorcycle battery clamped to the aluminium floor between the driver's knees. Fuel came from a drum-tank mounted in front of the "pelvis," and oil from a Francis-Barnett fuel-tank sitting saddle-fashion on top of the steering-column above the driver's knees. This car may have been the first in the movement to have twin brake-cylinders operated off one pedal—a device installed in mid-1948. Latterly the rather flimsy Fiat chassis has been strengthened by light-alloy channel members fixed diagonally below the driver's seat. These run roughly from the rear thwart to the pelvis and cross at a kingpost common to both, below and in the centre of, the structure. They seem, surprisingly, adequate. The Fiat differential was one specially made locally during the war, with the "breakable half" turned from mild steel. Fregona, who has his own workshop well equipped (he is in the trade, with Hall as his foreman) welded up the ports in the diff. and greased it through a nipple and gun. The body tail is short, simple and light, held on with a hefty strap.

After completely blowing up three Triumph T.100 engines, Fregona bought the demonstration Gold Flash bike, sold the bits, and put the engine in the Cub. Then he bought a new A7, so that he could race in "500" and larger class events at will. Unfortunately he forgot in the first try-out that the B.S.A. gears work the reverse way to the Triumph . . . the valvegear got stuffed down the piston's neck. Spares have not yet—many months later—arrived. . . .

M.G.s easily beaten

The 650, however, is a terrifying vehicle, and even in standard form, mildly polished inside, can clean up TC and TD M.Gs. It is quite usual to find a TC or TD with as much as 10 seconds start in handicap hill-climbs where fast times are about the 33 to 44 seconds mark. Even then, the 500 or 650 will put up a faster time. The Cub weighs, I believe, about 620 to 650 lb. Originally the drive from the Triumph gearbox went upstairs to a layshaft and down to the diff. This gave final chain adjustment. The fitting of the B.S.A. units, however, has allowed a direct drive to be arranged, and the diff. is now built, as is the back axle casing, of bits of Austin and Fiat scrap, with a neat adjustment arm of two steering knuckles with right-and-left-hand threads to give the unit a movement on the final chain. At present the motor mount is an inverted channel of steel on which the unit sits, the channel being upswept at the front to the old-type "link." The rear end of the channel is held by a pivot-bolt to the bottom of the diff. discs.

Fregona, by the way, developed, with Hall's help, the use of the S.U. float chamber to an Amal carburettor for pump feed, and this was installed as far back as 1948.

The combination of "Freg" and the Tiger Cub has proved startlingly successful and the car is, relatively, the "Cooper" of S. African D-Class

Fregona, with Tiger Cub, in action last year during a meeting at Maritzburg.

racing. It has now been found that, Hall tells me, the rigid back axle tends to lift slightly on bends (when the diff. sets up spin), and this is to be replaced by an independent structure now in fabrication.

The Wishart Special

Another amateur-built car—probably one of the most beautiful made anywhere—is the Wishart/B.S.A. This has been the spare-time sole occupation for nearly two years of Mr. A. G. Wishart, a Durban advertising employee who is one of our very rare amateur-builders. Not an engineer, he has his own lathe, welding plant, etc., at home, and does all his own work. Almost everybody else here either has the job "done out" and merely does the assembling of bits in person, or is in the trade and uses his own workshop or a pal's. Wishart took Technical College night classes to learn to machine and weld.

He is a keen model airplane enthusiast and built his car first of all in balsa (7in. long), to scale of 1in. to 1ft. He then sought an engine—eventually finding a 1948 B.S.A. A7 in a wreck in S. Rhodesia—1,200 miles away from his home garage. He designed the chassis on his own, thinking it all out himself, and used Cooper wheelbase and track sizes.

The scheme is a sort of combination of J.B.S. and Cooper, as will be seen in the photograph. Wishart procured a quantity of 1¼in. by 18 s.w.g. steel tube—he has no idea of its technical specification or possibilities. He made up two welded pelvises of 18 s.w.g. steel plate, to taste, and concocted a sort of tubular basket from one to the other.

The springing is Cooper-type, using Fiat Cub wishbones and front fittings, mated to Morris 8 brakes (spares more easily and cheaply procurable than are Fiat) and Cub steering, mounted on a drilled angle-pylon welded inside the front pelvis. At the back, he has Morris 8 drums and backplates, with "blisters" welded on to the backplates to act as mountings for the transverse spring and Fiat wishbones. Diagonal upward shock-absorbers, tubular, are fitted at each end.

The rear stub-axles are of truck half-shafting, the short universally jointed half-shafts are Austin 7 shafts cut down, and the fixed central (sprocket) shaft is made out of the remains of Austin Seven sideshafts, plugged at the ends with hunks of old truck shaft, welded in.

The Wishart is perhaps the only car in the world to have spoked Fiat Cub wheels (the spokes were attached by Wishart, using Morris Minor hubs). As seen in the photographs, they look most beautiful. Rude rumour has it, however, that they are both heavier and weaker than the original—which is perhaps why Wishart used Morris Minor back wheels complete, drilling the hubs and rims lustily. (Like me, he believes in "tuning with a drill"). The dry-sump oil-tank holds about two gallons and fits round the seat and behind it, low down. Perhaps a unique feature are drip-feeds from a special tank on the rear pelvis, which lubricate the final chain and the fuel pump cam on the back axle. (I do not think anyone else has ever thought of this . . . cunning!) Wishart, by the way does his own panel-beating on a sack in the back yard. Most of the body frame is of surprisingly strong aluminium tube of about ¾in. diameter. Workmanship throughout is impeccable and the finish of the machining

Chassis of the Wishart, one of the South African cars described here by Harrington-Johnson.

and welding of the highest order. The painstaking care and skill of the whole job is worthy of the highest praise—especially considering that Wishart is a young amateur who has not had an engineering training. Even such details as the pedals are tubular and welded—and Wishart has even gone to the length of turning his own clevis-pins. Braking is hydraulic to all four wheels, with the Morris handbrake by cable as standard to the back. A somewhat Kieft-like " spider " of tubes has been devised to allow of adjustment of the final chain. Front chain, of course, is shoe-adjusted within the B.S.A. unit. This last has been " blown on " but the owner is " going canny " at present.

The Wishart has just undergone its first road test—always the greatest thrill for the constructor—and is causing some puzzlement by slight directional uncertainities at the front end. Latest gen suggests, however, that in a copy of *Iota* he discovered the uses of inverse backwheel camber on Coopers, and the Wishart/B.S.A. is now au point.

Another most interesting 500 is the Lawhart, probably one of the most interesting 500's produced anywhere. Basically simple, it was attractively finished and, while not spectacular in performance, it proved unexpectedly reliable.

The car was produced in 1949 by a garage mechanic, K. G. Hartley, of Durban, as a sports two-seater. He secured the square-tube backbone chassis of a D.K.W., stripped it down and installed rather longer transverse front springs than usual—giving a marked crab-track.

Where the D.K.W. unit used to live, he inserted a modified Lawrence charging plant motor—the " general donkey-engine " of the Catalina flying boats used from S. African bases in the Indian Ocean theatre during the war. Not being in the Air Force, we can only speak from hearsay, but the engine has been claimed to pump out the bilges, operate the flaps, retract the wing-tip floats, operate the winch, and any other odd jobs. It is about "the biggest 500 ever built," and comprises an alloy mounting plate about 3ft. 6in. in diameter out of which poke two tiny air-cooled cylinders with fixed heads. The actual c.c. are a mystery—it is reported that they are 488 c.c.—but the unit is fitted with two twin-spark polar-inductor magnetos, each apparently firing a plug in each cylinder—cross-wise. The engine has a fearsomely elaborate set of fuel and lubricant filters, and a geared cord-and-pulley starter at a very inconvenient angle (for car users).

Hartley scrapped the induction and exhaust systems, fitting two motor-cycle Amal carburretors (touring models) and two straight-through brass pipes. He knocked up an alloy sheet chain-case and drove the D.K.W. transmission by a chain from the original power take-off of the Lawrence motor—the fan and flywheel side. It was all rather awkward to get in, but it was done in the end.

Well-finished engine

The Lawrence motor is stated on its maker's plate to give 10 b.h.p. at 4,100 revs. Rumour says that if you take the governors off, the flat twin will hit about 8,000. Its standard compression is somewhere over 8:1, and inside you'd swear someone had pinched a set of B.R.M. spares. Very rarely will you see an engine so beautifully finished outside a factory racing establishment. The two-throw crank, the short, heavy-webbed steel rods, are machined and polished literally like glass. The big ends are enormous and the rods very much too heavy for speed. Curiously, the webs are at right-angles to accepted British practice (i.e., the open end of the webs faces the direction of rotation so that, looking at a rod side-ways, it seems solid. I don't know why this should not work, except that the rods weigh, with lead bronze big end bushes, about 18-19 oz. each). The stubby alloy pistons have a "flat peak" on top. Detail work inside the engine would make even an old-time racing Douglas enthusiast jealous. There is, however, a persistent rumour that the porting (or the cam-contours) are not flexible enough for road use and that, while it will spin like mad, it lacks pick-up.

Second prototype

Hartley is now building Number Two—he sold the first Lawhart—as he has another Lawrence motor (you could buy 'em for £25 apiece just after the war—if you could imagine what to do with them . . .) The chassis of this has cardan-shaft tubular side-members, independent front suspension using lower wishbones welded out of lengths of steering-arm and pivoting on steering arm "knuckle joints," and the back end looks most unusual. Roughly it is "sort of Kieft" . . . anyhow, it has a solid centre axle shaft bearing a sprocket and an immense Opel car brake drum, hydro-operated. At the ends of this shaft—level with the chassis side-members—are universal joints, with short outer-shafts to the hubs.

Coaxial with the universals are the " knuckle joints " of more steering-arm parts, forming wishbones on which the back wheels swing.

Below the axle and parallel with it are short stubs extending from below the chassis. From these, rubber shocking-cord will be lashed round the swing-axle bearer-housings to spring the car. The movement will be limited by upward-inclined tubular shok absorbers. Hartley admits that if he had seen the diagrams of the Kieft earlier, he would have altered almost everything. He didn't. The result is a possibly unique structure, with swinging axles—about 14in. long—at the back, slung direct on shock-cord—no Bowden wire, here!

On this model the Lawrence motor will drive through an ex-Levis B.A.P. Burman gearbox, mounted wrong-way-round—the Lawrence drives from the right-hand-side of the crankcase in this case.

Cooper victory in South Africa

AGAINST opposition which included Basil Beall's E.R.A., M.Gs., Chris Ferguson's Cooper, Fregona's Tiger Cub and other specials, Arthur Mackenzie (Cooper Mk. V) won the 100-mile Fairfield Handicap at Durban on January 20th. His average speed for the 33-lap race was 84 m.p.h. Mackenzie only recently took delivery of the Cooper, which had not previously been entered in a race.

Half-Litre Club's Annual Meeting

THE Committee Room of the R.A.C. will be the scene of the Half-Litre Car Club's Annual General Meeting on Saturday, February 23rd, at 2.30 p.m. The main items on the agenda are the Club's account and report and the election of directors and officials.

The Club's report on last year's activity discloses that successful race meetings held during the season added over £420 to the capital fund, so that the Club now has in hand over £1,300. During 1951, of course, the reputation of the Club was greatly increased at home and abroad. The price of fame, however, is reflected in the statement that " the anticipated loss incurred [£105 11s.] at the annual dinner and dance was due to the necessity of inviting the Press and official guests who had done so much for the Club."

With the exception of H. R. Godfrey and R. J. Trevellick, the retiring directors will offer themselves for re-election, including K. A. Gregory, who is retiring from the post of Club Secretary in order to manage the professional affairs of Stirling Moss. Ken Carter is thought to be a likely successor.

Trevellick's retirement from the board is caused by pressure of business; he cannot spare the time to travel regularly from Birmingham to London to attend meetings. He will remain secretary of the Midlands Centre. Unless another Midlands member steps forward for election in Trevellick's place this important area (which contains an unusually high proportion of amateur constructors) will not be represented on the Half-Litre Club board.

"GETTING ON TO THE MEGAPHONE"

Racing Correspondent

ELSEWHERE in this issue P. Harrington-Johnson describes some of the efforts of the South African amateur constructors. By profession H.-J. is a journalist—he is night editor of the *Natal Mercury*—but he is also one of the pioneers of the 500 c.c. movement in South Africa. His own car is depicted in the accompanying picture, to which he attached the following :—

" This picture gives you an idea of the tail construction—one of my own pet brainwaves which the car has had *ab initio*. The frame is of ½in. aero steel tubing and the tail hinges upwards and forwards, being kept up by a ¼in. aluminium rod fashioned like a buttonhook, which lives in the headrest and telescopes out to grab hold of the rim of the steering-wheel. It can just be seen in the picture, muffled by some rubber tube to check its rattling when the car is going. As can be seen, it allows everything but the steering to be fought with—and do we fight, brother?

" The funny looking carb. is a battered Type 27 fitted with a special float-chamber of our own devising. This has a top-feed top off a B.M.W. Bing. To this, in place of the pipe, is screwed a special nipple brazed to a length of 2in. copper ex-pipe off my old Magnette, which is closed at both ends by brazed discs of copper. Into this small drum is brazed an intake and outlet pipe nipple, connected respectively to the feedpipe from the back axle pump and to the nose tank, respectively. This allows the Amal float to deal with the pressure from the pump (normally too great for it) and the carb. is thus an " organised leak " off the pipe from the pump back to the main tank. The overflow is provided back to the tank as a counter to excess pressure. The system also allows the car to run for a few seconds at a standstill. In practise it works very well on the move but it is the bane of hill-climb starters as the J.A.P. *will* fluff out at the most

This South African special was built by Harrington-Johnson, who mentions features of its construction in the accompanying letter.

Weight-reduction can be carried too far. Or perhaps the neat hole drilled through this piston (during one of last season's meetings) was the result of a too-weak mixture.

Photograph : Geoffrey Goddard

embarrassing moments. I eventually climbed down and installed a copper one-gallon header-tank which is coupled the same way on a return pipe but gives much better results. The S-shaped device on the oil-tank is a hefty hunk of odd iron bent this shape to mount the Matchless oil-tank. We could not get an oilfeed to work properly any other way, as it had to have a " head " and a shortish line. As can be seen, the chassis side-member has been filled in with a flat strap stay—there is one each side in a flattened V form, to stiffen the members (they bent once—but then I weigh 210). Yes, that's me in the overall.

" The petrol-pump can actually be seen behind the oil-tank. The curious behaviour of the seat upholstery can be explained because it is hung on the seatback (one with the tail), I mean, in one piece, including the scoops for air, by a hoop of aluminium rod selftapping nailed in place. The nose is the tank. The dent is from the day when the car was on a tow rope and the brakes melted at speed. Aluminium does not rip, praise be.

" The car emerging past my posterior is S. Africa's one and only E.R.A., property of one Basil W. Beall, and his also is No. 25, just behind the Fidgit."

André Loens, who last season raced the prototype J.B.S., is the latest recruit to the ranks of Kieft owners, and his forceful driving should be well suited to the Bridgend car. Almost any evening that one cares to call on the Merton workshops of Ray Martin, Ray and Don Parker can be found working on the special Kieft that the latter is building up for his own use. Don is treating this as an evening and week-end job, but the car is making splendid progress.

Martin's main preoccupation is the rebuilding of the prototype Kieft, which is now owned by Stirling Moss. A recent visit found the car being reassembled after a complete strip, incidental work including the cadmium-plating of the chassis frame. The Moss equipe strongly deny that this has any connection with the recently reported thefts of large consignments of cadmium, which the newspapers loudly proclaim as atom material. Standing alongside the Kiefts is the chassis of Les Leston's J.B.S. which has undergone considerable changes under Martin ministration.

G. A. Henrotte of Eltham is building, with the assistance of his father, his own 500. He describes the design as conventional, with wishbones at the four corners top and bottom. The chassis is of 2½in. diameter tubes; the engine will be either J.A.P. or Norton. The car will be ready in about two months for racing this year.

Johnnie Lockett, famous for his successes as Norton's No. 2 rider, is reported to be retiring from the two-wheeled scene—a news item which may be connected with another prophecy in this issue.

J.B.S. cars will be prominent during the coming season. Peter Collins will race as a one-man "team" for the J.B.S. works, and several other British drivers will soon take delivery from Feltham. Export orders include two cars for Finland, and three more will be shipped to America during the next few weeks.

Stirling Moss expects 500 c.c. racing to occupy about a third of his 1952 programme. Driving his own Kieft, he will take part in about four main half-litre events at home and eight abroad. The rest of his time will be taken up by Jaguars and "a new British Formula II car." If the car turns out to be as successful as its driver, we can look forward to great things.

Ecurie Richmond plans for the season ahead no longer end in a question mark. In half-litre events Brandon and Brown will definitely drive new Mk. VI Cooper-Nortons; their Formula II cars will also be Coopers.

Ian Burgess has hopes of entering the Formula II sphere. He will also be seen driving a new Cooper and a prominent marque of sports-car.

Denis Taylor has recently acquired R. W. A. Frost's J.B.S.-Norton, to which he is fitting a roll-bar. His Iota has been bought by a neighbour —Jim Gregory, former Cooper-operator, who is the proprietor of Bellegrove Autos.

Bill Lowe is disposing of his Mk. IV Cooper and has bought D. W. Powell-Richard's Kieft; he is raising the front cowl and modifying the steering of his new car, and is also fitting a roll-bar.

George Wicken is awaiting delivery of a Mk. VI Cooper, while M. G. (High-Flash) Thomas has bought a "Mk. 5½" car from the Surbiton works—a lightweight Cooper, basically a Mk. V, but fitted with several of the newer Elektron components now standard on the Mk. VI.

Increased costs of materials are reflected in some of the current prices for production cars. With J.A.P. engine, the new Kieft is priced at £800; Coopers quote £708 with J.A.P. engine for the Mk. VI, £620 without engine. The same price—£550 less engine—is quoted for both Arnott and J.B.S. The basic price of the Iota is £525 *with* Speedway J.A.P. engine (£440 less engine).

Bob Gerard will follow up his 1951 entry into Formula III racing during the season ahead. He will probably drive both his Mk. V of last year and a new Mk. VI now on order. In larger-car events, E.R.A. and Frazer-Nash will fill the brackets following the name "Gerard" in the 1952 race-results.

John Habin is anxiously watching the progress of a car of new design. More news of this machine will be given in another issue.

The R.A.C. has so far refused to be drawn when enquiries have been made as to their plans for a Grand Prix meeting (assuming such a race will be run at all now that Pall Mall no longer has the lease of Silverstone). Rumour has also been busy with the possible fate of the Tourist Trophy. If this race is run to the suggested S.M.M.T. eligibility clause, which merely requires that to qualify as a production sports car provision must have been made for the manufacture of 25 cars, it will again be a pity should no one produce a team of half-litre cars. On the handicap formula used for the Dundrod races to date, a 500 would have an excellent chance of victory.

Though the B.R.D.C. have begun preparations for their annual *Daily Express* race meeting by issuing the regulations for the International Trophy only, it seems certain that there will be a Formula III even mixed into the even more ambitious programme. The fact that the International Trophy is to be for Formula II machines has fairly fanned the flames of controversy as to the fate of the B.R.M. and other Formula I cars; but it seems that in this case, anyway, the fault lies with the main Formula I teams, who failed to give a satisfactory reply when asked what they intended to do about a racing programme. Very likely B.R.M. did not know, whilst Alfa have also been very cagey and the 4½-litre Ferraris may well be in the United States for Indianapolis.

Stop Press: Stirling Moss and Peter Collins will work as a team this year. The partnership is on an administrative basis only, and they will not drive the same type of car.

A multi-cyclinder 500 c.c. engine may be produced by one of the by one well-known manufacturer of racing machines as a subsidiary enterprise to the development of a new Formula II car. While British enthusiasts long for a multi-cylinder engine, the Italian Gilera motorcycle concern, chief protagonists of the four-cylinder 500, are spending this winter developing a twin o.h.c. single for motorcycle racing. Gilera, it is reported, do not intend to abandon their famous four-cylinder engine, but they believe it is possible to obtain better performance on a twisty circuit with a single—because of the improved bottom-end torque. It is apt to recall that the only time a British multi has won an important race was in 1950, when Frank Aitken's Triumph-engined Iota was victorious in the Grand Prix meeting at Silverstone.

Scottish hopes will rest again on the J.P. and, all being well, a com-

March 1952

INTERVIEW with STIRLING MOSS

Pictured here in the Kieft prototype in which he won five important races last year, 22-year-old Stirling Moss is regarded by many as the finest British racing driver. At the time of writing, he is taking part in tests of the B.R.M. at Monza.

Photograph: Geoffrey Goddard

What first aroused your interest in motor-racing?

As far back as I can remember I was interested in fast motor-cars. When I was about 16 I ordered a 500, but the old man soon stopped that and bought me a sports-car instead. Once I mentioned to him the idea of becoming a professional and he told me not to be a fool (in those days I was studying dentistry—that was before I went into the hotel business).

And when did you start racing?

I started—not actually in racing—with a Cooper at Prescott in May, 1948. A few weeks later I had my first success at the Stanmer Park Hill-climb, near Brighton.

Which event do you remember best?

It's difficult to say, because various races stand out for different reasons. For sheer enjoyment, I should say the T.T. in both 1950 and 1951—or, perhaps most of all, the first race with the Kieft at Goodwood last year, because it realised so many hopes and rewarded so much effort on the car. Probably the hardest race to be placed in was that at Zandvoort in the H.W.M. My biggest "dices" were against Brandon in the 1949 Silverstone and in the H.W.M. against Villoresi at Monza.

What cars have you driven?

I've actually raced the 328 B.M.W., Cooper 500 and 1,000, H.W.M. one- and two-seaters, the Jaguar XK120 and 120C, Frazer-Nash and Kieft.

How valuable is 500 c.c. racing as a training-ground for the young driver?

It's more than a training ground—it's an opening, the finest there is. Half-litre racing offers more races and therefore more chances of gaining experience. It teaches you balance and gives you opportunities to study the techniques of other drivers, the effects of slipstream, etc. But although the 500 teaches track-craft, it doesn't bear much relation to bigger cars such as the B.R.M. from the driving viewpoint. The difference doesn't lie in the maximum speeds but in the amount of power available. At 100 m.p.h., for example, the B.R.M. is much more of a handful than a 500 travelling at the same speed—even though the B.R.M. is using only part of its power, while the 500 is flat out.

Many people are interested in your "relaxed" driving position. Did it come naturally or did you develop it?

I suppose you could call it the "Italian" position; I thought a lot about this and, to me, it seems the logical position. The farther away from the wheel, the more control you have—as the arm is moving through a bigger arc. And the more comfortable you can get, the more chance you have of repeating a fast lap every time instead of putting up one good time and finding yourself completely exhausted from the effort.

Is the ability to drive well enough, or should one also have a good mechanical background?

I don't think one needs a lot of mechanical knowledge to start with, but you're bound to pick it up if you do a lot of driving—by asking questions and storing up the information. Obviously one must be able to sense the reactions of the car, know the effect of tyre pressures and be able to read plugs and oil pressure, etc.

Do you intend to do much 500 c.c. racing this year?

Yes, a lot—over 20 international 500 c.c. races, all in the Kieft, and probably over 50 events all told. I shall keep on driving 500s because I enjoy it—and that is my main reason for racing, even though I now scrape a living out of it. The atmosphere of 500 c.c. racing is very friendly.

What is your ultimate ambition?

I don't really know how to answer that, but I would like to win the Gold Star again this year.

Stirling Moss made his entry into motor racing four years ago—at Prescott, in May, 1948, when he put up a promising performance in this cream-coloured Cooper.

FROM OUR POSTBAG

Cyril Kieft on Cheaper Racing

Cyril Kieft, well-known manufacturer of the Kieft car, expresses some original ideas on the subject of 500 c.c. racing in the following letter (a copy of which has been forwarded to the Committee of the Half-Litre Car Club). The letter contains a new scheme for making possible cheaper racing, in addition to some definite statements on the merits of Kieft cars—past and present. On reading the letter, some readers may be prompted to cross swords with Mr. Kieft; we hope that they will do so through "Iota's" correspondence page rather than catch the first train to Bridgend.

As an enthusiast of motor and motorcycle racing, I have recently been amazed by the interest created by Dick Caesar's recent article, *Five Hundreds for the Poor*.

I do not think that a "500" Specials class could be worked on a basis to satisfy all constructors, because of the difficulty in finding a dividing line which would ensure satisfactorily the elimination of racing engines and chassis, etc. Once one has produced a successful racing car, there are so many drivers who want the best that it is impossible to refrain from taking an order to make another—and then you are in the business, whether you like it or not.

In my own case, I bought a Marwyn in 1949 and was so disappointed that I decided it was easy to design and build something better myself. Having my own engineering and drop forging business, I decided that it would not take long to produce a Formula III racing car at least 200 lbs. lighter than the Marwyn by using entirely different means of suspension and a light alloy chassis.

It took one racing season (1950) to make the car the most reliable Formula III racing car. In that year it took from the French and Italians fourteen International records at Montlhéry. Although twelve of these records have since been taken by a car with an aerodynamically designed body, I am pleased to say that the 200-mile 500 c.c. class record is still held by us at 86.99 m.p.h. in a standard Formula III type car, weighing still more than 200 lb. above the minimum allowed under the Formula.

After our successful trip to Montlhéry, Stirling told me he thought he could persuade some of the most experienced "back-room boys" to design and build a prototype "500" which would definitely be superior in both design and performance to any other production models. The results of this are now well known, and the only feature in the new design which had been used in a Kieft before was the use of Metalastic torsion units for the front suspension.

"Outstanding superiority"

The new Kieft, Type C52, which was so successfully driven by Stirling, was soon in demand by the leading drivers, because of its outstanding superiority over all other makes. A number of the new design features are being copied by other manufacturers and constructors.

My reason for giving a brief history of the Kieft racing car is to prove that I do not think it possible to make 500 c.c. racing cars to *win* without the expenditure of a reasonable capital sum, especially in view of the speed at which development takes place.

In Dick Caesar's article, I do see his good intentions and wholeheartedly agree that there *must* be a class for the enthusiastic constructor who is, wisely, going to limit his expenditure to, say, £400 in materials and labour. I am therefore prepared to offer the Half-Litre Car Club a trophy and prizes for a race, which I think should satisfy the needs of the constructors who wish to see the banning of double knockers, etc., by introducing the following specifications:—

Two or four-seater sports car with engine capacity under 500 c.c. in full road trim, having four road wheels and running on standard pump fuel. No engine to be installed of which a similar type has been used by a motor or motorcycle manufacturer in their racing machines during the last twenty years.

The car must be in full road trim and driven to the Meeting, with mudguards, lighting equipment and capable of starting without having to be pushed. Electric or mechanical kick or hand starter must be used and the cars can have their engines started before the race and not have to use the Le Mans type of start, which might possibly penalize the kick or hand lever type of starters.

In order to ensure that the class does *not* get out of hand, the entrant of the car must be agreeable that if his car obtains a place, he will allow it to be auctioned after the race, with a reserve of, say, £500; this reserve can only fluctuate with the rise in general market prices of new cars.

The above specification details are sufficient to enable the enthusiasts to decide that they can use their knowledge and skill to produce a fast, reliable and cheap sports car which gives them an equal chance of producing the *winner* in their particular class.

If the Half-Litre Club will allocate one race of 30 mins. duration at its Brands Hatch meetings later in the season, and there are at least eight entrants, I will be happy to provide suitable trophies for the first three places.

I am sure that the above Formula will adequately satisfy the constructors and designers of "Cheap Cars to Race." Perhaps the outcome may be the finding of another Austin or Nuffield to add to the famous names who have succeeded in building up a business by satisfying the demands of Mr. Everybody, who needs cheap transportation on four wheels.

If the committee of the Half-Litre Club are prepared to support my offer by making available a date in September, I am sure the boys will be satisfied and produce a most interesting variety of machines.

LUXEMBOURG and EIFELRENNEN

Notes by " JAY " *on two Continental Formula III events*

TOWARDS the end of the month of May there are two important Formula III events which are pretty close to one another and would make an ideal trip for both competitors and spectators. In view of this a few notes about the meetings, apart from the actual racing may be of interest.

As is the custom, the Luxembourg G.P. is being held on Ascension Day, May 22nd, a Thursday. Last year the race was held for Formula III cars and although monopolised by the British it was a great success. Consequently the organisers have retained Formula III classification for this year. This race is run over a triangular circuit of 2.35 miles in length and the long straight, on which the start and finish are situated, runs alongside the Luxembourg aerodrome. Although the circuit is generally spoken of as being at the town of Luxembourg, the capital of the Grande Duchy, it is actually about 6 kms. outside, so it is rather essential to have some sort of transport, or at least to know where the competitors are staying so that lifts might be cadged.

Habitation around the circuit is rather sparse, although there is one hotel at the paddock hairpin, situated at the beginning of the finishing straight. While being quite a reasonable hotel and restaurant it suffers from being the only one close at hand and consequently is continuously overcrowded and understaffed.

In the town of Luxembourg itself there are plenty of hotels at all prices, just as there are restaurants, but if the golden rule for eating is adhered to— pick a place that displays its menu and prices outside and study them before going in—one need not be ruined. Remember also that the price quoted for accommodation is almost certain to be for the best room, so argue your way down to something that will do just for the night.

Assuming you are staying in the town and are going to the circuit for practice, you will find it fairly easy to get in the best places without the right sort of passes, but do not be misled into thinking it will be the same on race day, for at continental meetings very formidable wooden barriers can appear overnight. At the Luxembourg meeting it is a good thing to go prepared with food for the day's stay, although there are plenty of beer tents.

An important point to bear in mind, whether spectator or competitor, is that there is very little shelter from sun or rain around the circuit. The paddock consists of a corner of the aerodrome and has a gravel surface with not even a hedge in sight. From the paddock, along the straight past the start and pits to the first bend, which is a very fast downhill right hander, there is virtually no cover at all and if it rains you will get very very wet, whatever you are doing. There are two or three grandstands opposite the start and pits but their only function is to provide a seat, the roof is only a token.

The pits, on the inside of the circuit are very temporary and only

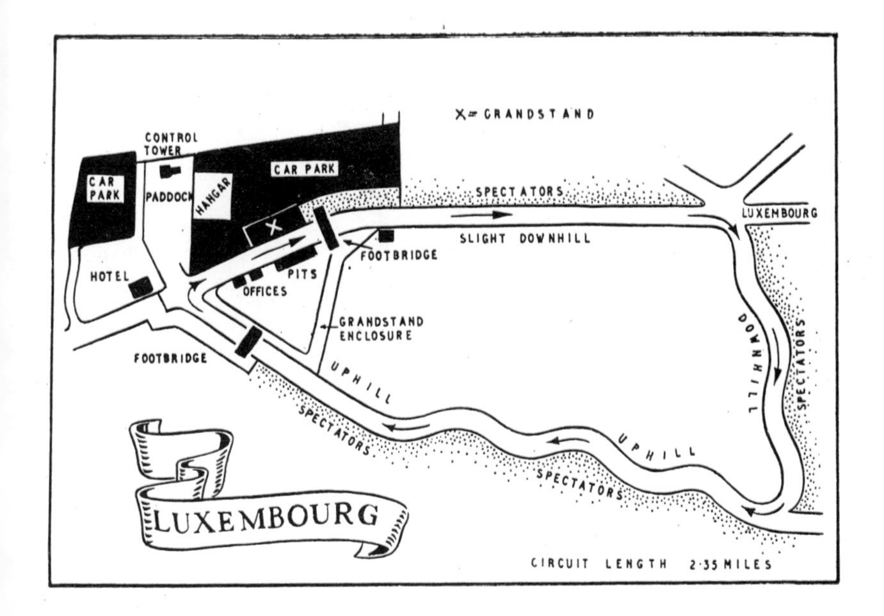

used for the actual race. For the competitor it is important to remember that you cannot get a car, trailer or van, behind these pits, they are built on the edge of the road, and fields slope away behind. All vehicles apart from the "racer" are left in the paddock, which is about a quarter of a mile from the start in the reverse direction of the course, so you can imagine the pandemonium if you arrive at the starting line having forgotten the plug spanner!

Location of the paddock is bad in some ways but good in others, one being that in practice your first lap can be timed with a flying start, though it does mean that your last lap will finish before you pass the timekeepers. While the roads are closed for practice or racing, it is possible to leave the paddock, but it is a very long way round the back roads to Luxembourg.

Last year there was a bit of a bother over the starting, for it was not made clear that you were expected to arrive at the line all ready to go, consequently some people arrived on soft plugs which caused confusion.

On Sunday after the Luxembourg meeting is the Eifelrennen at Nürburgring, which is about 90 miles almost due north, near Adenau. During the season two big meetings are held at the Ring, the May meeting being the Eifel races and the July meeting is the German G.P. At the Eifelrennen there are usually races for all types of machinery and Formula III are included.

The surrounding countryside is very hilly and the 22 km. circuit runs up and downhill, through some of the finest forest country you could wish to find. The whole atmosphere of Nürburgring is one of efficient organisation with the competitor of first importance. The paddock, a very fine concrete affair, is surrounded by lock-up garages and is situated,

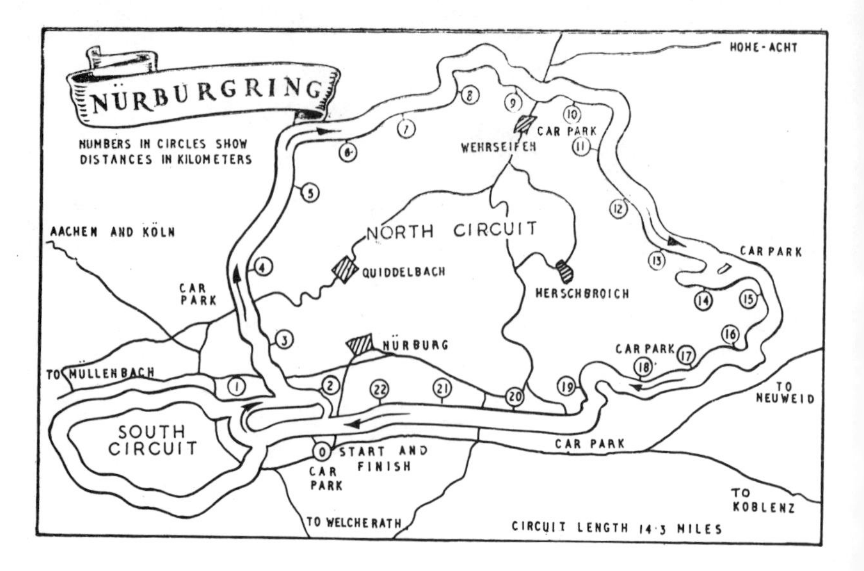

very wisely, on the outside of the course. In a field adjoining the paddock is an area reserved for the fuel and oil people and all manner of accessories.

The way to the start is through a tunnel under the track (controlled by traffic lights), it is not very wide and brings you up a ramp to the starting area, which is as big as an aerodrome runway. You pass the three-storey timekeepers building and come to the pits, which are two-tier concrete structures, but which do not accommodate vehicles, all transports being left in the paddock.

From the pits the circuit runs in a big loop and returns immediately behind them, with only a wire netting fence in between. At the end of the pits the road turns left and winds away across country, but if you have just set off on a practice lap and want it timed officially you do not have to cover the 22 kms., because just before the road turns left there is a gate on the right which brings you out at the exit of the tunnel on the track side. You can set off and pass the timekeepers with a flying start. Similarly, you can finish a lap with a flying finish, drive round the loop, up behind the pits and through the gate, going then either down under the tunnel or hairpin back to the pits. All this is most convenient for the competitor, though any attempts at setting up a lap record for this short circuit are frowned upon.

It is usual to give each competitor a small card, and if this is handed in at the control tower after practice all the lap times recorded by the holder will be written on it.

For the spectator there is an enormous grandstand opposite the pits with a fine view of the starting area and the " loop," while away to the right, mounted on top of the parapet to the entrance to the paddock tunnel is a large cupboard. On race day the cupboard opens to display the number of each car as it starts the final two kilometre straight leading to the starting area. In front of the stands are the usual score boards, while loudspeakers, in German, French and English, give details of the progress of the leaders from various parts of the course.

The Nürburgring is about as fine a racing circuit as you could wish to attend, but it has its drawbacks. The biggest is that it attracts upwards of 400,000 spectators, which means that accommodation in the few villages nearby is limited, and again restaurants are always full, although there is a large one on the ground floor of the main grandstand. The nearest town, or to be more precise large village, is Adenau, which is about 14 kms. from the paddock, diametrically across to the other side of the circuit. The easiest approach is via the circuit, turning off where it crosses the public road just outside the town. The towns of Bonn and Koblenz are not far away and are both quite large.

From about the middle of the afternoon on the day before the actual race all traffic near the circuit is very strictly controlled and if you have not got an official pass life becomes difficult. At Nürburgring distances are very great and it is fatal to be in a hurry, unless you are actually on the circuit. After practice it is possible to pay a small fee and drive round the circuit, an experience not to be missed, but there is no free service for pulling you out of the hedge! Nürburgring, like Luxembourg only more so, is a circuit to visit with a vehicle, or at least with someone who will give you a lift. Only the very strong and very enthusiastic are advised to try and walk from the nearest railway station.

These two meetings, coming close together as they do, would make an ideal pair for a "continental visit," though it would be quite strenuous. Between them they give a good insight into continental racing, one being a typical "local" meeting held on a fête day on normal public roads, and the other a wonderful example of racing on the grand scale at what must surely be the finest racing circuit in the world, aided and abetted by a super-organisation, not tied up in red tape. Luxembourg is a delightfully free and easy country, entry from Belgium is not controlled and Belgian francs are freely accepted, but entry from Germany requires a visa. However, since control is in the hands of the Belgians and English the numerous formalities are not really frightening.

OMISSION IN MARCH ISSUE

We apologise for an error which occurred in last month's issue. On page 22 in the article entitled "Chain Transmission," there is an ommission after the last line. The entire last paragraph should read as follows :—

"A roller chain consists of nothing more nor less than a large number of bearings held together by side-plates, all manufactured to precision limits. The clearances between bearing surfaces are determined as a result of many years of experience; some indication of the accuracy of manufacture is shown by the fact that on 50in. length of ½in. pitch chain of first class precision make (this size is used on the primary drive of any typical "500") the *total* permissible variation in length is from −0 to + .075in., and that such a length contains no less than 500 components.

HALF-LITRE CLUB NEWS

by the Secretary

AN interesting social evening of the Club took place at the "Albert," at Kingston, on Monday, April 7th, when Mr. Bryantson, of Firestones, presented some excellent films.

The 1952 racing season started at Easter in glorious weather, and the Club's International "London Trophy" Race was a great success. I have received compliments from a number of people who say that the race and heats were run off in a most efficient manner. John Gale, the Clerk of the Course, should be given special praise as he was responsible for the organisation of the meeting on race day.

I have just received the lap speed sheets and give hereunder some details which will be of interest to drivers. The fastest recorded lap of the meeting was put up by Stuart Lewis-Evans, a 22-year-old 7¾ stone driver, at 52 secs. dead. This is a speed of 69.23 m.p.h. and a record for the circuit. Other laps which broke previous records were: Paul Emery, 52.2 secs., at 68.97 m.p.h.; Harold Daniell, George Wicken and Norman Gray, all at 52.4 secs., at 68.70 m.p.h.

Perhaps I should remind readers that a new and smoother surface has been laid during the winter months, which might tend to improve last year's speeds, and speeds have always been faster at Brands when the east wind is blowing, as was the case at Easter.

After the Easter Meeting some 160 members and friends attended the Club Dance and prize giving at Clearways Country Club, West Malling, which was also a very great success.

Arrangements are progressing for the International August Bank Holiday meeting at Brands Hatch, which will be sponsored by the *Daily Telegraph*. It is hoped that higher prize money will be put up than has ever before been offered in a 500 c.c. race. Members are therefore asked to keep this date free and support this Club event in full strength.

Regulations for the Club's Snetterton Meeting are now published and any members who have not already received them should let me know as soon as possible, as entries close on May 10th. Snetterton is 96 miles from London on the A.11 road. For Formula III cars there will be two heats each of 27 miles and a final of 81 miles. Also there will be a "Formula Libre" Race of 81 miles. The date of the meeting is Whit Saturday, May 31st, and racing starts at 1.30 p.m.

I have received many requests from members for car badges. The Club badge has been redesigned and supplies should be ready in about a month when members will be advised.

I would like to remind members of an important rule in the General Competition Rules of the R.A.C. When there is more than one race meeting taking place on the same day it is strictly forbidden to enter two races with the idea of deciding later in which one to drive. Some drivers do not seem to be aware of this, and a breach of this rule would almost certainly lead to the suspension of the driver concerned. Copies of the General Competition Rules of the R.A.C. may be purchased from the R.A.C., price 2s. 6d.

K. E. CARTER.

DAILY EXPRESS SILVERSTONE

Formula III race full of surprise

Photograph: G. Goddard.

A shattering roar, a cloud of spray and the 500's are away on their 45-mile battle at Silverstone.

WITH the flags of all nations fluttering in a typical airfield breeze and with British, Italian, Swiss, German and Belgian cars and drivers in the paddock, there was a truly international atmosphere at Silverstone on May 10th when the *Daily Express* staged their finest meeting to date. What a pity the international flavour was confined to the Formula II, sports, and touring-car events; nevertheless, the 500 c.c. race was good value and full of surprises.

In the early morning there were some heavy showers, but the rain stopped before the first event and thereafter the weather remained dry with sunny, although quite cool, periods.

Soon after 10 o'clock the 35 cars for the Formula III race started off on their warming up lap. Non-starters were Ken Wharton, whose Erskine Staride was not yet ready, Frank Bacon (*F.H.B.*) and Peter Collins (*J.B.S.*), who had decided to concentrate on the Formula II race with his H.W.M.

At 10.15 a.m. precisely they were off and the pack snarled its way on the first lap of the 45-mile battle. On their first appearance it was Stirling Moss in the lead, taking a beautiful line through Woodcote on the wet track. Some distance behind was Charles Headland, followed by Alan Brown driving Charles Cooper's lightweight Mk. VI car, and Don Clarke (*Cooper*) who had been credited with the fastest practice lap on Thursday. George Wicken had retired at Copse on his first lap.

Moss still led on the second lap, but Brown was now behind him with "Dick" Richards (*J.B.S.-Norton*) third and Stuart Lewis-Evans (*Cooper-Norton*) fourth. Clarke had retired and Headland had fallen back with

THE FRAZER-NASH Mille Miglia
IS FITTED WITH

Hydraulic **SUSPENSION CONTROL**

NEWTON & BENNETT LTD

VALETTA RD., ACTON, LONDON, W.3 'PHONE: SHEPHERDS BUSH 3443 (4 LINES) GRAMS: NEWSORBER, EALUX, LONDON

Pit Patter

Bill Whitehouse, fit again after his Snetterton crash, is seen here at Brands Hatch on June 22nd discussing the incident with IOTA'S Roy Pearl and Douglas Armstrong.

Photograph: G. Goddard

Laurence Bond, designer of the Bond 500 and Bond Minicar has now added engine designing to his activities. This latest effort is a 500 c.c. single cylinder racing unit with rotary valves and it is at present being tested by a very well known Midlands motor cycle manufacturer. It is giving over 70 b.h.p.!

Gordon Bedson, designer of the Mackson 500, informs us that the Mackson team as such no longer exists, and that any of the cars seen in competition this season will be private entries. He also informs us that he is engaged on modifying the chassis design of the Kieft 500 for Cyril Kieft, and will be responsible for incorporating them in Stirling Moss' car, which will be turning out at Silverstone on July 19th.

George Wicken wasn't really in the mood for motor racing at Brands Hatch on June 22nd. He was passenger the night before in a friend's Sunbeam-Talbot, which rolled over on to its roof in swerving to avoid a motorcyclist. Inverted motoring took them a further 100 yards until the car struck the bank on the opposite side of the road, rolled back on to its wheels and continued in the orthodox manner. Not the best sort of thing to occur before going motor racing.

The Seaman Trophy is presented annually by the Half-Litre Club to the member who gains the highest number of points in Formula III races on the Continent. Points are awarded on the following basis : 6 for a win : 4 for 2nd ; and 2 for 3rd place. Previous holders were K. E. Carter in 1950 and A. E. Brown in 1951.

Italian Ferraris are using not only British alcohol-based fuel—Shell, of course—but we hear excellent reports from the racing team of the alcohol resisting paint produced by Modern Industrial Finishes and now used on all the cars.

Ken Carter, Secretary of the Half-Litre Club, unfortunately hospitalized himself and severely bent his Cooper when practising for the Crystal Palace " private race " on June 26th. He was approaching the end of Terrace Straight when a half-shart broke and tore off a brake pipe. Ken then found himself in the unenviable position of having a corner to negotiate at about 90 m.p.h. without brakes! He positioned the car as best he could to slow it before it left the road and then " took off " over a bank narrowly missing a tree and landing on a pile of rocks. He remembers nothing after leaving the road until he came-to sitting in the Cooper,

CRYSTAL PALACE AGAIN

Scenes from the June 26th try-out illustrate that it is a true road circuit

There is a possibility that motor racing may be resumed at the Crystal Palace, a circuit which will be remembered by many of our readers who witnessed racing there pre-war. The recent "race" was put on not only to let the drivers test the condition of the circuit, but for members of the L.C.C. Parks Committee to experience race atmosphere and also to take recordings of the volume of noise at different points outside the circuit. Their verdict was that although some local residents might be inconvenienced, the noise could not be considered serious enough to stop further investigations into the question of a possible limited number of race meetings being held there each year.

Top to bottom, left to right. 1. The "start" with Norman Gray (Cooper-J.A.P.) temporarily leading the field. 2. George Wicken (Cooper-J.A.P.) the "winner" leads Sir Francis Samuelson (Cooper-Norton) through one of the many hairpins. 3. What's this? Mike Hawthorn tries John Cooper's Cooper-Norton for size. 4. Same man gets the Formula II slant on the circuit with his Cooper-Bristol. 5. Les Leston (Cooper-Norton) and Paul Emery (Emeryson-Norton) do a "Brands Hatch" (see page 22).

SNETTERTON

Close racing on June 28th

THE Eastern Counties Motor Club had a better deal from the weather clerk on June 28th than did the Half-Litre Club a month previously. This time the sun shone with tropical intensity, and a large crowd saw some very close racing besides keeping the refreshment vendors very busy.

Pre-race paddock activity was enlivened by R. A. R. Bell's Iota-J.A.P. being towed round and round by a Jeep in ever decreasing circles, while Bill Powell-Richards stood on the back of the Iota surf-board fashion to determine the cause of the car's reluctance to start. The last-named driver's Kieft-J.A.P. had broken the gearbox mountings in practice and was to be a non-starter. Les Leston had broken the 500 c.c. lap record in practice at a speed of 77.8 m.p.h. in his Cooper-Norton, not the Leston-Norton as entered. The 10-lap Formula III race was event three in a programme full of variety, and fourteen cars went to the line. R. A. R. Bell's Iota-J.A.P. was a non-starter, the trouble having been traced to a duff magneto.

The start itself was rather incredible to watch, because, as the cars came up from the pre-race grid to the starting positions proper the front row stopped and the rest were still rolling when down came the flag. The " back row boys " were able to shoot through the still stationary front row. After one lap, however, the " favourites " were to the fore again with Leston leading Parker (*Kieft-Norton*) and Wicken (*Cooper-Norton*) and the " dicing " just couldn't have been closer. Wicken worked his way to the front by the second lap and Leston was in third place with Parker holding his second position.

The pace among the leaders was really too hot for the crowd to take much notice of the progress amongst the back markers, but all the same D. S. Shale (*Kieft*) and R. Paulson (*Cooper*) were having quite a dust up. On the fourth lap Parker took Wicken just before the paddock, and so the fight for first place went on with first Leston back in the lead on the next lap and Parker third, and then Don leading again on the sixth lap.

In the midst of all this excitement a U.S.A.F. gentleman arrived in a jet fighter and proceeded to give an aerobatic display at very high velocities. There was an awful lot to watch at once. By the seventh lap Parker was still out in front, but Leston had taken Wicken's second place. George had over-revved somewhere in the heat of battle and clipped a valve, losing him a few hundred revs.

The positions did not change after that although Leston was " breathing on Parker's neck " for the rest of the race, and indeed on the last lap was so close that the final issue was in doubt right until the drop of the flag.

Don Parker found the top of his carburettor hanging off at the finish. " Dick " Richards (*J.B.S.-Norton*) limped in after everyone else with a deranged gear control, the bolt having dropped out of the selector arm.

The Formula Libre race also provided a close finish. Tony Gaze, who had dominated this 15-lap scratch race with the ex-Whitney Straight-Bira 2.9-litre supercharged Maserati, was caught on the last lap by Kenneth McAlpine in the 2-litre Connaught, and they came up to the finish absolutely "neck and neck." At the flag it was the unsupercharged car that was just ahead. It transpired the "Maser" started to run out of fuel on the last lap and was misfiring slightly.

Many more finishes like that and it would pay competitors to fit hand-controlled telescopic bonnets!

(June 28th) **SNETTERTON** **Eastern Counties M.C.**

500 c.c. Race (10 laps) : 1, D. Parker (Kieft-Norton), 71.5 m.p.h.; 2, L. Leston (Cooper-Norton); 3, G. Wicken (Cooper-Norton).

Fastest lap and new 500 c.c. record : D. Parker, 78.4 m.p.h.

Results of Recent Events

(June 28th) **SILVERSTONE** **Midland Motoring E.C.C.**

500 c.c. Race. Heat 1 (8 laps) : 1, C. Headland (Kieft-Norton), 62.63 m.p.h.; 2, T. Leigh (Cooper); 3, C. A. N. May (Cooper-J.A.P.).

Heat 2 (8 laps) : 1, R. G. Bicknell (Revis-J.A.P.), 62.67 m.p.h.; 2, P. W. Nuckey (Cooper-J.A.P.); 3, T. J. Clarke (C.B.P.-J.A.P.).

Final (8 laps) : 1, C. Headland (Kieft-Norton), 64.55 m.p.h.; 2, R. G. Bicknell (Revis-J.A.P.); 3, T. J. Clarke (C.B.P.-J.A.P.).

(June 14th) **SILVERSTONE** **Bugatti Owners' Club**

500 cc. Race. Heat 1 (5 laps) : 1, C. Headland (Kieft-Norton), 70.07 m.p.h.; 6 mins. 53.2 secs.; 2, D. Truman (Cooper-J.A.P.); 3, T. Leigh (Cooper).

Heat 2 (5 laps) : 1, T. Clarke (Iota), 66.69 m.p.h., 7 mins. 14 secs.; 2, P. W. Nuckey (Cooper); 3, C. Lones (Iota).

Final (10 laps) : 1, C. Headland (Kieft-Norton), 13 mins. 48.8 secs.; 2, C. Carter (J.P.-Norton); 3, T. Leigh (Cooper); 4, C. Smart-Jones (Cooper).

(June 28) **BO'NESS HILL CLIMB** **Scottish S.C.C.**

500 c.c. : 1, N. Sanderson (Cooper), 37.80 secs.; 2, A. McGlashan (Cooper), 40.22 secs.; 3, D. Prosser (Cooper), 40.31 secs.

De Dion Suspension for J.B.S.

IN view of the current arguments in our correspondence columns over the merits of swing-axle and wishbone rear suspension, it is interesting to hear of a manufacturer making a different approach to the problem.

Charles Bottoms has adapted one of his J.B.S. cars to De Dion type rear suspension. This conversion has been carried out on a standard J.B.S. chassis, and, as can be seen in the illustration, the spring unit brackets are welded on to what would normally be the top wishbone carriers. The spring damper units, which are of Girling manufacture, now number one per side and are of a larger diameter than the twin types fitted to the standard chassis. Each damper unit contains a two-rate coil spring which provides a very soft ride.

The De Dion tube of 14 s.w.g. mild steel 1⅝in. in diameter is bolted up in three sections and is located by a " Paxoline " block sliding in a 1⅝in. wide slot. This three-piece construction is used for ease of replacement in the event of mishap. It will be noticed that a trunnion bearing is embodied in the De Dion tube to obviate the torsional stresses imposed on it. The radius arms are constructed of 14 s.w.g. mild steel tubing ¾in. in diameter, and pivot at the chassis end on a self-aiigning ball race. On production models this race will be adjustable.

With the new layout, each drive shaft is 3in. longer and in consequence universal joints cannot " bottom."

This adaptation has resulted in the complete car weighing some 15 lbs. more than the standard model, but Charles Bottoms is confident that he can make the production De Dion car (to order only) lighter than the standard model. S. W. Creamer has fitted one of these J.B.S. De Dion layouts to his own Creamer-J.A.P., and Charles Bottoms would like Formula III car owners to know that he can undertake the fitting of similar rear ends to a variety of cars.

LATEST MAGNETO FROM LUCAS

Racing type with rotating magnet

POST-WAR developments in motorcycle racing engines, giving higher maximum speeds and more severe torsional vibration, have placed an increasing strain on the magneto. Indeed, the limit is being approached beyond which it would be unreasonable to hope for reliable operation from a unit consisting of rotating windings, condenser and other parts installed in a necessarily compact and comparatively light component.

Consequently, a new Lucas magneto has been developed to meet the increased revs. of racing motorcycle engines. The important difference, as compared with other types, is that the windings, condenser and contact breaker are not made to rotate, so eliminating the need for slip ring and carbon brush pick-up. The only rotating part is a small, compact rotor and shaft assembly supported in ball bearings at either end; the assembly comprises a magnet with laminated pole shoes, and a shaft which is located and retained in the magnet bore by zinc-base metal cast around the ends of the magnet. By making use of this rotating-magnet design, a simple but extremely robust construction is made possible. Moreover, the small diameter of the rotor reduces the intertia loading on the engine and drive, an important factor in the quest for rapid acceleration.

Features of the Magneto

Stator laminations are cast integral with the one-piece aluminium body, and the laminated core upon which the coil is wound fits across the upper ends of the stator laminations to complete the magnetic circuit. Since the coil does not rotate, adequate insulation of the secondary winding presents no problems. The compactness of the rotor, already described, is achieved by the use of Alnico magneto steel, an aluminium-nickel-cobalt alloy with exceptional magnetic properties. An extension of the rotor shaft carries a hardened steel cam to operate a normal rocker-type contact breaker, the design of which easily permits magneto speeds of the order of 6,000 r.p.m., i.e., 12,000 engine r.p.m. On the other hand,

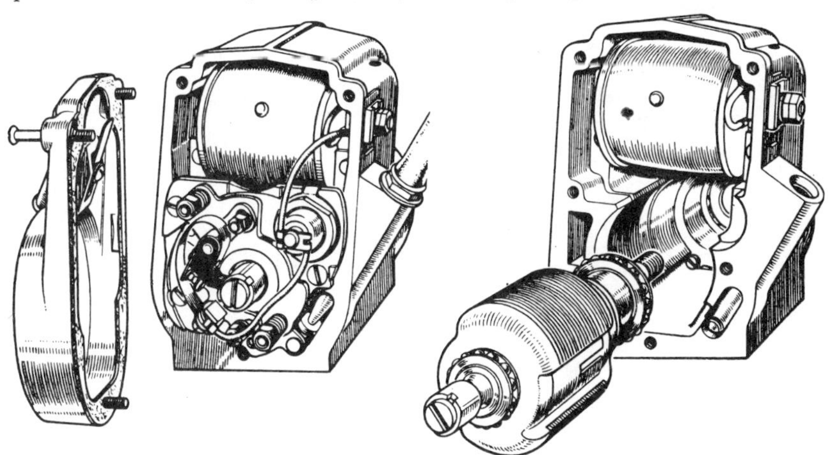

The Lucas racing magneto model SRR1. The left-hand picture shows the end cover removed exposing the contact breaker mechanism, and to the right the rotor and coil arrangements are illustrated.

the magneto has also exceptional slow-speed sparking performance, an essential feature where good starting and quick " get away " are of vital importance.

Manufactured in single- and twin-cylinder form, these magnetos can be arranged for either base or flange fixing. Asymmetrical rotor poles on the single-cylinder unit reduce to weak strength the " idle " spark produced at each revolution.

The condenser employed in this magneto is a metallised paper type, in which the electrodes consist of a very thin metallic film deposited on a paper strip, instead of separate metal foil which is relatively thick. Not only does this effect a saving in bulk, but even more important is the fact that such a condenser is " self-healing." Should the dielectric break down (which, in other condensers, would cause ignition failure), the heat of the spark would vapourise away the metallic film around the point of rupture, so preventing a permanent short circuit. Improved impregnating wax and a new type of rubber seal assist in making the condenser thoroughly reliable under any conditions of service.

Special attention has been paid to the problem of water-proofing, the only joint being that between the aluminium body and the moulded cover at the contact breaker end. This cover carries a high-tension pick-up in the form of a spring blade which makes contact with a " tapping " on the coil winding. On the twin-cylinder magneto, a rotating electrode fitted to the camshaft distributes the high tension supply to each plug in turn. Ignition timing is controlled by means of a lever-operated Bowden cable which rotates the contact breaker assembly on a spigot concentric with the cam.

These magnetos are, at present, available only to motorcycle manufacturers.

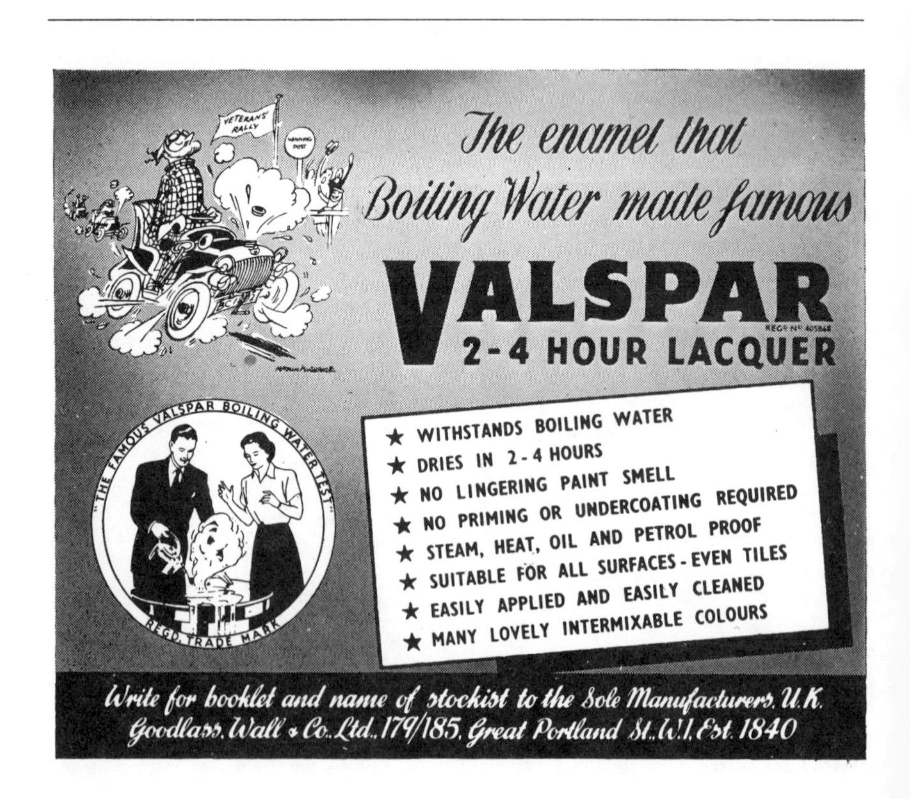

THE BEART-COOPER

A modified design to be known as the Mark VIIA

NEWS of successful Formula III cars and motorcycles powered by Beart-prepared engines has become an almost commonplace occurrence, but news of a complete 500 c.c. car built by this busy little establishment at Byfleet in the shadow of the old Brooklands Track is news indeed.

We mentioned the car briefly in the December issue of *Iota*, and now that construction is rapidly approaching completion more details can be released of this interesting project.

Based on a Cooper Mk. VII, the whole car has been constructed with the approval and indeed the co-operation of the Cooper Car Company, so much so that it has been designated the Cooper Mk. VIIA by the

The simplicity of the car can be appreciated in this view. The lowered seat position will be noticed, also the two three-gallon fuel tanks, and the flexible exhaust pipe section and mounting. An engine driven fuel pump is to be fitted.

works. The frame is basically Cooper, being constructed of the standard 1¼in. mild steel tubing of 17 s.w.g., but with tubular upright cross members welded in instead of the perforated steel strip used on the Surbiton chassis. The position of the driver's seat is 3in. lower than on the standard production, and a three gallon fuel tank is located under the driver's legs between the chassis members. Another three gallon fuel tank is " scuttle " mounted on a framework of welded triangulated tubes. The combined capacity of these two tanks is deemed sufficient for the duration of the races that Beart has in mind for the car, and in consequence the normally fitted side tanks are dispensed with and a body of chassis width can be employed with a very slim profile and small frontal area.

The engine, a Beart prepared Norton " Featherbed," is mounted in dural plates with the gearbox, as on the racing motorcycle, and the " unit " is mounted in the chassis 2½in. further forward than standard, and is retained by ten nuts and bolts of 70 ton steel. Nuts and bolts of this tensile strength are employed throughout the car, even to the wheel nuts, and every nut subject to vibration is split-pinned.

Careful attention has obviously been paid to the mounting of the exhaust system with a view to eliminating fracture caused by vibration. The exhaust pipe is welded to the top chassis tube on two short brackets and has a section of flexible piping inserted at the exhaust port end. This should not only absorb vibration, but should prove a boon when the cylinder head has to be removed quickly. It is possible to remove the finned exhaust port nut, pull the flexible pipe away, leaving the exhaust pipe proper in situ, and the way clear for cylinder head removal.

An innovation in the eyes of half-litre car enthusiasts is the use of a chainguard on the upper and lower run of the primary chain, the oil

It is evident from this head-on view of the Beart-Cooper that frontal area has been kept to the minimum. For the first tryout, three leaves only will be used in the front spring. Spring dampers had yet to be fitted when this photograph was taken.

for this hard-worked component being supplied by its own light alloy oil tank, weighing just a few ounces. The rear sprocket is of the split variety allowing ratio changes to be effected without disturbing the drive shaft universal joints.

Very light tubular supports are used for the mounting of the rear Girling shock absorbers, the front ones had not yet been fitted when this visit was made. The body work also was in an unfinished state, but the panelling that had been carried out by Wakefield and Sons of Byfleet indicated that the finished job would be very pleasing to the eye. The car is to be completely undershielded, and no air intakes will be fitted for the initial tryout. It is hoped that the engine will run cool enough without these as it is the intention to keep the body as slim and smooth as possible.

In the tradition of the Beart racing motorcycle equipe, the Mk. VIIA will be finished in light green enamel, and will be entered in about seven meetings this year. Again following the pattern of his bicycle policy Beart does not believe in entering too many events, but rather in spacing his meetings and having the car (or bicycle) right. Alan Brown will drive the car at Goodwood and Eric Brandon at Silverstone. We look forward to seeing this car in competition.

INTERVIEW with

CYRIL KIEFT

A pioneer manufacturer of 500 c.c. cars, Cyril Kieft's plans now include Formula II and sports cars as well.

What prompted you to become a racing car manufacturer?

I have been a keen follower of both motor and motorcycle racing since pre-war days, and when the 500 c.c. car racing movement got under way, it seemed to me that a " one make " monopoly was not a good thing. I think that my entry into the field of manufacture was instrumental in preventing design stagnation.

It is noticeable that your early 500 c.c. racing cars employed wishbone type suspension at the rear, but the later and current design have swing-axles. What is the reason for this?

Although I had enjoyed a good deal of success with my original type of car including the breaking of 13 world records at Montlhéry in 1950, I felt that the swing-axle design evolved by J. A. Cooper, Ray Martin and Dean Delamont was superior. Accordingly I acquired this design and produced it. It was at least 50 lb. lighter than my original type, and this of course was mainly due to the simplicity of the rear suspension layout.

Your recently announced sports/racing car has reverted to wishbones at the rear. Do you consider they suit sports cars better than swing-axles?

Actually the Kieft sports/racing car has been designed by Gordon Bedson who has joined the board of my company and who will also be responsible for the design of the Formula II Kieft. I cannot say very much about either of these cars at the present.

What is the reason for the centrally disposed steering wheel on the Kieft sports car?

This was entirely due to my spectating at the Nurburgring last year. I noticed that the German Veritas with fully aerodynamic bodies and virtually central steering were miles an hour faster through the left hand bends than the Ferraris with their right hand steering. I think that for a course which employs left and right corners the central steering arrangement is the best compromise.

May we ask what form the Formula II car is going to take?

I can only tell you that this car is going to be very light and is at the moment showing great promise.

We recently published a photograph of your 650 c.c. B.S.A.-engined road car. Do you intend to produce this car commercially?

I am not interested in the commercial side at all. I have a business of my own which takes up the greater part of my time, and my interest in motor racing is purely from the sporting side.

My main idea is, and always was, to build cars which could win races. I am perfectly willing to talk to anyone who is interested in marketing the road car as a commercial proposition.

You have been answered officially by the Half-Litre Club on your proposal for road car races. What is your reaction to the arguments?

If the minority still feel they are not being catered for by the Club, I would like to say that my offer to provide a trophy, etc., still holds good. I feel that this country needs a high-performance car of under 750 c.c. to compete with the Renault and D.B. and racing on these lines would be an ideal method of developing this type of car.

Has the move of your factory premises from Bridgend to Wolverhampton benefited you in any way?

Yes. Wolverhampton is an extremely good area for labour of the right type. I now have men working for me who have been in the motor and motorcycle industry for many years.

So far, you are the only car manufacturer to announce that the Turner 4-cylinder engine can be supplied and fitted in the 1953 models. Can you tell us any more about the Turner-engined Kieft?

The Turner engine is giving every reason for optimism in its tests, and a Turner-engined Kieft should be running at Goodwood on Easter Monday. W. E. Ford will be the owner/driver.

How many new Kieft's 500's shall we see racing this season?

There will be four new cars. Don Parker and André Loens will both be driving their last year's cars and both will be powered by my own "double knocker" Norton engines, which will be prepared by Steve Lancefield. Billy Nicholson will be driving my own car which has of course the "works" prepared B.S.A. twin engine.

Photograph: Norman Burnitt

Don Parker in his Formula III Kieft. This was one of the most successful racing cars in 1952 irrespective of formula. Fourteen races were won and thirteen course records were set by this particular car.

Monthly Round-Up

IT is amusing to note how the cycle of motoring fashion revolves. Twenty years ago, to give their cars that svelte look, owners hid their wire wheels with discs. Now, in the United States, where many people are getting "Continental car minded," an accessory manufacturer is offering clip on "wire wheels" to hide the discs. These are made in stainless steel with 40 spokes and are supplied with or without a dummy "knock-on" cap. They clip on in place of the usual hub caps, or nave-plates, as they are known these days, and give the "Chevvy" that Modena look, or so the advertisements would have us believe.

An entirely new business has come into being as a result of the American enthusiasm for sports cars and for motor racing, and it is now possible to buy American-made accessories ranging from polished aluminium rocker covers for the TD. M.G. to cuff links bearing the Jaguar or M.G. emblem.

Budding Hawthorn

It is obvious that Enzo Ferrari is looking well ahead (as always) and planning for the 1954 Formula I. It is then that Lancias plan to return to formula racing and the rumour that Alfa-Romeos are working on a supercharged 750 c.c. car, plus the new found speed of the 6-cylinder Maseratis, indicate that there will be a dearth of front rank drivers—even in Italy. Hawthorn will do well to spend at least a season with the Modena concern, as he must accumulate a wealth of experience, driving in company with such experienced masters as Alberto Ascari, Luigi Villoresi and Guiseppe Farina.

Mike Hawthorn must feel highly satisfied (and so must his very keen father) that, after only one season of racing with Grand Prix type cars, he has been given a wheel in the official "works" Ferrari team. This constitutes some sort of record, since even the great Dick Seaman raced for several seasons with M.G., E.R.A. and Delage cars before he was offered a place in the 1938 Mercedes-Benz team, which occupied much the same position in Grand Prix racing then as Ferrari does to-day.

He will not expect to win many races, however, since Ferrari is naturally keen on an Italian driver winning the World Championship. Perhaps when Mike has experienced real Grand Prix racing there may be a serious British Formula I challenger for him to drive. It is significant that he has been able to insist that his Ferrari is finished in British racing green.

Alpine Sports

In just a few days time the 1953 Monte Carlo Rally will have started, and with the British entry of 113 outnumbered only by the French entry of 150, our chances of repeating the 1952 success seem to be pretty bright. Altogether there are 440 entries from twenty-two countries.

Sydney Allard, last year's very popular winner, is again starting from Glasgow and again is driving a 4.4-litre Ford V8-engined Allard Saloon. Stirling Moss, who finished second last year at his first "Monte" attempt, is starting from Monte Carlo and is again driving a Sunbeam Talbot. It is a great pity that Mike Hawthorn will not be taking part as planned, but his first drive for Ferrari will be on January 18th, when he takes part in the Argentine Grand Prix.

April 1953

CASTLE COMBE

New Martin Specials' good showing

Photograph : G. Goddard

John Brown (Martin Special) leading Don Parker (Kieft-Norton) through Camp Corner in the first Formula III heat. He was ultimately passed by Parker, but the new Martin Special showed great promise.

ALTHOUGH deprived of a few of the top-flight drivers, due to the Goodwood practice on the same date, the Bristol M.C. and L.C.Cs. meeting at Castle Combe on April 4th was far from being dull.

It was noteworthy for the successful debut of the new Martin Specials driven by John Brown and Dennis Taylor, the latter driver winning the 10-lap Formula III Final from the redoubtable Don Parker whose last year's Kieft-Norton sported a new slimmed body.

The first race of the day at 1 p.m. was a 6-lap heat for 500 c.c. racing-cars and was run in brilliant sunshine although a cold wind prevailed. The starting grid order was :—

J. Brown (Martin Spl.)	J. Ebdon (Iota)	J. H. Bennett (Cooper)	C. Lones (Cooper)
B. E. Bradnack (Cooper)	D. Truman (Cooper)	D. Parker (Kieft)	S. W. Creamer (Creamer)

John Brown was first away, displaying immense acceleration with his new Norton-powered Martin-Special, he was followed very soon by Don Parker who quickly worked his way through from the second row. Don Truman was left on the line with his new Cooper Mark VII with the new type suspension, but got going when the field was pretty well out of sight.

Brown led in good style for two laps, but was overtaken on the third lap by Parker with Clive Jones holding third place with his newly-acquired Cooper, christened Tiger Kitten III. From then on Parker increased his lead, whilst on the fourth lap at Quarry Corner Lones was passed by Bertie Bradnack looking surprisingly small for his 17-odd stones in the new Cooper Mark VII (with normal type suspension).

Truman, who was by now circulating fairly well back, did not appear very happy with his new car. J. H. Bennett was getting through Camp Corner very quickly indeed. Finishing order—Parker, Brown, Bradnack.

Heat II, another 6-lap heat, was Event Three on the programme at 2 p.m. and the weather was still fine although clouds were menacing. The grid order was:

I. L. Bueb (Arnott)	A. A. Butler (Cooper)	J. K. Brise (Cooper)	G. G. Smith (Kent-Smith)
D. Taylor (Martin Spl.)	V. Worlock (Cook Spl.)	P. Thornton (Cooper)	D. Boshier-Jones (Kieft)	D. Gray (Cooper)
	A. J. Nurse (Cooper)		C. Headland (Kieft)

John Brise made a terrific getaway and led for two laps, but Dennis Taylor, who handling of his new Norton-powered Martin-Special through Camp Corner was really worth watching, took the lead on the 3rd lap and was never again challenged. Poor Brise retired on the 4th lap with a suspected con-rod breakage. Ivor Bueb who was in 3rd place for the 1st lap with the "works" Arnott went out with a broken primary chain.

Charles Headland moved into 2nd place when Brise retired and held it until the end, but the "scrap" which held everyone's interest was between Austin Nurse (*Cooper-Norton*) and Gerald Smith (*Kent-Smith*). Nurse, who weighs around 18 stone, was driving magnificently and so for that matter was Smith, whose Kent-Smith was powered by an elderly single-cam Norton motor. Smith finally finished in 3rd place, but Nurse was close behind. Don Gray, who has used J.A.P. motors for so long, finished fifth in this heat and was using a twin-cam Norton engine in his Cooper MarkV for the first time. Finishing order—Taylor, Headland, Smith.

Race 6, the 500 c.c. Final was a 10-lap affair, the grid being:—

D. Parker (Kieft)	D. Taylor (Martin Spl.)	J. Brown (Martin Spl.)	C. Headland (Kieft)
G. G. Smith (Kent-Smith)	A. J. Nurse (Cooper)	D. Gray (Cooper)	B. E. Bradnack (Cooper)
C. Lones (Cooper)	A. A. Butler (Cooper)	P. Thornton (Cooper)	J. H. Bennett (Cooper)
S. W. Creamer (Creamer)		J. Ebdon (Iota)	D. Truman (Cooper)

It was obvious from the positions on the starting grid that the final would be a good race and a good race it was with Parker whipping into the lead at once, followed by Brown and Smith. By the third lap Parker was well out in front and Taylor had moved into third place, going on to the grass at Camp Corner in his efforts to catch up.

Brown, driving very fast, dropped to third place on the 4th lap when his magneto cut-out switch began to give bother, and he finally spun off—a great pity. By this time Nurse and Smith had renewed their earlier battle and were really mixing it, Nurse's Cooper showing unusually good acceleration out of Camp Corner for such a heavily laden car. The suspension on Smith's car finally collapsed but he finished fourth behind Nurse, nevertheless. Creamer's Creamer Special was well back, the motor sounding very flat, had the car been lapping quicker it would have been easier to judge how well the new De Dion back-end was behaving. Sprint specialist J. Ebdon retired on lap 8 with oiling troubles on his Iota, now powered by a single-cam Norton.

On the 9th lap the order was Parker, Taylor, Nurse, Smith, and it looked like another victory for Parker but, as he missed a gear on Quarry Corner, Taylor seized his opportunity and was past in a flash to win by about four lengths. A good race and an excellent showing by the new Martin Specials and heavyweight Nurse. A large black cloud which had been threatening throughout the race broke just as the 500s finished and the last race—a sports car handicap—was run in a blinding hail-storm.

(April 4th, 1953) **CASTLE COMBE** **Bristol M.C. and L.C.C.**

FORMULA III

Heat 1 (6 laps, 11.04 miles): 1, D. Parker (Kieft-Norton), 74.96 m.p.h.; 2, J. Brown (Martin-Norton); 3, B. E. Bradnack (Cooper-Norton).

Heat 2 (6 laps, 11.04 miles): 1, D. Taylor (Martin-Norton), 74.93 m.p.h.; 2, C. Headland (Kieft-Norton); 3, G. Smith (Kent-Smith-Norton).

Final (10 laps, 18.40 miles): 1, D. Taylor (Martin-Norton), 76.58 m.p.h.; 2, D. Parker (Kieft-Norton); 3, A. J. Nurse (Cooper-Norton); 4, G. Smith (Kent-Smith-Norton); 5, D. Gray (Cooper-Norton); 6, B. E. Bradnack (Cooper-Norton). Fastest 500 c.c. lap: D. Taylor, 78.85 m.p.h.

Results of other classes on page 120

PIT PATTER

No, it is not an A.J.S. Formula III car, but one of two cars that have been built by M. Bousquet of Casablanca, French Morocco. Powered by standard single-cylinder A.J.S. engines, they finished 1st and 2nd on their first appearance at Tunis on March 29th.

Our Cover Picture. This is a fine action shot by T. C. March of Les Leston negotiating Runway Hairpin at the Brough meeting on April 3rd, 1953. Leston is obviously putting all he knows into getting the Cooper round without a time-wasting slide. This photograph brilliantly illustrates how much concentration is necessary to race a motor car successfully.

The Draguignan International Formula III Meeting is the latest continental event to be cancelled. This race which was to have taken place on May 17th has been called off owing to material and financial difficulties which cannot at present be overcome, the Automobile Club du Var informs us.

Johnny Goldschmidt, whose Lea-Francis-engined "Performance Special" is now going so well, is seriously thinking of purchasing a Formula III car as well. He likes to partake in as many races as possible at any one meeting and thinks this is the answer.

Piero Taruffi, driving his 500 c.c. Guzzi-powered Italcorse, set up a new Class I record on April 17th. Using the famous Via Appia for the run he covered 50 km. at 103.413 m.p.h. The record was previously held by Bill Aston (*Aerodynamic Cooper-J.A.P.*) with a speed of 99.3 m.p.h.

Shell-Mex and B.P. Ltd. are making a free issue of interference (radio and television) suppressors to all Shell and B.P. service stations, which stock Shell X-100 motor oil. Each motorist who fills up his sump with X-100 will be given a suppressor, which can be fitted in a few moments.

The Bugatti Company of Molsheim are negotiating with the Maserati brothers to make the sports version of the O.S. C.A. under licence.

B.R.M. plans are progressing for the new 2½-litre car, although they may be raced under a different name when the new Formula I commences in 1954. Raymond Mays has said that the new engines have been bench-tested and that work was proceeding on the new chassis and body. The existing 1½-litre supercharged cars will be driven this season by Ken Wharton and Reg Parnell, although Fangio and Gonzalez have also agreed to drive in races yet to be nominated by them.

Silver City Airways are to operate two new air ferry services for cars, passengers, and cycles with effect from May 15th, 1953. The new services will be from London (Gatwick) to Le Touquet, and Southampton to the Isle of Wight. The new London-Le Touquet service will operate twice daily with new Bristol Superfreighter aircraft, seating 20 passengers and accommodating up to 3 cars and several cycles and motorcycles. Time 40 minutes, passenger fare £4 single, £7 4s. return, single fare for a small car £10 10s.

Brands Hatch is to be the scene of a special Coronation Meeting on May 24th. Invitations have been sent out to the sixteen fastest Formula III drivers to compete in one race. This should really be worth watching.

A Club to be known as the Brands Hatch Racing and Social Club is to be formed, and will have many useful functions, one of which is to train marshals for racing events. Any enthusiasts who are interested, write to J. Pritchard, 9 Kingdon Road, London, N.W.6.

The B.A.R.C. meeting at the Crystal Palace Circuit on Whit Monday (May 25th) is to be an international event. Practice for this meeting will take place on Saturday, May 23rd.

P. J. ("Steve") Stephens has recently joined the staff of Pearl, Cooper Ltd. as Advertising Manager of MOTOR RACING. He was at one time a familiar figure at the circuits with the Rolls-Royce mobile book-shop—an idea he was instrumental in starting when managing F. & E. Stoneham's, the well-known London booksellers. A keen motor-racing enthusiast, he built and raced his "750 Stoneham" with success last season, and has recently written a book, "Building and Racing my 750," which was reviewed in MOTOR RACING last month.

Redex have now instituted a racing service, and their specially equipped van will be in attendance at most race meetings. Many well known drivers are now using this service, and W. J. Holloway, the Competitions Manager, and L. Marshall, the racing mechanic, will be pleased to give further details of this service either at the circuits or at their High Road, Chiswick, London, W.4, premises.

Granville Grenfell, Constructor of the Grenfell Suspension Special, is busy at work designing, and producing a six-speed gearbox for Formula III cars.

Interviews with well-known personalities, a regular feature in this magazine since February, 1952, has been discontinued temporarily. The series will be resumed at the end of the racing season.

Mike Erskine is now producing the Staride Mark III without body, price £450 complete with nose-panel

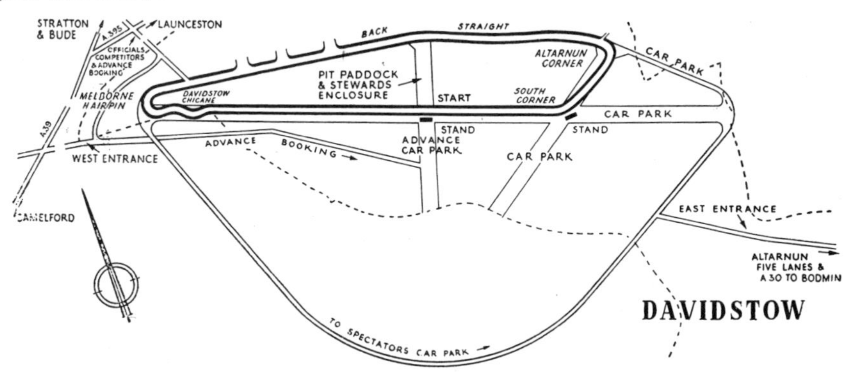

The very fast Davidstow Circuit near Launceston, Cornwall which will be the scene of a Formula III and Sports Car Meeting on Whit-Sunday (May 24th).

TECHNICAL SIDE

By Philip H. Smith, A.M.I., Mech.E.

RACING-ENGINE DESIGN

Philip H. Smith, A.M.I., Mech.E., is a Chartered Mechanical Engineer and a Chartered Automobile Engineer who has made a close study of high efficiency internal combustion engines. He is the author of three books, THE SPORTS CAR ENGINE, SPEED FROM THE SPORTS CAR and TUNING AND MAINTENANCE OF MG'S. This is the first of a series of monthly technical articles by Mr. Philip Smith who is to be a regular contributor to MOTOR RACING.

WITH the season's racing programme getting nicely under way, this is an excellent time to take stock of engine development and to assess British chances for the future. We can justifiably commence by considering the situation in the smallest G.P. class—that for 500 c.c. engines. This is a category pioneered by British enthusiasts, and one in which this country has been on top from the beginning.

The reason for this happy state of affairs is not difficult to find: power units, gearboxes, and transmission systems have been adapted almost without alteration from motorcycle units, and these latter already represented the last word in racing development in the sphere of two-wheelers. At long last, however, continental makers have shown signs of providing very formidable opposition to our motorcycle supremacy, as was shown in 1952, when out of five World Championships (based on the aggregate results of the Classic races) Italian machines secured three, including the class of particular interest to Formula III enthusiasts, that for 500 c.c. machines, annexed by the famous 4-cylinder Gilera.

Formula III Design

It has been evident for some years that the supremacy of the single cylinder 500 c.c. engine was bound eventually to come to an end in the face of development of fast-revving multi-cylinder power units. Because of the long start enjoyed by the single, it has been able to hold its own with remarkable tenacity and, in the two-wheeler sphere, has succeeded by virtue of sheer reliability on the odd occasions when the characteristics of the circuit favoured the multi-cylinder to a more than usual extent. It was only in 1952 that the 500 c.c. single showed definite signs of having reached its zenith in power production.

As far as racing cars are concerned, the type is obviously going to be a prime favourite for a long time to come, if only on the score of simplicity and ease of tuning and maintenance in the hands of the amateur speedman. Apart from that, it is in any case the only type of engine available in quantity. Probably in due course a few of the more experienced continental (and possibly British) drivers will find themselves provided with factory-built multis of the latest racing type.

The remarkable pitch of reliability, combined with high power output, to which the single-cylinder engine has been brought, should serve as an object lesson to all concerned with the design and building of racing machinery. Unfortunately there are far too many signs that full advantage is not being taken of the varied experience built into the type, which is available for all. The virtues of the single come from two quite simple factors—rigidity and high thermal efficiency. It is agreed that these two features are more easily obtained on the single than on any other type. Mixture distribution problems are non-existent, ports and valves are of adequate size, and the combustion chamber area is the minimum possible for any given cubic capacity. Intake and exhaust pipes can be designed to give the greatest benefit from column inertia of the moving gases, effecting, in fact, a degree of supercharging by this means at certain periods of the r.p.m. range.

Mechanical Rigidity

The crank assembly of the single, utilising heavy inside flywheels carried between closely-spaced ball and roller bearings in a very rigid housing, ensures that the full value of the expansion stroke is applied to crankshaft rotation. The liberal use of ball and roller bearings throughout the engine is also a factor in cutting down frictional losses. Thus, as an appliance for extracting the utmost power from a given weight of fuel, the single is supreme. Its drawback is of course the inherently outrageous balance. Many words can be written on the subject of balancing a single, but the fact remains that it is purely and simply a matter of trial and error. That the type has managed for so long to hold its own, and even to produce just a few more revolutions, and corresponding "horses" each year is due to a vast amount of data accumulated over the years, concerning, amongst other things, the percentage of reciprocating weight to be applied to the flywheels opposite the crankpin. When arriving at this figure, all sorts of peculiar things have to be taken into consideration. Even the method of mounting the engine in the frame exerts some influence, and the mere changing of an engine from one frame to another has been known to set up such unbearable vibration that rebalancing has become necessary.

It is this failing that puts a limit on the revving capacity of the single, and which reduces to an undesirably small portion of the power curve the part over which really smooth running can be obtained. At the same time, the use of extremes of valve timing to take full advantage of gas column inertia and "megaphoning," though productive of high power output, limits this also to a very small proportion of the power curve. Basically, therefore, the single, though in its way a very fine example of engine design, is dogged by two faults as its output is increased—its narrow r.p.m. range (and consequent lack of low-speed torque) and its inability to rev beyond a certain limit.

Over the years, of course, designers of singles have obtained their few extra revolutions periodically by a methodical shortening of the stroke, while keeping the piston speed more or less constant. Obviously there is a limit to which this can be carried, which would appear to have been just about reached.

Multi-cylinders—The answer

Division of the engine's cubic capacity amongst a number of cylinders will at once throw the problem open again, since, with a rational arrangement of multiple cylinders, not only may a better balance be expected, but very much higher r.p.m. for the same piston speed. We know that a 100 mm.-stroked single will turn over quite happily at 6,000 revs or so. How pleasant, therefore, to produce a multi with 50 mm. stroke at 12,000 r.p.m. for the same piston speed, and twice the power; always providing that we can maintain the same expansion pressure in the cylinder as before.

The key to the problem is in the last few words. The same cylinder pressures, in the present stages of development at any rate, are not being

Reliable power over the years. The highly developed "double-knocker" Norton single cylinder here seen installed in one of Moss' early Coopers.

Photograph: Guy Griffiths

reached. Before considering the multi from this angle, however, it will be interesting first to think about its mechanical construction; in particular, why it is that its reliability at really high speeds (as evidenced in the Classic motorcycle races) is still on the unpredictable side, in comparison with the single.

That great engineer, Sir Henry Ricardo, has written with truth that multiplication of components, each one doing its rightful job, is far and away preferable to attempting to make one part do several things; the more complicated layout will in fact be more reliable because each item is designed for its particular task and is therefore well up to it. There is no reason at all why this home-truth should not apply to the small-capacity multi-cylinder racing engine. Any lack of reliability therein must be looked for elsewhere than in the mere fact of having say eight valves instead of two.

The answer probably lies in one word—experience. Everything that

Continued on page 220

can be broken on the single has already been broken during its forty odd years of racing. The multi is now reaching a similar stage. As far as the small "four" is concerned, its main faults in past years have been in the valve gear. This comprises a large number of microscopic parts, each one actually stressed somewhat less in proportion than on the corresponding single, but requiring stern testing under racing conditions to bring them to maturity. Then of course there is another factor—the human one. The assembly and adjustment of a large number of small components demands real concentration and infinite patience.

The layout of cylinders alternative to the single had consolidated itself

The Triumph parallel twin, an example of a type which the author considers unlikely to challenge the single - cylinder engine in Formula III.

at the beginning of this year on something of a national basis. Italy has gone for the four-in-line, the famous wide-angle two Moto-Guzzi being definitely obsolescent, with an intriguing liquid-cooled four-cylinder in its place to form a future challenge to the fabulous M.V.-Agusta and Gilera "fours." Germany is keeping somewhat in the background for the moment, but the extremely rapid B.M.W. horizontally-opposed twin is known to be very much about the place, and there are rumours of German four-cylinder engines.

The parallel-twin-cylinder engine is in many ways admirable for the normal sports motorcycle or light car. It possesses a very real commercial virtue in looking like the type of engine which the average purchaser has come to regard as correct—upright cylinders on a drum-type crankcase. Its induction and exhausting arrangements, and its valve gear are easily and rigidly accommodated and not complicated in operation. Finally, its torque is excellent and a commendable degree of smooth running can be obtained, thanks to the doubling of the number of power impulses compared with the single.

None of the foregoing points, however, actually produce more power. For that we need more r.p.m. than with the single, with expansion pressures on a par with that type. In the next article it will be shown why these are not being obtained, and why there is no particular reason why they should be.

To be continued

Scottish Notes

WITH Charterhall fresh in our memory we cannot but give our native drivers a pat on the back. Ron Flockhart drove an inspired race and effectively held off the B.R.M.'s challenge for the first six laps in Formula Libre. His brilliant performance gladdened our hearts when he went on to win convincingly over the rest of the field.

Reverting to the Formula III race, congratulations are due to Rob Gerard, whose convincing victory accrued from a combination of faultless driving, meticulous preparation, and a very good motor. Leslie Thorne drove extremely quickly and well until eliminated by clutch trouble. His performance showed a vast improvement on that apparent at previous meetings. The local challenge faded out when Ninian Sanderson broke an axle shaft and David Swan suffered gearbox trouble. With Thorne also out the picture owing to a broken clutch cable it was left to David Blane to annex a place behind the immediate leaders. David was driving Joe Potts's latest experimental car with De Dion type rear-end. It looked very steady in action but might benefit from softer springing.

Messrs. McKay, Gordon, Mauritzen, and other Scots continue to gain experience. They will obtain race placings sooner or later, although for some of them the best short cut would be acquisition of a "double knocker."

A Scottish Club may yet obtain a circuit to balance the loss of Crail and Turnberry. Nothing further can be said at the moment lest negotiations are prejudiced.

Wretched luck again dogged Charlie Graham. His immaculate light-weight Cooper Special froze to the starting line at Charterhall with a seized clutch.

Circuit racing in Scotland has an unwelcome rest until the International Meeting at Charterhall on August 15th. In the interval we must content ourselves with the Hill Climbs; Bo'ness on June 27th and Rest-and-be-Thankful on July 4th.

Re-shuffle Department. Ninian Sanderson has turned over his Mark VI Cooper to Peter Gordon and David Swan has acquired the writer's similar car.

ALEX. McGLASHAN.

HALF-LITRE CLUB NEWS

by the Secretary

20, William IV Street, Charing Cross, London, W.C.2.

DURING the past few weeks a certain amount of publicity has been given to the association known as the Brands Hatch Racing and Social Club, especially on the Brands Hatch circuit whilst the Half-Litre Car Club have been organising race meetings. It is reported that one of the objects of this club is to recruit marshals for race meetings organised by the Half-Litre Car Club, and the committee have requested me to place before the members certain facts.

Firstly the Half-Litre Car Club are in no way associated with this new association, and wish to state here in this column that in future as in the past all marshals and helpers needed at our race meetings will be drawn from the marshals' list held by the club's chief marshal, R. S. Ridgeway, 51, Broxholme House, Harwood Road, Fulham, S.W.6. Any member who wishes to help in an official capacity at any race meetings will be very welcome and should contact Mr. Ridgeway direct. Whilst on this subject, I hope members in the Midlands will be particularly forthcoming, especially in view of the fact that the Club Silverstone is to be run on August 22nd. This meeting is primarily intended for those of our members who do not live in the south, and I certainly hope that sufficient help will be forthcoming to run the meeting.

In stock at the moment are a quantity of the new club blazer badges which are being sold at 11s. each. In view of the fact that members who have requested details of this particular item are far too numerous to reply to individually, I am taking the liberty of using this column to let members know that these are now available. We also have a small quantity of car badges at 30s. each and a quantity of lapel badges at 5s. each. All these are available on request to the secretary at the club office.

K. A. GREGORY.

NEW MEMBERS

W. HOWARD, 198, Knutsford Road, Warrington.
B. TYE, 81, Hitchen Hatch Lane, Sevenoaks.
Miss M. URQUHART, 19, Crook Log, Bexley-Heath.
M. BUDD, "Silver Trees," The Gateway, Woking.
M. MORLING, The Chimes, College Avenue, Maidstone.
E. MORLING, 15, Gabriels Hill, Maidstone.
W. LANCASTER, 136, High Street, Macclesfield.
R. GEE, Swanley Village P.O., Swanley.
D. COTTER, 97, Belgrave Road, Westminster, S.W.1.
R. LAMB, 24, Slyne Road, Lancaster.
V. S. WARD, 9, Eltham Park Gardens, Eltham, S.E.9.
A. SHARP, 16, Lexham Mews, W.8.
K. STEVENS, 75, Hurlingham Road, Bexleyheath.
H. POVAH, 3, Drewstead Road, S.W.16.
G. SAUNDERS, 14, St. James Road, Surbiton.
A. COWLEY, Broadlands Cottage, Camden Park, Tunbridge Wells.
H. PHILLIPSON, Windy Harbour Lane, Bromley Cross, Lancs.
J. FERGUSON, 32, Queensway, Derby.
J. HALL, 53, The Grove, Gosforth, Newcastle-on-Tyne.
J. NICHOLSON, Davidsons Garage, Scotland Road, Penrith.
D. TRUDGILL, 143, Landseer Avenue, E.12.
I. RABY, 27, Clifton Hill, Brighton.
J. KNIGHT, 3, Ashmere Grove, Brixton, S.W.2.
C. E. BASTIN, St. Ishmaels, The Cross, Cheddar.
W. ELSTON, c/o Ravensthorpe Manor, Boltby, Yorks.
T. BREWER, 30a, St. Johns Road, Tunbridge Wells.
W. PARRY, 31, First Avenue, Acton, W.3.
J. BRIERLEY, 211, Halifax Road, Rochdale.
G. PLACE, Ravensthorpe Manor, Boltby, Yorks.
R. HUTTON, 26, Princes Court, Wembley.
P. TAYLOR, 7, Hillside Avenue, Wembley.
J. ABBOTT, "Uplands," Hartley Road, Altringham, Cheshire.

"Montlhéry" Arnott

Proposed August record attempts

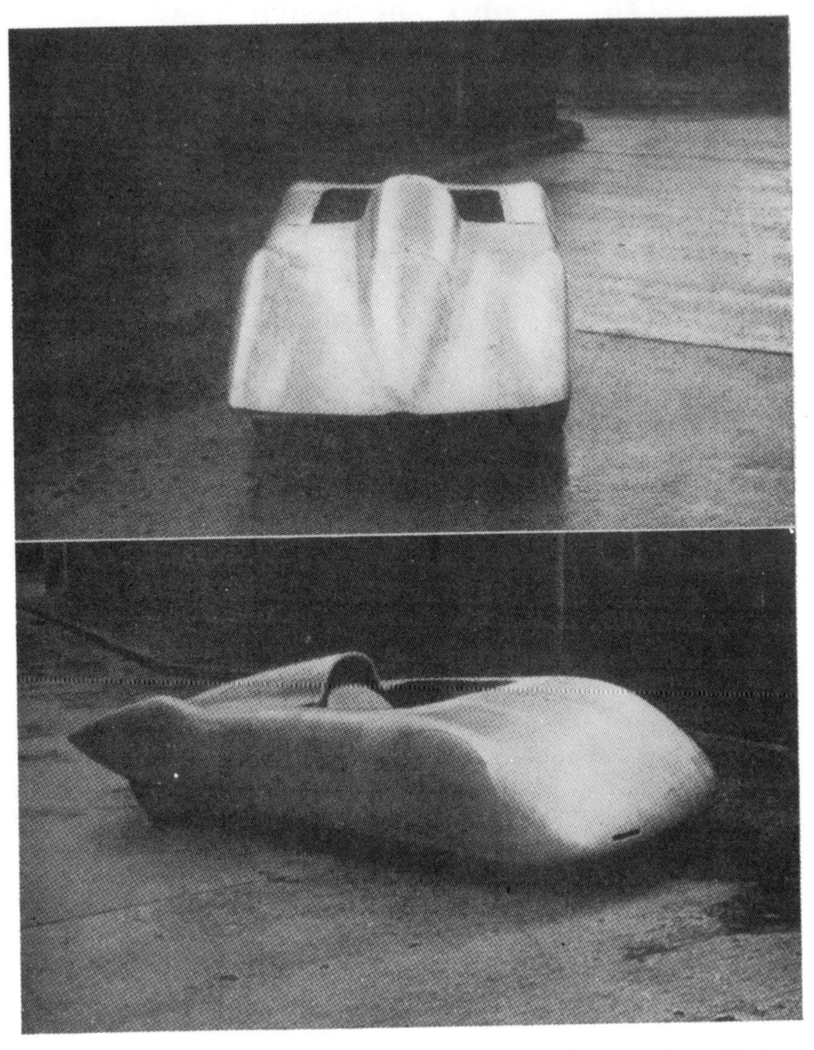

The clean lines of the aerodynamic Arnott can be appreciated in these two views. The panel-work was not completed when these photographs were taken. The driver's compartment will be covered by an aluminium panel to which will be fitted a Perspex " bubble." Arnott's hope to make attempts on Class I and J records at Montlhéry near Paris on August 10th. The driver will be G. G. Smith, and 350 and 500 c.c. Norton engines will be used for the attempts.

KENT'S BEST

Don Parker wins *Daily Telegraph* Trophy for second successive year

Entries

1 H. L. Daniell (Emeryson-Norton).
2 W. H. Lowe (Kieft-J.A.P.).
3 D. Taylor (Martin-Norton).
4 I. Burgess (Mackson-Norton).
5 C. W. A. Heyward (C.H.S.-J.A.P.).
6 R. F. Mayne (Cooper-J.A.P.).
7 P. Emery (Emeryson-Norton).
8 P. A. Taylor (Arnott-J.A.P.).
9 A. Cowley (Cooper-J.A.P.).
10 H. R. Povah (Cooper-J.A.P.).
11 L. Leston (Leston Spl.-Norton).
12 D. Parker (Kieft-Norton).
14 G. G. Smith (Kent-Smith-Norton).
15 B. A. Heyward (C.H.S.-J.A.P.).
16 G. Rolls (Kieft-Norton).
17 R. D. Biss (Cooper-Norton).
*18 R. K. Hutton (Arnott-J.A.P.).
19 C. D. Headland (Martin-Norton).
20 P. A. Seymour (Cooper-J.A.P.).
*21 R. Owen (Hill-J.A.P.).
22 P. A. Luke (Cooper-J.A.P.).
23 R. A. Anderson (Cooper-J.A.P.).
24 J. Russell (Cooper-Norton).
25 V. P. Labrum (Labrani-J.A.P.).
26 J. Rolls (Kieft-Norton).
27 R. T. Spreckley (Cooper-J.A.P.).
28 V. J. Firm (J.B.S.-J.A.P.).
29 N. Berrow-Johnson (Martin-Norton).
30 H. W. Walker (Walker-J.A.P.).
31 J. K. Brise (Arnott-Norton):
32 J. Rowsell (Cooper-J.A.P.).
33 D. H. R. Gray (Kieft-Norton).
34 P. Drummond (Cooper-Norton).
35 P. Thornton (Cooper-J.A.P.).
36 I. E. Raby (Cooper-J.A.P.).
37 A. Zains (Cooper-J.A.P.).
38 S. W. Creamer (Creamer-J.A.P.).
39 G. Wicken (Cooper-Norton).
40 R. C. Smith (J.B.S.-J.A.P.).
41 C. H. Coulson (Cooper-J.A.P.).
42 L. Lewis-Evans (Cooper-Norton).
43 S. Lewis-Evans (Cooper-Norton).
44 J. Brown (Martin-Norton).
45 P. Jopp (Emeryson-Norton).
46 F. Hobart-Smith (Martin-Norton).
47 R. E. D. Harrison (Cooper-J.A.P.).
48 R. G. Bicknell (Staride-Norton).
49 H. A. Frow (Cooper-J.A.P.).
50 G. A. Henrotte (Ettorne-J.A.P.).
51 L. Wood (Arnott-Norton).
52 H. Otterbein (Simca-Surva).
53 F. Antonelli (Volpini-Gilera).
54 M. Chazalet (Volpini-Gilera).
55 L. Beels (Cooper-J.A.P.).
56 B. Hutchinson (Cooper-J.A.P.).
57 R. Brise (Arnott-J.A.P.).
*58 A. Loens (Kieft-Norton).
59 W. Ford (Cooper-J.A.P.).
60 Kuhnke (Cooper-J.A.P.).

* Asterisk denotes non-starter.

THE natural amphitheatre of the Brands Hatch Circuit was packed with cars and spectators for the International Meeting there on August Bank Holiday Monday. In perfect sunny weather this *Daily Telegraph* sponsored event, the fourth of the series, was run off smoothly under the organisation of the Half-Litre Club.

The enormous crowd saw Brands Hatch expert Don Parker win the main event of the day, the 40-lap Final of the *Daily Telegraph* Trophy, for the second year in succession. He went ahead at the fall of the flag and was never challenged; his Lancefield-tuned engine displayed immense power and reliability. His car was so obviously the fastest on the circuit that by half distance he had built up a 10-second lead and although he steadily increased that lead he was driving well within his capabilities and no lap records were broken.

Les Leston finished second after a fierce battle for that position with Stuart Lewis-Evans during the first 10 laps. Lewis-Evans kept in third place until the end and Charles Headland held fourth place for the entire race.

There was a bad crash immediately after the start as the field swept into Clearways. Gerald Smith got out of control and his car rolled over several times, but he was not seriously injured. Reg Bicknell who was following Smith managed to avoid him but was rammed amidships by J. Rolls. Both these drivers were only slightly hurt.

Don Gray had hard luck in this race; he was holding 5th place after 35 laps, the Kieft going well, when the carburettor dropped off and not unnaturally he retired. George Wicken finished in 5th place after covering most of the race with a broken clutch cable.

Earlier in the day, Parker, Bicknell, Stuart Lewis-Evans and Leston had each won a heat of The August Sprint Race and also a heat of the *Daily Telegraph* International Trophy

Race. In addition to these races, Parker won the 10-lap Final of the August Sprint Race.

The international entry consisting of the Cooper-J.A.P.'s of Dutchman Lex Beels and American B. Hutchinson, the Volpini-Gileras of Frenchmen F. Antonelli and M. Chazalet, the 4-cylinder Surva of Frenchman H. Otterbein and the Cooper-J.A.P. of German Kurt Kuhnke were interesting but none were fast enough to qualify for any of the finals.

André Loens, who finished second in the *Daily Telegraph* race last year, was unable to compete this year as he crashed badly in practice when his car lost a rear wheel. He was not seriously hurt but the car was completely wrecked.

A very popular item with the crowd was a handicap event styled "demonstration"

Continued on page 337

Left to right, top to bottom. THREE HAPPY DRIVERS. *Stuart Lewis-Evans, Les Leston and Don Parker who came third, second and first respectively in the "Daily Telegraph" Trophy Race.*
P. A. Taylor looks doubtfully at the engine of his Arnott during heat 4 of the "Trophy" Race. His car had caught fire in an earlier race and also at the two previous Brands Hatch meetings!
F. Antonelli in his very neat Gilera-powered Volpini. Although beautifully finished, these Italian-built and French-driven cars were no match for the British machines.
L. Lewis-Evans grits his teeth as he has a private battle with H. W. Walker in heat 3 of the August Sprint Race. He finally took third place after a very tight finish. Note the "bent" front tyres.
Don Parker poses for the photographer after a very busy day of motor racing. His Kieft covered 67 racing miles. Note that Parker favours the old-type Dunlop racing tread on his rear tyres.
Les Leston leading the field in heat 3 of the "Trophy" Race. He won this race but had a stern struggle in the early stages with J. Russell (No. 24) who was right on form. Don Gray (33) finally finished 2nd with Russell 3rd. Bob Brise can be seen in the "works" Arnott-J.A.P. on the extreme left and Dennis Taylor brings up the rear of the group.

RACING PLUGS

by I. K. GOUGH, B.Sc.(Eng.),

Automotive Development and Test Engineer.
K.L.G. Sparking Plugs, Ltd.

One of the hardest stressed components in motor racing to-day is undoubtedly the sparking plug, and this article by an expert will be of interest to competitor and spectator alike.

RACING plugs stand in the same relationship to touring ones as do racing to touring engines. The same basic principles and components are used but developed to a point of higher duty with, often, different materials to deal with the more strenuous conditions.

But before considering racing plugs as such, a summary of basic plug design principles should not come amiss. Fundamentally, of course, the function of the plug is to provide a spark, but to do this consistently and without introducing any secondary and undesirable effects, a number of conditions have to be satisfied. Itemising the most important for brevity:

(a) There should be at no time any easier path to earth for the H.T. current than across the spark gap, under all conditions of operation. This demands, in particular, insulation which maintains its dielectric properties at elevated temperatures and is resistant to thermal and mechanical shock.

(b) As with the other components of the engine, the plug must undergo a measure of cooling so as to maintain a safe operating temperature. This must not be too high or pre-ignition will result, nor too low or deposits from combustion will build up excessively and cause tracking of the spark to earth instead of allowing normal sparking. In figures, the electrodes and insulator tip should be in the range 500°-600° C. for touring conditions (called the self-cleaning temperature), with the pre-ignition danger zone at 850° C. in racing, just as with such components as exhaust valves, it is generally customary to run rather hotter than with touring engines for higher efficiency as relatively short life is regarded as normal; the danger zone must be carefully guarded against, however, for pre-ignition in a racing engine is calamitous.

(c) The construction of the plug must be such that it remains pressure tight under engine operating conditions, otherwise the passage through it of hot combustion gases will completely upset the cooling function and bring about rapid failure.

Enlarging on these items, it can be said (a) that the insulation is probably the biggest single item of plugs which has undergone change with the years. Early racing plugs embodied mica insulation, and the name K.L.G. has long been associated with such plugs, dating from the days when Kenelm Lee Guiness made them for his own use. However, good as mica is, it has limitations and is now outmoded. From the racing viewpoint, the continual changing from hard to soft plugs and vice versa necessitated by the rather poor oil resistance of mica plugs was a definite disadvantage.

Nowadays, ceramic materials have been developed to such a high degree that they have virtually displaced mica. Their chemical inertness, high thermal strength and conductivity enable the " business end " of the plug to be opened up to the gases, compared with mica technique, giving better scavenging of the spark gap and therefore cleaner pick-up and better cleaning of the gas space of the plug itself, so that soft plugs are needed

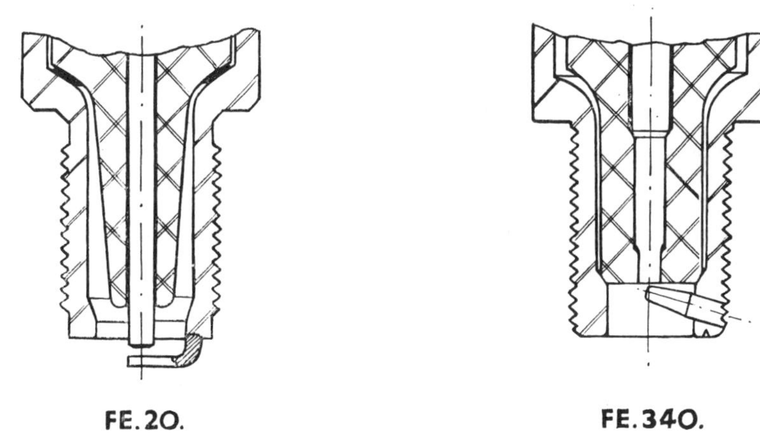

The left-hand illustration shows a K.L.G. type FE.20 sparking plug which is of the " soft " variety whereas the right-hand illustration shows a " hard " racing type.

much less, sometimes not at all.

Item (b) introduces the all-important subject of plug heat value, and a little more detail here is well worth while. Whether any given engine is cool running or hot running, the appropriate plug will be one which will conduct away little or much heat respectively to the cooling system in order to remain working in the safe range of temperature. This means that there must be ranges of plugs of progressively increasing heat value (or ability to cool themselves to the optimum temperature range) to cater for engines of progressively increasing standard of specific power output and tune.

In the definition of ranges of plugs, those for cool running engines are generally referred to as " hot " or " soft " whilst those for hot running ones are " cold " or " hard." This is not universal, however, for sometimes a " hotter " plug is taken to mean one which will stand more heat, i.e., the

Continued on page 382

inverse of the general definition. However, any system of identification should compare one plug with another rationally in terms of its heat value, i.e., its ability to withstand heat. Different manufacturing firms have their own ways of classifying the heat values, and it is often difficult to compare plugs of one make with those of another. In the case of K.L.G. plugs, a letter coding system is used to define the thread size and reach, and a numerical suffix denotes the heat value. Thus a plug suffixed 20 is a very hot plug for a cool engine, and one suffixed 100 is cold for a hot, say, super-sports engine. For racing, even cooler plugs are used, and these are classified in the range 220-340 for clear differentiation from normal commercial production, representing, in direct heat-value number comparison with the commercial range, 120-240.

Gas capacity

The main control feature of the heat value of a plug is its gas capacity. By this is meant the volume inside the body surrounding the working end of the insulator into which hot combustion gases pass. For a soft plug, this capacity is large so that the " business end " is kept hot enough to burn off combustion deposits, which are heavy in the case, say, of a slow-running paraffin engine, particularly if it is using a lot of oil through wear, as is often the case. Conversely for a hard plug, the capacity is very small, for in the case, say, of a fast-running racing engine the rate of heat input to the plug is so high, and temperatures likewise, that only a fraction of the hot gases must be allowed inside the plug compared with a soft plug to maintain the optimum operating temperature.

The technique involved in decreasing the gas capacity gives progressive shortening of the exposed portion of the insulator and lowering of the seating between it and the metal body, which forms the pressure-tight joint of the assembly and the path for heat to flow away from the insulator to the cooling system. For racing, this low seating position is important so that the rapid input of heat can get away quickly. Two sketches illustrate the point.

Now a few points on those differences in detail distinguishing racing from touring plugs as with racing and touring engines mentioned at the beginning of the article.

The greatest problem with racing plugs is getting rid of the heat rapidly and so avoiding pre-ignition, involving at the same time progressive shortening of the insulator nose which reduces the electrical shunt path and makes the plug more sensitive to oiling up. Any means which can increase the flow of heat to the cooling system will enable a slighter, softer, and therefore more oil-resistant plug to be used than would otherwise be the case. To this end, high conductivity materials for the central electrode and the highest possible conductivity of the insulator as compared with touring plugs are desirable. Conversely, of course, it follows that for the different condition of touring plugs, racing plug materials and techniques are not necessarily best for those conditions.

The latest K.L.G. ceramic racing plugs utilise Hylumina insulators, formerly known as S.749. This material represents the ultimate in plug insulation to-day; it possesses very high thermal, mechanical, and electrical properties and good thermal conductivity. The central electrode is internally of high conductivity material tipped with erosion-resistant alloy to give low gap burning rate and thus avoids the electrical strain on the ignition system that would otherwise result from a higher rate as the gap increases.

For racing use, engine manufacturers usually determine a basic type by test bed running, but actual racing conditions may require a slightly different heat value, generally on the softer side. If there is no basis to start on, a very hard plug is the best to try first as at worst it will only oil up, whereas, if too soft, pre-ignition may result and damage the engine. In this way one can come down progressively and with safety in heat value until the optimum type is reached. This can be recognised—assuming the engine is in good shape and with reasonable carburation—by the plug insulator nose having the merest film of deposit over it following a clean engine cut after a practice run.

When the plug type has been thus settled, the effect of carburation adjustments can within limits be judged by the appearance of the plug; the complete absence of deposit and a rather stark, hot appearance denoting a weak mixture, and darker deposit to the ultimate of lamp black appearance signifying progressive richness.

Finally, in this matter of plug selection, there is no substitute for experience, as with all aspects of racing so much depends on knowing at a glance whether the plug looks "right." K.L.G. are always pleased to give advice either "on the spot" when servicing actual races or when enquiries are addressed to the company. With proprietary racing engines, the correct plugs are known from previous experience for most conditions, and a recommendation can generally be made on application.